Technology and the Decline in Demand for Unskilled Labour

NEW HORIZONS IN THE ECONOMICS OF INNOVATION

Series Editor: Christopher Freeman, *Emeritus Professor of Science Policy, SPRU – Science and Technology Policy Research, University of Sussex, UK*

Technical innovation is vital to the competitive performance of firms and of nations and for the sustained growth of the world economy. The economics of innovation is an area that has expanded dramatically in recent years and this major series, edited by one of the most distinguished scholars in the field, contributes to the debate and advances in research in this most important area.

The main emphasis is on the development and application of new ideas. The series provides a forum for original research in technology, innovation systems and management, industrial organization, technological collaboration, knowledge and innovation, research and development, evolutionary theory and industrial strategy. International in its approach, the series includes some of the best theoretical and empirical work from both well-established researchers and the new generation of scholars.

Titles in the series include:

Technology and the Decline in Demand for Unskilled Labour

A Theoretical Analysis of the US and European Labour Markets

Mark Sanders

Entrepreneurship, Growth and Public Policy Group,
Max Planck Institute for Research into Economic Systems,
Jena, Germany

and

Utrecht School of Economics,
Utrecht, The Netherlands

NEW HORIZONS IN THE ECONOMICS OF INNOVATION

Edward Elgar
Cheltenham, UK • Northampton, MA, USA

Published by
Edward Elgar Publishing Limited
Glensada House
Montpellier Parade
Cheltenham
Glos GL50 IUA
UK

Edward Elgar Publishing, Inc.
136 West Street
Suite 202
Northampton
Massachusetts 01060
USA

A catalogue record for this book
is available from the British Library

Library of Congress Cataloguing in Publication Data

Sanders, Mark, 1972-
  Technology and the decline of unskilled labour demand : a theoretical analysis of the US and European labour markets / by Mark Sanders.
      p. cm. -- (New horizons in the economics of innovation series)
  Includes bibliographical references.
  ISBN 1-84542-132-9
  1. Unskilled labor. 2. Technological innovations--Economic aspects. 3. Labor market--United States. 4. Labor market--Europe. I. Title. II. New horizons in the economics of innovation
  HD5706.S246 2005
  331.7'98'0973--dc22

                                                      2005040015

ISBN 1 84542 132 9

Printed and bound in Great Britain by MPG Books Ltd, Bodmin, Cornwall

TABLE OF CONTENTS

LIST OF TABLES

LIST OF FIGURES

LIST OF APPENDICES

AVAILABLE IN .PDF AT WWW.MARKSANDERS.NL

ON NOTATION

CHAPTER 1

w_H/w_L	relative wage, high over low skilled
L_H/L_L	relative employment, high over low skilled
sh_{ujt}	share of unskilled in the wage bill of sector/industry/firm j at time t
as_{jt}	share of sector/industry/firm j in aggregate wage bill at time t
$u_{H,L}$	high and low skilled unemployment rates

CHAPTER 2

Some standard conventions on notation apply. Bold print signifies vectors (small letters) of matrices (capital letters). Usually the letter signifying a single element in the vector or matrix is also used to denote the vector or matrix, such that x_{ij} is an element of the m by n matrix X that consists of m row vectors x of length n. The symbol d is used to signify total, the symbol ∂ for partial derivatives. Furthermore the following symbols have been used:

y	output
i	index of final goods
n	number of final goods
t	time
$f(.)$	production function
x	intermediate input
j	index of intermediate inputs
m	number of intermediate inputs
p	price
$u(.)$	utility function
c	consumption
Σ	sum of elements over index
g	growth rate
sh_j	share of input j in total costs

CHAPTER 3

Again some general conventions apply in this chapter. For example a dot over a variable signifies the derivative of that variable with respect to time. A star over a price or quantity signifies an equilibrium price or quantity that may or may not be exogenously given. The following symbols were used:

r	rate of return on risk free assets
E	expenditure on consumption
e	the number e
log	the natural logarithm
ρ	the subjective discount rate
τ	time as an iterator under the integral sign
$U(.)$	direct utility function
P	price of one unit of utility (such that $U(.)=E/P$)
Y	total income
A	the stock of assets
α	parameter in the CES-utility function
σ	elasticity of substitution
mc	marginal costs
π	profits
tc	total costs
w	wages
l	labour employed
v	value of an innovation
a	productivity parameter in the innovation function
L^*	aggregate exogenous supply of labour
$L^{R\&D}$	aggregate demand for labour in R&D
L^D	aggregate demand for labour in production sector
L_x^D	aggregate demand for labour in intermediate production
K	physical capital stock
$K^{R\&D}$	aggregate demand for physical capital in R&D
K^D	aggregate demand for physical capital in final output production
K_x^D	aggregate demand for physical capital in intermediate production
Δ	discrete change
$S(.)$	savings function
X	intermediate goods or inputs
px	price of input X
V	value of an innovation
$R(.)$	innovation function
θ	the intertemporal elasticity of substitution in the utility function
bx	exogenous productivity parameter

$A_{H,L}(.)$	endogenous technology parameter augmenting high or low skilled labour
$\chi_{H,L}$	price of sub-intermediate that is complementary to high or low skilled labour
$\sigma_{H,L}$	elasticity of the demand for sub-intermediates H and L.
β	output elasticity of labour in the production of final or intermediate output
ψ	exogenous parameter representing marginal costs for sub-intermediate production in table 3.4
$R_{H,L}$	Research and Development resources employed in intermediate sectors H and L
δ	knowledge spillover parameter in the innovation function

CHAPTER 4

σ_{SR}	short run (given technology) elasticity of substitution between high and low skilled labour
σ_{LR}	long run (steady state) elasticity of substitution between high and low skilled labour
φ	knowledge spillover parameter in the innovation function
ψ	knowledge spillover parameter in the innovation function
χ	knowledge spillover parameter in the innovation function
ζ	knowledge spillover parameter in the innovation function
γ	output elasticity of R&D resources in innovation function
λ	switch parameter for product life cycle
v_t	random normally distributed error term

CHAPTER 5

$U_x(.)$	Partial derivative of the direct utility function with respect to x
$L_{H,L}^S$	High and low skilled labour available for employment
ω_{MIN}	ratio of minimum to high skilled wage
$V(.)$	value function for worker
ω	bargaining power of the worker
$\Pi(.)$	value function of the employer
$A_{H,L}$	outside option for the high and low skilled worker
$s(.)$	survival function
σ_{sw}	elasticity of the survival probability with respect to the wage
$B_{H,L}$	benefit level for high and low skilled
$U_{H,LO}$	acceptable or ineffective level of unemployment

$m_{H,LO}$	minimum mark-up of wages over unemployment benefits
$\rho_{H,L}$	replacement rate for high and low skilled defined as the ratio between an exponentially weighed reference wage and unemployment benefit levels
$\delta_{H,L}$	exponential weights in the reference wage for high and low skilled
$e_{H,L}$	effort level for high and low skilled
$e(.)$	effort function
$e_1(.)$	partial derivative of the effort function with respect to its first argument
N	stock of employed
U	stock of unemployed
P	population
o	share of employed that find a new job
s	share of employed that are separated from their job
r	share of employed that retires
m	share of unemployed that is matched to a job
d	share of unemployed that leaves the labour market discouraged
v	inactive population that enters the labour force through unemployment
e	inactive population that enters the labour force through employment
$M(.)$	matching function
$se_{U,V}$	search effort of unemployed (U) and employers (V)
$S_{H,L}$	separation rate in the high and low skilled sector

CHAPTER 6

$M(.)$	mark-up function
$U_{H,L}$	value of unemployment for high and low skilled
$w_{H,L}^{RES}$	reservation wage for high and low skilled
V_{it}	random normally distributed error term
$\varepsilon_{H,L}$	wage elasticity with respect to effective unemployment
UB	upper bound
LB	lower bound
$ltu_{H,L}$	share of long-term unemployment in unemployment for high and low skilled workers

CHAPTER 7

$G(.)$	government objective function
r^*	target return to education
U^*	target unemployment rate
T^*	target growth rate
$\eta_{1,2}$	exponential weights of targets 1 and 2 in the objective function
T	total consumption tax revenue
τ	consumption tax rate plus 1
T	total labour tax revenue
$t_{H,L,R}$	labour tax rate plus 1 for high and low skilled and research and development workers
t_0	level parameter in the tax function
t_1	progression parameter in the tax function
Σ	total expenditure on innovation subsidies
$\sigma_{H,L}$	subsidy rate plus 1 on innovations for high and low skilled sector
B	total cost of unemployment benefit scheme
D	deficit

PREFACE

In his 2002 book *The Rise of the Creative Class* Richard Florida welcomes the scientist, the engineer, the architect, designer, writer, artist and musician as members of a new and rising class. But what of those who are not members? What of the sales people and office clerks? What of the workers with low or no skills? With the rise of the creative class, the working class seems to have fallen on hard times. Rising unemployment and falling (relative) wages for the less skilled indicate that their labour market position has deteriorated markedly. But what is driving these processes of skill de- and revaluations over time?

That question motivated me to embark upon a project that resulted in the PhD thesis that underlies this book. As in so many PhD projects, the quest for an answer raised many new questions. But the initial ideas are still alive. As this book will argue, technical change is at the core and the good news is that it does not lie beyond our (policy makers) control.

To arrive at this conclusion I will present the various steps that make this hypothesis plausible. Starting from standard assumptions and simple models I gradually develop a model in which technological change causes cycles of high and low demand for skilled and unskilled labour respectively. In doing so this book should also allow the non-experts to develop a feeling for the modelling strategies and more importantly the underlying intuition. In addition the model itself allows one to make sense of the recent trends in developed countries' labour markets. As we take a closer look at the nature of technological change and the many interactions between labour markets, technology and policy variables, some rather unorthodox policy implications may even emerge.

Of course this book could not have been written without the encouragement of family and friends and the crucial inputs of Prof. Dr. Joan Muysken, Dr. Adriaan van Zon and many others who have, consciously or not, helped me develop the arguments below. I should also thank Prof. Dr. Harry Garretsen in particular for encouraging me to submit my thesis for publication and Edward Elgar Publishers and Prof. Dr. C. Freeman for accepting it in their catalogue and his series respectively. A final "thank you" is due to my employers, the Max Planck Institute in Jena, Germany and the Utrecht School of Economics, Utrecht, the Netherlands, for enabling me to prepare the manuscript, which is always more time-consuming than anticipated.

Mark Sanders, Utrecht/Jena, February, 2005

Chapter 1:

General Overview: Facts and Hypotheses

The position of low skilled workers on the labour market has deteriorated significantly over the past three decades. Their employment rate, and to a larger or lesser extent their wages dropped in OECD countries over the 80s and 90s. This has been a major concern to economists and politicians in all industrialised countries. Starting from the standard supply and demand framework, the deterioration cannot be explained by the observed supply movements as the relative supply of low skilled labour generally decreased. Hence demand must have shifted significantly. A major puzzle now presents itself: What has caused the apparent collapse in low skilled labour demand and what can explain the different labour market responses throughout the OECD? Solving that puzzle is a prerequisite for formulating policies to improve upon the present situation and prevent further deterioration in the future.

This book will address that puzzle. It first develops a theoretical framework that explains the shift in demand as well as the different ways this shift has manifested itself in the OECD. Then policy implications are considered. This introductory chapter provides the empirical background that inspires much of the theoretical work presented later on. An additional advantage is that such facts are very accessible. By combining facts and theory in an intuitive way this chapter can serve both as an introduction to and as an overview of the entire book. To serve this purpose best it is structured, as the main body of the book itself, in 3 parts.

Part I of the book develops a basic theoretical framework that yields two hypotheses to explain the drop in relative demand. Both attribute the relative demand shift to skill-biased technical change. The results are derived under the assumptions of an exogenously given inelastic labour supply and labour market-clearing wages. As in the OECD these assumptions are least violated in the US, and this chapter first presents the US facts and figures that are relevant in constructing and evaluating the hypotheses of Part I.

In Part II of the book the theoretical framework is extended by introducing unemployment. Unemployment is particularly relevant in European countries. Section 2 of this chapter therefore summarises facts and figures that relate to the European situation. In contrast to the US,

1

they experienced high levels of unemployment but also had more stable relative wages. It is only natural to assume that the two phenomena are linked and a trade-off exists. It will be argued below, however, that introducing unemployment is insufficient to explain the facts and some additional hypotheses, developed within the general theoretical framework, are formulated to explain the main EU-US differences.

Part III analyses both the implications of policy on and the policy implications of the resulting theoretical framework. Policies aimed at income redistribution, the labour market or innovation will interact in this framework. Moreover, different policy stances could help to explain the observed differences in labour market trends. To benchmark this part of the analysis, Section 3 will provide some facts on income, labour market and technology policies in Europe and the US.

The appendices to this book, that were not included in this edition, can be downloaded free of charge from www.marksanders.nl. These appendices provide background information that is not essential for understanding the main text.

1.1   TECHNICAL CHANGE AND THE DEMAND FOR LABOUR: THE CASE OF THE US

The United States have received the bulk of attention in both the empirical and theoretical literature on the deterioration of the low skilled labour market position. This focus is justified because developments in the US have been most pronounced and dramatic in the OECD. Despite continued increases in the average educational level of the American worker, low skilled wages decreased, in relative but even in absolute terms, as did their employment share (Card and DiNardo (2002)).

Figure 1.1 shows the ratio of high over low skilled labour supply, measured by fulltime equivalents in the labour force, and the ratio of their hourly wages. The graph shows that the relative supply of college-educated workers has increased. According to these data, the relative supply of high skilled grew at an average 4.4 percent annually in the 70s and fell to some 2.6 percent annually in the 80s. The graph indicates a further slowdown in the 90s to about 1.7 percent annually. On the right axis the college to high school wage ratio (males) is plotted. Starting in the 70s at about 1.4 it first shows a drop to about 1.3 followed by a steep rise from 1979 until 1987 with some stabilisation around 1.6 in the early 90s. Autor, Katz and Krueger (1998) studied an even longer period and concluded that relative demand and supply have gradually increased since the 40s.

Figure 1.1:   RELATIVE WAGES AND RELATIVE SUPPLY IN THE US
High over Low Skilled Labour, 1967-2000

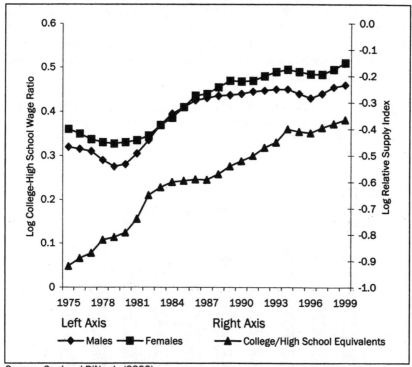

Source: Card and DiNardo (2002).

But supply accelerated in the 70s and while demand picked up in the mid 80s and continued to rise throughout the 80s, relative supply growth fell back to more moderate levels by the start of the 80s. This caused the strong relative wage responses illustrated above.

Beaudry and Green (2002) identified the underlying trends in the wage *levels*. For the entire period 1976-2000 they find a steady rise in the real wage level of the college educated. The movement in the relative wage is predominantly determined by a sharp drop in the real wages of (less than) high school educated over the early 80s, followed by a stabilisation over the 90s. The evidence thus suggests that the demand for low skilled workers has collapsed over this period.

The shift in relative demand poses a clear policy challenge since it severely eroded the standard of living for already vulnerable groups in the US. To meet that challenge it is crucial to understand what has caused the shift. A useful first step is to consider the evidence in more detail. Firms demand labour to fill jobs. Therefore a shift in aggregate demand can be the result of shifting from low to high skilled jobs in many firms, from low to high skilled firms in many industries, from low to high skilled industries in many sectors and finally from low to high skilled intensive sectors. It can therefore be considered a shift in the labour demand over skilled and unskilled activities.

Figure 1.2:   COMPOSITION OF THE UNITED STATES LABOUR FORCE[1]
Composition in 1983 (Bar); Growth Rate over 1983-1991 (Line)

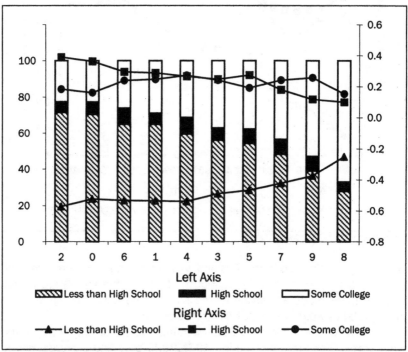

Source: CPS Monthly Outgoing Rotation Groups.

The exact level at which the shift has occurred provides a first indication of possible explanations. In Figure 1.2 the average change of low skilled labour intensity, measured by the wage bill share, over the 80s is presented for 10 sectors in the US economy. It can be verified that all sectors saw the wage bill share of low skilled decline but some more than others.[2]   A more detailed look at the numbers shows that large differences exist within these sectors as well. Obviously it is not convenient to present Figure 1.2 for more detailed industrial classifications. Shift-share analysis provides a more elegant way of separating between and within industry shifts in skill intensity.[3] In this procedure one simply decomposes the aggregate drop in low skilled labour intensity in a 'within-' and a 'between-sub-aggregates' (industries) component.[4]

Table 1.1 expresses these terms as a share of the aggregate shift for the US. It shows that about 80% of the shift in aggregate skill intensity is due to within industry shifts over the 80s.

Table 1.1:   DECOMPOSITION OF THE SHIFT IN EARNINGS SHARE
United States, 1983-1991

	<HIGH SCHOOL	>HIGH SCHOOL	COLLEGE
WITHIN	0.79827	1.05006	0.78797
BETWEEN	0.20173	-0.05006	0.21203

Source: CPS Monthly Outgoing Rotation Groups.

These numbers correspond reasonably well with those found in for example Autor, Katz and Krueger (1998). Dunne, Haltiwanger and Troske (1996) decompose at the establishment level and find lower within percentages.[5]

Having located the shift in demand as a general within-industries phenomenon even at the 3-digit level industry classification, one has eliminated any explanation that predicts that some sectors or industries are affected while others are not.[6] The cause of the aggregate demand shift apparently lies in firm characteristics that explain the *within* industry (*between* firm) variation. At the same time it is also clear that many firms must have been affected simultaneously across industries and sectors, to produce a significant aggregate shift.

An important trend in the US economy that started in the 70s, continued through the 80s and 90s and that affected firms in all sectors and industries, has been the introduction and rapid diffusion of information and communication technology (ICT).[7] Figure 1.3 illustrates that the penetration rates of the personal computer at work almost doubled for all skill groups in the US. Diffusion followed a traditional S-shaped pattern and was rapid in the mid 80s, levelling off in the early 90s for all skill groups.[8] It can also be observed in Figure 1.3 that high skilled workers clearly used the PC more intensively over the entire period.[9] Empirical research has shown that this positive correlation between the skill intensity of demand and computer use does not only exist over time at the aggregate level but also across sectors, industries and firms in panel and cross-section data.[10]

Figure 1.3:   THE DIFFUSION OF PERSONAL COMPUTERS
United States, 1984-1997

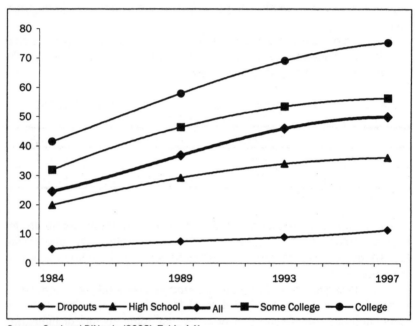

Source: Card and DiNardo (2002), Table 1.[11]

In addition, the literature shows that other proxies for the use or production of new goods and processes, in short innovation, are positively correlated to the skill intensity of production.[12] The observed correlation of skill intensity with such proxies for technical change at sectoral, industry and down to the firm and establishment level has led to the popular *Skill Biased Technical Change Hypothesis* (SBTC-hypothesis). This hypothesis claims that, due to the widespread introduction of skilled labour using technologies, the skill intensity of labour demand has increased at the firm or even job level. Many have found evidence that is consistent with this hypothesis and a consensus is forming on the pivotal role that new technology has played in causing the observed relative demand shift in the US.[13]

This consensus, however, is built upon indirect evidence that eliminates most alternative hypotheses that have been considered and raises a new and more fundamental question rather than providing the final answer. If technical change was biased over the 80s, one may wonder *why* it was biased. Understanding this will shed light on whether the resulting deterioration of the low skilled labour market position is a permanent or transitory phenomenon, whether or not policy responses are in order and if so, of what kind. The key is to determine to what extent the bias in technical change was the result of behaviour that can be manipulated, rather than beyond the reach of policy makers. To answer these questions, a closer look at the sources and dynamics of biases in technical change is required.

1.1.1 PERMANENT BIAS BY DESIGN

Economists have long realised that technical change is the work of man, and does not fall like *'manna from heaven'*.[14] Many if not most of the innovations that generate technical change today are conceived and developed by people in R&D facilities, universities and firms. The empirical evidence to support this claim is mounting and by now it is a generally accepted fact that technical change is the result of deliberate action by, to some extent, economically motivated agents.[15] These agents may be induced to develop one technology over another, which implies that biases in technical change are also the work of man. Very early on in the debate, John Hicks (1932) coined the term *'induced bias'* to refer to this idea. If innovations are biased against low skilled labour by design, than policy may try to affect agents' decisions to develop or abandon certain projects. However, explaining the observed bias as a deliberately designed feature of new technologies poses quite a challenge. In Hicks' conception, the observed drop in relative wages would, all else equal, induce a bias *towards* low skilled labour.

There are ways around this paradox but they require a very precise formulation. Acemoglu (1998, 2002a) has shown that a supply-shock, such as the accelerated increase in the supply of high skilled labour in the early 70s, can induce biases that cause relative low skilled wages to fall below the pre-supply-shock levels in the long run. The argument is that the increased availability of high skilled labour induced innovators to direct their efforts towards high skilled labour using innovation during the 80s.

A simple demand and supply schedule as in Figure 1.4 can illustrate the mechanism. The rightward shift in the vertical supply curve represents the increase in the relative supply of high skilled labour. Starting at point *A*, relative wages drop (*A-B*) for the high skilled in response to this shock. As technology responds, the demand schedule is shifted up, increasing relative wages (*B-C*). The insert on the right depicts the resulting change in relative wages over time. At this point it is important to note that, because Acemoglu assumed technical change to be skill-specific and irreversible, his conjecture yields induced biases in technical change that permanently shift demand away from low skilled workers.

Figure 1.4:   THE INDUCED INNOVATION HYPOTHESIS

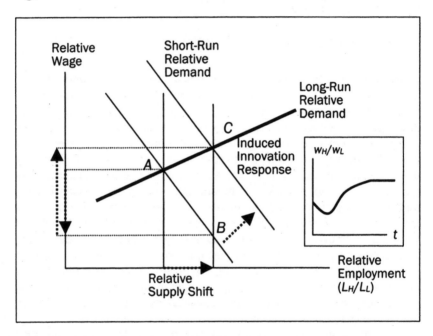

Further details follow in Chapters 3 and 4. Following Aghion (2001) this hypothesis will be referred to below as the *strong market size effect*, as the size of the market for high skilled complementary technologies induces this technological response.

1.1.2 TEMPORARY BIAS BY NATURE

A second explanation presented in Part I also goes back in the literature at least to Schumpeter (1934). It accepts the fact that technology is man-made but there are some relevant aspects in the *dynamics* of technical change that were not considered in the argument above.

Observe for example in Figure 1.3 that PCs are diffusing among low skilled workers as well. And even though they still lag behind, the ratio of high to low skilled penetration rates of computer use has been falling since the late 80s, indicating that the low skilled workers are catching up. The development and introduction of user-friendly interfaces has no doubt contributed a lot to this 'trickling down' of computer use and it seems that ICT-related products and services are becoming less skill intensive over time. This is not a unique feature of ICT. There is little historical evidence to support the claim that the skills-composition of the labour required to operate or produce a new technology is stable over time.

Indeed many case studies (e.g. Ehlen and Marshall (1996)) show that innovations do not 'freeze up' after invention or commercial introduction but continue to evolve, both shaping and adapting to their environment as they mature. In this case-study literature some common dynamic regularities emerged, which led economists to formulate the concept of a *product life cycle.*[16]

The existence of a product life cycle would imply that the use of new technologies is correlated with high skilled labour intensity not because the technologies are intentionally biased but merely because they are new. Bartel and Lichtenberg (1987) empirically validated this point that was first raised by Schultz (1975) and features prominently in all product life cycle models.

Audretsch (1987) showed that on average the skill intensity of labour demand moves from high to low as products age. Xiang (2002, p.1) recently found that: *'the average skilled-labor intensity of new goods exceeds that of old goods by over 40% and they account for about 30% of the rise in relative labour demand'.*

The product life cycle thus provides an interesting alternative explanation for the observed positive correlation between innovation indicators and skill intensity.[17] Not less so because it predicts that the shift in demand is temporary and can eventually be reversed. In Figure 1.5 the introduction of an innovation, biased or not, shifts the demand curve outward initially but back as innovations mature.[18] If a wave of innovations hits the economy, as arguably was the case when ICT was introduced economy wide in the 80s, then the aggregate effect is an initial outward shift that increases relative wages. As the wave matures, the initial shock is followed by a gradual return towards the initial position.[19] One could refer to this as the *life cycle explanation* for skill-biased technical change.[20]

A crucial point to be noted is the fact that relative wages increase more in the short than in the long run. As the new technologies mature, the initial natural skill bias is reversed.

Figure 1.5:   **THE PRODUCT LIFE CYCLE**

It can be argued that this maturing process is not entirely automatic and exogenous, but, like innovation itself, driven by innovative activity in R&D

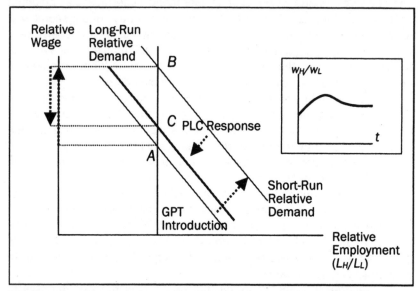

laboratories. Chapters 2 and 3 provide more details on how technology moves over the cycle. In Chapter 4 the implications for short term and steady state responses are analysed in a model that assumes a product life cycle exists.

1.1.3 CONCLUDING REMARKS

The two competing explanations offered above can easily be reconciled. The relative supply shock in the US may have induced innovators to focus on skilled labour using innovations, resulting in the ICT revolution of the 80s. The newness of the related products and services prevented these sectors from absorbing large numbers of low skilled workers and aggravated the already built-in skill bias.

Moreover, in that period traditional industries were shedding low skilled labour due to a severe recession and consequently the position of low skilled workers in the labour market deteriorated rapidly. Anderson (2001) presents evidence that over the mid and late 90s the wave of ICT-related innovations matures and the relative wage effects are partially reversed.

At this stage it should be noted that in particular the life cycle explanation has not been put forward in this debate as explicitly as it will be in Part I of this book. It will position the above arguments in the literature, extensively discuss the required modelling tools and develop a mathematical model that is analysed and simulated to refine the explanations offered above. The formal analysis will show that both the market size effect and life cycle dynamics exist under a variety of specifications and the model can be calibrated to reproduce the US stylised facts presented above.

1.2 TECHNICAL CHANGE AND THE LABOUR MARKET: THE CASE OF THE EU

The American relative wage changes are not representative for the entire OECD. In this section the focus is on formulating hypotheses to explain the differences. First consider the supply side. One can observe in Table 1.2 below that the increase in the share of skilled labour in the labour force was quite comparable in Europe and the US.

Table 1.2: RELATIVE LABOUR SUPPLY TRENDS IN THE OECD

COUNTRY	PERIOD	LOW (Secondary)	HIGH (Degree)	% P.A. CHANGE IN HIGH/LOW
FRANCE	1970	68.9	4.9	10.7
	1993	23.4	17.3	
GERMANY	1978	20.5	9.6	6.4
	1987	15.6	12.8	
UK	1973	55.7	16.4	8.6
	1991	28.2	36.8	
US	1970	37.5	15.7	7.5
	1991	14.5	28.2	

Source: Colecchia and Papaconstantinou (1996), Table 1.[21]

The numbers in Table 1.2 do not account for large differences in educational systems but more carefully designed studies using literacy scores also find that the rise in the relative availability of skilled labour is comparable, even when taking such differences into account.[22] In most European countries, however, relative supply has developed more gradually than in the US. The acceleration in the mid 70s in the US, attributed by Acemoglu (2002a) to the Vietnam draft laws, obviously did not occur in Europe. Sanders and ter Weel (2000) conclude that in contrast to developments in the United States and several other Anglo-Saxon countries, relative wages remained stable or even fell in many Continental European economies.[23] This wage stability in spite of comparable relative supply shifts can mean one of two things. European countries were not hit by the same demand shifting technology shocks that the US has experienced, or European labour markets responded differently to these shocks. Part I will argue that the former is perhaps too easily dismissed whereas others have argued that the latter is perhaps too easily adopted.

On the demand side, the downward trend in relative low skilled employment is also concentrated within detailed industries in Europe.[24] Moreover, the shifts in employment seemed to have occurred within the same industries throughout the OECD.[25] Globalisation and rapid international technology diffusion are therefore usually assumed to have shifted demand in both the US and Europe. In addition the latter hypothesis is supported by the obvious (negative) correlation of wage stability with a host of labour market flexibility indicators and, arguably as a consequence, unemployment levels. That hypothesis, which Mühlau and Horgan (2001) refer to as the *trade-off hypothesis*, is therefore by far the more popular one.[26]

1.2.1 THE TRADE-OFF HYPOTHESIS

The trade-off hypothesis basically claims that European low skilled workers paid for the relative wage stability with high unemployment. Simple cross-country regression of earnings inequality on a host of labour market flexibility indicators indeed suggests there is such a trade-off.[27]

An upward sloping relative supply curve can be the result of workers' trade-off between supplying labour and consuming leisure. Intuitively, as their relative wage rises, workers are more inclined to supply their labour, causing relative supply to rise at any given composition of the working age population. In this case unemployment is voluntary. Alternatively the upward sloping supply curve may be the result of collective wage bargaining and unemployment is involuntary.[28]

Note that in Figure 1.6 a quantity response (horizontal) reduces the necessary (vertical) relative wage adjustment. This quantity response is a change in relative employment given the relative stocks of skilled and unskilled labour, either due to changes in relative participation or unemployment rates. The slopes of both curves, given by the elasticity of relative demand and supply with respect to relative wages, determine how the burden of adjustment is shared between wage and quantity adjustments. Flat curves imply that any given demand shock generates large quantity and small wage movements. The trade-off hypothesis now relies on European curves, in particular the supply curve being flatter; i.e. more elastic than in the US. Inflexible labour market institutions in Europe are generally held responsible for this combination of low wage flexibility and persistently high unemployment levels.

Figure 1.6:   **THE TRADE-OFF HYPOTHESIS**

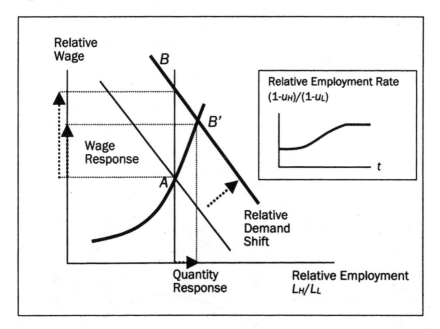

However, there is little evidence to support the claim that demand or supply elasticities differ a lot across countries. The elasticity of relative demand is largely determined by the elasticity of substitution between high and low skilled labour. Freeman (1986) and Hamermesh (1993) for example concluded that this elasticity probably lies between 1 and 2 in most of the countries in the empirical studies they survey. Freeman and Schettkat (2000) find 1.5 in a joint Germany-US dataset. That result is insignificantly different from estimates by Bound and Johnson (1992) and Katz and Murphy (1992) for the US at 1.7 and 1.4 respectively and by Beissinger and Möller (1998) for Germany at 1.8. Hence there is no empirical or theoretical reason why this elasticity should be assumed to differ a lot between advanced countries.

On the supply side the evidence shows a little more international variation. Still participation on the labour market has yielded estimated elasticities of supply between 0 and 1, with the bulk around 0.1.[29] For involuntary unemployment, most empirical studies, for example Blanchflower and Oswald (1990, 1994b), Card (1995), Blanchard (1998), find an elasticity of between -0.01 and -0.2.[30] Many of these studies control for educational level and conclude that the elasticity of wages with respect to unemployment is equal between skill groups and across countries.[31]

The evidence offered above is too weak to reject the popular and intuitively plausible trade-off hypothesis, but the case for rejection is much stronger when one considers that a key prediction also lacks support in the data.[32] That prediction, illustrated in the insert in Figure 1.6, is a rise in relative employment rates.

Figure 1.7:   RATIO OF LOW OVER HIGH SKILLED UNEMPLOYMENT RATES

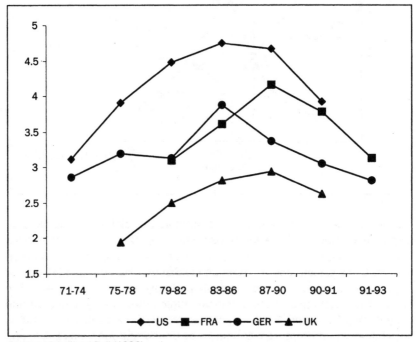

Source: Nickell and Bell (1996).

To explain wage stability in Europe while maintaining the hypothesis that a US size relative demand shock has occurred, implies that relative participation and/or the unemployment ratio must have risen faster in Europe than in the US.[33] The evidence on relative labour force participation excludes the possibility that Europe absorbed a US-size demand shock by voluntary unemployment.[34]

Figure 1.7 clearly illustrates that the unemployment ratio is lower in Europe and shows a remarkably similar pattern, moving up over the late 70s and early 80s and down again towards the 90s.[35]   Both contradict the predictions of the trade-off hypothesis and this pattern suggests that there is very little trade-off between *relative* wages and *relative* unemployment in adjusting to technological shocks. The implications of this obvious fact for the trade-off hypothesis have frequently been overlooked.

1.2.2 THE ADJUSTMENT AND LAGGED ADOPTION HYPOTHESES

Having dismissed the trade-off hypothesis there are few other explanations that would reconcile the data with a standard demand and supply framework.[36] One very straightforward one, however, is that Europe has experienced a more moderate relative demand shock. The evidence in Blanchard (1998), Howell and Hübler (2001) and Mühlau and Horgan (2001) suggests that there is some merit in this explanation. They conclude that while most of the OECD countries experienced comparable relative supply shifts, Anglo-Saxon countries, the US in particular, experienced a larger relative demand shift causing wage inequality to increase.[37]

A first explanation may lie in the more gradual relative supply increases in many European countries. As relative wages reflect the tension between technology driven relative demand shifts and education driven relative supply shifts, a less erratic relative supply increase may allow technology to keep up in the race, preventing large relative wage adjustments.[38] This hypothesis explains relative wage stability in the transition to a new equilibrium but is clearly at odds with the claim that technical change is a global process. The moderate demand shift hypothesis requires one to address why similar technologies affected relative demand in different countries differently or alternatively why some countries developed and adopted different technologies than others in spite of technology spillovers.

The latter could be labelled the *induced adoption hypothesis*, as it closely resembles the induced innovations hypothesis above. Acemoglu (2002b) argues that European employers demanded less skill-biased technologies as high and binding minimum wages for low skilled workers ensured they would reap the full benefits of productivity gains in those jobs.[39] The existence of a product life cycle, however, also implies that similar technologies may affect different countries differently. Europe clearly experienced an explosive diffusion of ICT technology in the 80s and 90s but lagged some years behind the US.[40]

Hence Europe did not choose to adopt or develop different technologies; they adopted the same technologies in a later stage of their life cycle. If new technologies mainly originate in the US and spill over with a lag, first to Anglo-Saxon and then to other OECD countries, then life cycle dynamics predict a pattern of decreasing biases towards skilled labour. One might label this the *lagged adoption hypothesis*. If it holds, the same life cycle dynamics that magnify induced skill bias in innovation in the US may moderate the transmission of such biases to Europe. For this hypothesis to be valid, it is necessary to show that the EU is lagging in developing new technologies and adopts them mainly from the US.

Figure 1.8:   GROSS EXPENDITURE ON RESEARCH AND DEVELOPMENT
in % of GDP, OECD 1981-1999

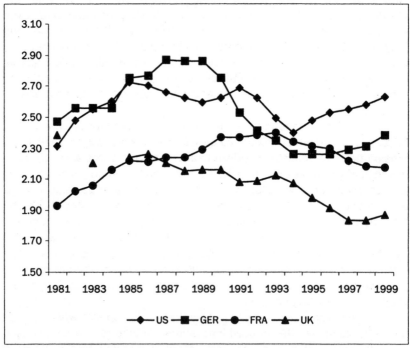

Source: OECD (2002a) Science and Technology Indicators, Appendix Table 4-40.

The data on R&D investments do not support this hypothesis at first sight. Figure 1.8 shows the gross expenditure on R&D as a percentage of GDP and the US is only slightly ahead of the Continental European countries.

The OECD (2002a) and European Commission, however, conclude that the EU is lagging behind the US in developing new technologies. Obviously a lot of relevant details are hidden in these aggregate numbers. In an elaborate empirical study on innovation and growth, Cameron (1998) presents several.

Table 1.3 for example illustrates that in the US, and to a lesser degree in the UK, business R&D labs are more active than their Continental competitors, at least well into the 80s. It gives the R&D intensities for manufacturing only. The main message from Table 1.3 is that there is a large share of government sponsored R&D in Germany and France, which is generally directed towards more basic and less applied R&D. In light of the lagged adoption hypothesis it is worth investigating whether government and basic R&D are typically increasing the countries' absorptive rather than their creative capacity.

Table 1.3:   **R&D INTENSITIES IN MANUFACTURING**

COUNTRY	PERIOD	BERD[41]
FRANCE	1973	3.4
	1981	4.3
	1990	6.5
GERMANY	1973	3.2
	1981	4.3
	1989	6.4
UK	1973	4.3
	1981	5.2
	1990	5.0
US	1973	6.3
	1981	6.0
	1989	7.2

Source: OECD STAN database, UK Census of Production, taken from Cameron (1998), p. 12, Table 5.

Also the sectoral composition of R&D expenditures is relevant. Business R&D in France and Germany was concentrated in mature industries such as chemicals and metal industry, whereas R&D in the US is much more concentrated in Computers and Electronics.[42] The UK takes an intermediate position. Table 1.3 would then suggest that, at least up to the mid-80s, Continental Europe was specialised in adopting (and adapting) rather than creating new technologies.[43]

On the R&D output side the lagged adoption hypothesis also receives strong support. The technology balance of payments in Table 1.4

strongly suggests that there is a net eastbound transatlantic technology transfer.[44]

Table 1.4:   TECHNOLOGY BALANCE OF PAYMENTS

COUNTRY	RECEIPTS in % of GDP		PAYMENTS In % of GDP		BALANCE in % of GDP	
	1990	1999	1990	1999	1990	1999
US	0.29	0.40	0.05	0.14	0.23	0.25
UK	0.21	0.43	0.28	0.22	-0.07	0.21
FRANCE	0.16	0.18	0.21	0.22	-0.05	-0.04
GERMANY	0.42	0.59	0.46	0.77	-0.04	-0.18
EU	0.30	0.52	0.39	0.64	-0.09	-0.13

Source: OECD TBP Database, May 2001.

The strong increase in payments in the US and the slight improvement of the receipts in the EU over the 90s indicate that the EU is, however, closing the gap as the ICT evolution matures. Again it is worth noting that the UK has closed that gap most successfully and has turned its deficit into surplus by the end of the 90s. Considering the evidence, however, it can also be argued that Europe has to maintain a considerable level of gross R&D investment to be able to adopt the flow of innovations from the US. If adoption, like innovation, is a costly activity, the adoption lag may be the result of rational waiting and can be linked to the fact that European firms would wish to adopt technologies that are less skill intensive. That behaviour would reconcile the induced adoption hypothesis of Acemoglu (2002b) with the above-proposed lagged adoption hypothesis.

1.2.3 CONCLUDING REMARKS

Based on the available evidence, this section has dismissed the trade-off hypothesis and formulated alternative explanations that built on the induced innovation and product life cycle hypotheses developed in Section 1.1. According to the lagged adoption hypothesis, European wage stability, much like US wage divergence, can be attributed to the dynamics and economics of technical change. The argument proposed here is that Europe experienced a more moderate relative demand shock because it selected less biased new US technologies and adopted them with a lag. This implies a more moderate demand shock and less relative wage pressure, even for given relative supply shifts.

Note that the trade-off hypothesis is rejected as an explanation for *relative* wage stability in Europe. The observed relation between wage and unemployment levels and labour market institutions is fully compatible with these hypotheses. The high levels of worker protection and institutional wage setting cause higher wage levels and unemployment rates for all skill groups in Europe. As such, however, they do not directly contribute to explaining relative wage trends, which leaves technical change as the prime suspect. Still institutional features could, through their impact on relative profitability, affect the decision what innovations to adopt at what stage of the cycle. An assessment of this potential feedback into technical change requires a more precise formulation of the labour market in the framework developed in Part I below. Part II of this book is dedicated to the introduction and analysis of the required extensions.

1.3 THE ROLE OF GOVERNMENT

The previous two sections made an attempt at explaining labour market trends in the OECD without explicitly addressing the role of government. In Section 1 it was argued that the US saw increasing wage inequality due to the rapid diffusion of a new general-purpose technology that was skill biased in response to the relative labour supply shock in the 70s. Section 2 argued that Europe managed to maintain stable relative wages, not by resisting wage pressure and accepting rising low skilled unemployment, but because relative demand increased more or less in line with supply. It did so in Europe because on the one hand biases spilling over from the US were moderated through induced-lagged adoption. On the other hand relative supply increased more gradually, possibly due to a more diligent educational policy, which limited the initial relative wage drop and following induced biases.[45]

The role of government in the economy, however, is not limited to managing relative supply through educational policies. It is part of the economy of a country much like consumers and producers are. In fact government expenditures account for as much as 50% of total GDP in the OECD area.[46] A large share of that percentage, especially in Europe, is spent on transfers through social security and subsidy schemes. Both the way in which these transfers are spent and the way in which they are financed can, intentionally or unintentionally, interfere in the transmission mechanisms sketched above. The government can affect the interaction between technology and the labour market by for example levying taxes, actively pursuing income policies, affecting labour market relations by providing unemployment benefits and social security or setting legal minimum wages, and finally by directly granting subsidies to R&D. As government policies in all these areas differ between the US and EU, a positive analysis of government interference may contribute to a more complete explanation for observed differences in labour market trends. Also, European and American administrators might have to pursue their goals differently when taking the interactions between the labour market, technology and their policy instruments into account.

Part III of this book addresses these issues. Before proceeding with that exercise, however, it is useful to benchmark the policies that will be evaluated there. Three sub-sections below present data on tax and income, labour market and science and technology policies on both sides of the Atlantic. The differences in these policies may on the one hand help explain different trends in European and US labour markets, whereas on the other it also sets the stage for evaluating policy proposals.

1.3.1   TAX AND INCOME POLICIES

The main thing that distinguishes the government from other agents in the economy is its power to tax people. As taxes are involuntary transfers of income, the ones bearing the tax will generally try to avoid taxation. Taxation thus alters behaviour. Economists usually assume that the government can levy neutral taxes. In that way all their policy proposals can be financed without distorting the efficient allocation of resources.[47] The bulk of government revenue, however, comes from highly distortionary taxes.

The pie charts in Figure 1.9 show that labour taxes, corporate taxes and consumption taxes are the key sources of revenue in both the US and EU.[48] Together they make up over 80% of total government revenue that on average amounts to some 35-40% of total GDP in the OECD.[49] These taxes drive a wedge between pre- and after tax prices, wages and returns and can therefore distort the allocation of production factors. Consumption taxes are least harmful in this respect. Although some consumption taxes are explicitly intended to affect consumer behaviour, the main purpose of these taxes is to raise revenue and a uniform rate is therefore often applied.[50] They reduce the after tax price a producer gets for his products. That reduces the overall demand for his products, but as all other producers face the same tax rates, there is no relative price effect.[51] Consequently, the return on all production factors involved is reduced in proportion to their contribution to the final product and relative factor prices also remain unaffected.

Figure 1.9: **THE COMPOSITION OF GOVERNMENT REVENUES**
Average (1979-1998) Shares in Total Government Revenues

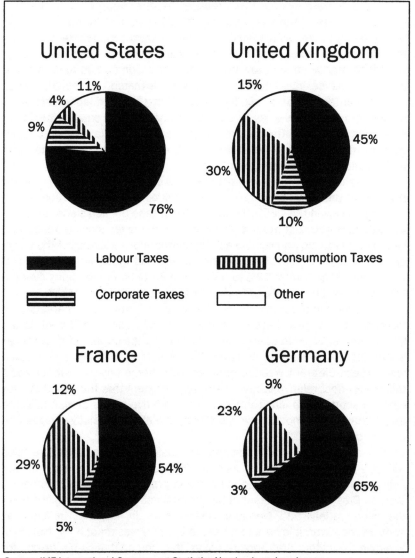

Source: IMF International Government Statistics Yearbook, various issues.

There are significant differences between the US and EU in this respect. In the US the consumption tax rates are about 5-7% whereas European countries typically charge a rate that is well above 15%, with Germany and the UK being in the lower ranks with 15% and France about average at around 20%.[52]

Corporate income taxes reduce the after tax profits (in the non-economic sense of the word, i.e. including the normal return on capital), which mainly increases the cost of capital and reduces the after tax return to investors. All else equal this reduces the supply of and demand for capital as producers shift towards other production factors and investors consume the savings they had otherwise invested. It has also been argued that the corporate tax discourages entrepreneurship, makes firms favour debt over equity as a source of finance and causes inefficient relocation of firms.[53] The distortions of the corporate tax are notoriously hard to measure but globalisation and tax competition cause the rates and revenues of corporate taxes to fall.

While corporate taxes still make up a significant share of total tax revenue in the US and UK (10%) it is a minor source of taxation that is eroding quickly in the OECD. Taxes on labour take the lion's share with on average over 50% of total tax revenue.[54] Personal income taxes and various other taxes and social security contributions paid out of the wage, drive a wedge between the take home pay and gross wage costs. This wedge rose slightly from 59% to 63% in the European Community over the 80s, whereas it has declined from 50% to about 38% in the US.[55]

Like corporate taxes the income tax distorts factor markets as it increases the relative price of labour. The key issue in this book is the labour market position of low skilled labour, so the impact of these taxes is particularly relevant as marginal tax wedges usually differ by income level. These different wedges between take home pay and labour costs therefore affect relative labour costs. To the extent that they do, they may cause a short- and a long-run response in relative labour demand. To the extent that they do not, the wedge affects the after tax relative wages and income distribution.[56]

Income taxes, in addition to raising revenue, therefore also reflect a country's stance on income distribution. A key indicator of the policy stance on income inequality is the progression in the income tax system. Progression implies that higher incomes pay more taxes.[57] Due to the wide variety and frequent adjustments in national income tax systems, however, it is hard to measure the progression of a tax system in a single indicator. Statutory rates in the personal income taxes, for example, typically show strong progression, particularly in Europe. Fixed ceilings in social security contributions, however, largely undo this progression.[58] The OECD (1995) provides a detailed international comparative analysis of trends in marginal and average tax rates at various levels of income. Table 1.5 gives an overview of the trends.

Table 1.5:   **TRENDS IN PROGRESSION**

COUNTRY	CHANGE IN MARGINAL TAX RATES in % points by income level (1978-1995)		
	66% of APW[59]	100% of APW	200% of APW
UNITED STATES	21.7	18.5	-4.6
GERMANY	-18.6	4.2	-5.4
FRANCE	10.9	1.1	3.0
UNITED KINGDOM	-4.5	-4.5	7.0
NETHERLANDS	8.9	-5.8	10.0
OECD AVERAGE	7.5	2.5	-0.1
OECD S.D.	0.7	4.8	4.7

Source: OECD (1998), Table IV.3, p. 161.

There is no clear pattern while changes are significant. Most countries reformed their tax systems quite dramatically over the 80s. In all countries these tax reforms aimed at broadening the tax base (eliminating tax deductions etc.) while improving incentives for people to work. Due to national political and legal circumstances, however, the reforms did not result in a strong universal trend towards increasing average rates while decreasing marginal ones. If anything it can be concluded that the reforms made most tax systems less progressive by increasing marginal rates for low income groups while cutting them in higher income brackets. No clear differences emerge when comparing Europe to the US.[60]

The progressiveness of a tax system can also be measured and compared by its results. If a tax system is very progressive, the after tax income distribution is flatter than the before tax income distribution. Figure 1.10 shows the percentage reduction in the Gini coefficient when comparing the pre- to post tax income distribution.[61] From these data it can be concluded that the EU on average had the more progressive income tax system.

The general trend in progression is up; the UK and US increased progression and converged on Germany and the Netherlands as they reduced it. Other European countries such as Italy and the Nordic countries, however, saw progression increase over time, widening the gap with the Anglo-Saxon countries. The regressive impact of tax reforms was apparently more than compensated for by the reduction in tax deductions and social security contributions. Overall Figure 1.10 shows that Europe had the more progressive tax system throughout the period under consideration.[62] Progression in itself will cause after tax relative wages to lie below before tax relative labour costs. If relative supply is inelastic, the taxes are fully borne by the employees and changes in the tax system will have no effect on relative profits.

Figure 1.10:   PROGRESSION OF THE TAX SYSTEM

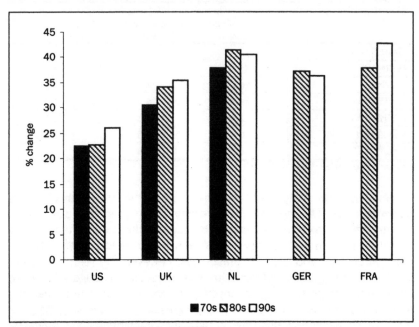

Source: Arjona, Ladaique and Pearson (2001).

Consequently one should not expect any impact on technical change and progression is the ideal tool for pursuing redistribution goals. If relative supply is anything less than perfectly inelastic, however, progression will cause quantity adjustments that affect relative profitability, causing a technology response. As progression makes high skilled labour artificially more expensive, the technology response will be to develop less skill intensive technologies.

Moreover, progression in the tax system will also limit the after tax relative wage shifts caused by the technical change it provoked. The increasing low skilled wage will be taxed at higher rates; the decreasing high skilled wage pays a lower one. Progression in the tax system therefore remains a powerful tool to stabilise and manage the after tax income distribution, especially if relative supply is quite inelastic. Given the absence of large relative quantity adjustments through unemployment and participation in Europe and the US, progression thus helps explain the observed different relative wage trends in Sections 1.1 and 1.2 above. Part III will address the impact of progression and income redistribution on the interaction between technical change and the labour market in further detail.

1.3.2 LABOUR MARKET POLICIES

In addition to tax and income policies, the government also plays a key role in the labour market. High levels of social security, worker protection and centralised bargaining structures all increase the bargaining power of the worker. It has often been argued that this caused high wage costs and high structural unemployment levels, particularly in Europe.[63] The OECD (1994a, 1994b) has analysed the labour market problems of the 80s in an elaborate study and formulated a comprehensive package of policy prescriptions in its *Jobs Strategy*. The core of that strategy has been summarised in Box 1.1 below.

Box 1.1:   **THE KEY POLICY RECOMMENDATIONS OF THE OECD JOBS STRATEGY**

---

1. Set macro-policies to make growth non-inflationary

2. Enhance creation and diffusion of new technology

3. Increase flexibility of working time

4. Nurture the entrepreneurial climate

5. Make wage and labour costs more flexible to reflect local conditions

6. Reform employment security provisions

7. Strengthen active labour market policies

8. Improve skills and competences through education and training

9. Reform unemployment and benefit systems to achieve equity in the most efficient way

10. Enhance product market competition

In particular points 2, enhancing creation and diffusion of new technology, and 9, the reform of social security schemes, show the relevance of the issues raised here. The former clearly establishes a link to science and technology policy discussed below whereas the latter links income distribution and labour market performance through benefits and the tax system. The system of social security benefits causes three labour market distortions.[64]

First benefits may cause a low employment trap by reducing the incentives to participate and search for jobs. This reduces the effectiveness of unemployed in competing for jobs and thereby increases wage pressure, particularly for low skilled jobs.

Second the benefit system may cause a poverty trap. As benefits are lost as income rises, the effective marginal tax rates are very high, again particularly at the lower end of the wage distribution. Increasing hours worked or investing in education or training therefore yield little additional disposable income, which reduces the upward mobility of workers and job competition from the bottom up.

Finally the costs of the system put a heavy burden on the budget. As that burden is largely financed out of labour taxes, the mechanism described above may reduce the general demand for labour and cause firms to substitute towards other factors of production.[65] As the hypotheses above link the labour market position of low skilled to technology through relative wages and employment, however, the most relevant aspect of the social security and unemployment benefit systems is their direct impact on the fallback position of skilled and unskilled workers, the insiders in the labour market.

Consider the unemployment and social benefit schemes in the US and Europe during the 80s. The level of benefits alone cannot measure the generosity of the benefit scheme. Entitlements, duration and the type of benefits received are clearly as important for evaluating the workers outside option. The OECD (1994b), Chart 8.1, provides a summary measure for benefit entitlements from 1961 to 1991 and for many countries in the OECD. This summary measure is an average of replacement rates at various earnings levels, family situations and unemployment durations. Subject to a host of qualifications the pattern that emerges is that Europe, and in particular Western Europe, had high levels in 1961 and increased its entitlements up to 1985. Southern European countries started out at much lower levels but generally caught up after joining the EU. The US on the other hand had low levels to begin with and after a moderate increase over the 70s cut back on benefit levels during the 80s, forcing in particular low skilled workers to accept wages that push them below the poverty line.[66]

The types of benefit systems are hard to quantify. The reader is referred to the case studies presented in OECD (1994b) for an excellent qualitative survey of social security systems. Summarising the main results presented there one might conclude that over the 80s both the US and the European systems have become stricter. Job search is obligatory and it is monitored more strictly. Eligibility has been made conditional on longer employment histories. Benefit levels are more directly related to previously made contributions, while they also tend to decline faster over time. As the *Jobs Strategy* still calls for further reforms in these directions, however, it seems that according to the OECD, those reforms were inadequate.[67] Overall it can be concluded that Europe had the more generous benefit system throughout the 70s and 80s and only started to seriously reform it in the mid 80s. The United Kingdom again finds itself in the middle between Europe and the US that ranks second in austerity after Japan.

The unemployment levels in Europe are closely correlated to the generosity of the benefit schemes and the OECD (1996) policy proposals suggest a causal relationship. The benefit system provides the outside option to those employed and also explains why real wage levels are generally higher in Europe. Moreover, relative wages seem correlated with the relative benefit levels.[68] Data for the 80s are hard to come by, but in a recent study on wages and benefits the OECD (2002b) presents benefit replacement rates at various levels of income. The ratio of the replacement rate in Europe over that in the US is 1.6 at low levels of income, but much higher ratios are found at higher income levels.[69] In the US benefits therefore seem less correlated with previous earnings than in Europe. Consequently the outside option for US high skilled workers is much lower relative to that of the low skilled than in Europe. This reduces upward relative wage pressure, which seems to contradict the observed high relative wages in the US.

Now consider the technology response. As replacement rates remain more stable over income levels in Europe, the outside option is high relative to their wage level for low and high skilled workers alike. In the US, on the other hand, that relative outside option is low but much lower for high than for low skilled. Thus high skilled labour will accept lower wages than they would otherwise have bargained for and innovation will be biased, causing relative demand to shift towards them. The US policies of reducing benefit entitlements and levels over the 80s may thus have contributed to a shift in relative labour demand, while maintaining high benefit entitlements for both skill groups in Europe has caused high general unemployment rates without seriously affecting relative wages or causing innovation biases.

1.3.3 SCIENCE AND TECHNOLOGY POLICIES

The above-proposed close linkages between technology and the labour market imply that science and technology policies interact with labour market and income policies. This link was also recognised in the OECD *Jobs Strategy* mentioned above. The OECD (1994a) concluded that technological change in general and product innovation in particular increases the demand for labour, despite the large structural changes that may be involved. Technologically advanced firms outperform the laggards in employment growth, the 'new' sectors accounted for a significant share of total employment growth. New technologies therefore did not seem to be biased against labour in general. Hence their policy advice under point 2 was to stimulate the innovation and adoption of new technologies. Policy makers and academics have almost universally accepted that advice and attention has shifted to how governments can support innovation rather than whether they should. In the light of the hypotheses put forward in Sections 1.1 and 1.2, however, the argument needs some refinement.

If technological change is biased towards high skilled labour, either by design or by nature, then stimulating innovation has equity and relative employment consequences, at least in the short and medium run. Increasing the rate of innovation increases the bias in relative labour demand, especially when it cuts the product life cycle short. If higher rates of innovation imply higher rates of obsolescence in existing mature products, low skilled workers compete for less and less jobs. Consequently the differences in science and technology policies may also contribute to explaining the labour market trends discussed above.

As science and technology policy is a relatively recent area of policy making, however, the detailed data required to evaluate this hypothesis are scarce and sometimes have not been collected during the 80s at all. Reliable and internationally comparable data for the 80s only exist on the expenditures on science and technology policy. The data on the effects of these policies are riddled with measurement problems and the tools for policy evaluation are still being developed.[70] But consider the evidence that is available.

It was already shown in Section 1.2 that European governments contribute a considerable amount to total R&D expenditure in their countries. These funds are mainly channelled through publicly financed research institutes and universities and aim at the generation of so-called basic knowledge. This basic knowledge is, hopefully and somewhere down the line, helpful in both product and process innovation. science and technology policy in Europe therefore arguably favoured both skill types equally. However, the policy stance has shifted. Increasing the share of business R&D is now the stated aim of many countries and regions, as that has been shown to spur innovation. Governments reduce their own R&D and channel funds to the private sector instead. In addition private sector funding of public research is on the rise. In 1981 some 2 and 3% of public research in higher education was funded by business in the EU and US respectively. In 2001 these numbers have doubled to over 6% and continue to rise.[71]

In the US the government's share in R&D was always smaller and the bulk of government funded R&D, especially during the Cold War, was spent on defence.[72] Tax exemptions and general R&D subsidies and outsourced defence R&D explain the high share of business R&D financed by government in the US.[73] The spillovers of military R&D to the civilian sector usually come in the shape of new products or services rather than basic knowledge. The Internet, for example, is a technology that spilled over from the military in the early 80s.[74]

In addition the propensity to patent and commercialise innovations is much higher at US universities and publicly funded research institutes. It is beyond the scope of this short survey to investigate whether these differences are institutionally, culturally or otherwise determined, but given that they exist, it is clear that publicly funded R&D yields much more commercialised innovation in the US than in the EU. If such innovations are new products and services clustered around a new, possibly skill biased general-purpose technology such as ICT, the science and technology policy in the US has contributed to the shift in relative labour demand. To the extent that science and technology policy has prepared and facilitated the adoption and maturation of those innovations, it has moderated the inbuilt and inherent product life cycle biases in Europe.

1.3.4 POLICY IMPLICATIONS AND CONCLUDING REMARKS

To evaluate if and how American and European administrators should adjust their policies in light of the interactions suggested above, one must first agree on their goals. If one agrees on the interaction of technology and the labour market and on the policy goals, then formulating policy is an almost mechanical exercise that boils down to choosing the most effective mix of instruments. Most of the debate in politics should therefore probably be spent on meeting these prerequisites. In this book, however, setting policy goals will not be addressed. In the final part it is merely assumed that the government aims to reduce income inequality, foster economic growth, reduce unemployment and has to balance its budget. Different governments give different priorities to each of them but in general all OECD governments care about all these issues. Given those priorities and under the assumption that technology and the labour market interact as has been hypothesised above, the normative analysis that concludes this book derives the policy implications. That analysis will verify what can be concluded on the basis of the above already.

If wage divergence is primarily innovation driven in the US, then both income policies and science and technology policy should be geared towards addressing that issue. More in general, since Tinbergen's (1975, p. 79) *race between education and technology* primarily determines the relative position of skilled and unskilled workers in the labour market, educational and science and technology policies should be additional policy instruments in managing the income distribution. As the strong market size effect of Section 1.1 claims that more education provokes more skill bias, however, one must be careful to argue for boosting education. In addition, as education has not been introduced in the analysis below, there are no clear-cut policy implications in that area. But if technology has won the race in the 80s, the US government should consider reducing the bias in innovation a bit. Given the product life cycle this implies stimulating adoption and maturation of existing technologies, rather than developing new ones. More European style science and technology policies could help to bring education (supply) and technology (demand) together.

In Europe on the other hand, the key challenge remains unemployment. But as the trade-off hypothesis is not supported in the facts and technology, not wage resistance, causes relative wage stability in Europe, policy makers do not face the dilemma that they are trying to avoid. The reforms of social benefit systems can be implemented to reduce overall wage costs and restore the demand for labour in general. The only pitfall that must be avoided in this operation is a shift in the relative wage bargaining position, as the resulting relative wage cost movements may provoke undesirable long-term technology responses.

European policy makers must also realise that current priorities in science and technology policy may have the equity implications they say they fear so much when social security reforms are discussed. The aims to strengthen the knowledge infrastructure and move towards a knowledge intensive economy require some rethinking as the equity implications have not been adequately assessed. It may well prove to be a blessing in disguise for European low skilled workers that these policies have failed to reach their objectives so far.

1.4 CONCLUSION: A GUIDE

This section concludes the overview of the issues in this book. This chapter presented the phenomena that require explanation and will be incorporated in a model below that aims to guide a policy response to labour market trends in the OECD. The remainder of this book will cover the three areas that require further analysis to do so.

To guide and evaluate an informed policy response one first needs a thorough understanding of the economy. The crucial relations to be understood are: The interaction between technical change and the relative demand for unskilled labour. The impact of wage setting arrangements in the labour market, that govern the link between supply, unemployment, wages and demand. And finally the impact of various policies on the entire system of economic interactions. These areas correspond to the three parts in this book.

Part I of this book will address the interaction between technical change and the demand for labour, assuming supply equals total availability and labour markets clear. Relative wages then only reflect changes in relative demand. The American situation as described in Section 1.1 is the empirical touchstone for the model in this part since its labour market institutions are generally assumed to least interfere with this market clearing process.

Part II builds European style labour market institutions into the theoretical framework to analyse their impact on technical change as well as the wage and employment consequences for the low skilled. The aim is to reproduce the observed trends in European countries and explain why European low skilled workers were not hurt by skill biased technical change, even though at first sight similar technologies have been introduced in Europe.

The models presented in Part I and II imply that income, technology and labour market policy become interrelated and may strengthen or weaken each other. Part III is therefore devoted to identifying the inconsistencies and complementarities and to the formulation of some policy proposals in these areas. This part introduces the idea that policy areas are likely to be linked and goals can be conflicting. If this part provides insufficient arguments to cause politicians to revise, than at least they should reconsider their technology, labour market and income policies upon reading it.

NOTES

[1] Sector classification is Standard Industry Classification (SIC) first digit: 0 agriculture and fisheries, 1 mining and construction, 2 primary industry, 3 advanced industry, 4 transportation and energy, 5 retail, wholesale trade, 6 financial services, 7 recreational and business services, 8 health, education and cultural services, 9 public administration.

[2] Note for example that the share of low skilled dropped fastest in business services (7) and advanced manufacturing (3). The share of high skilled, on the other hand, rose fastest in the mining and construction industry (1), followed by transport (4) and advanced manufacturing (3).

[3] See for example Berman, Bound and Griliches (1994), Machin (1995), Autor, Katz and Krueger (1998) and Machin and Van Reenen (1998).

[4] Shift-share analysis computes:

$$dsh_{u} = \sum_j dsa_j \bar{sh}_{uj} + \sum_j \bar{sa}_j dsh_{uj}$$

where d means a change over period t, sh_{ujt} is the share of unskilled in the wage bill of sub-aggregate j at time t and sa_{jt} is the share of sub-aggregate j in the aggregate wage bill. A bar over the variable indicates the average over the period considered. The first term on the right hand side can be interpreted as the shifts caused by *between* industry shifts in the wage bill, whereas the latter term captures the shifts *within* the industry. Those shifts in their turn can be decomposed in either between firms or within firm shifts. See Sanders and ter Weel (2000) for a survey of the evidence.

[5] This is partly due to entry and exit from the sample but also indicates that much of the aggregate shifts is due to between firm or establishment shifts within narrowly defined industries.

[6] This for example eliminates the so-called trade hypothesis. That hypothesis claims that increased trade with low skilled intensive non-OECD countries may have caused the American economy to shift from low skilled import competing industries to high skilled export oriented industries over the 80s. As the evidence shows little support for that hypothesis it is now generally accepted that increased trade has played a small contributing role at best. See also Hellier and Chusseau (2002) for a recent survey of the controversy.

[7] See for example Greenstein (1994)

[8] Reliable data on the use of computers on the job exist only since 1984 (introduction of the PC) so the full S-shape is not visible in the data. The drop in the diffusion speed in the early 90s and the fact that in 1970 the use of computers was negligible implies that the S-shape must describe the diffusion pattern.

[9] Low skilled workers do catch up since the late 80s.

[10] See for example Bound and Johnson (1992), Levy and Murnane (1992), Katz and Murphy (1992), Juhn, Murphy and Pierce (1993), Krueger (1993) and Katz (2002).

[11] A third order polynomial was fitted to connect data points.

[12] Surveys of empirical literature, for example Johnson (1997), Machin and Van Reenen (1998), Berman and Machin (2000) and Sanders and ter Weel (2000) consistently draw such conclusions.

[13] See Sanders and ter Weel (2000) and Card and DiNardo (2002) for a critical review of the evidence.

[14] This was how Joan Robinson expressed her critique on the neo-classical theory of growth that assumed technical change progressed at an exogenously given rate (see Kenney (2003)). Economists have always realised that technology was man-made but they were very late to incorporate this obvious fact in mainstream theory. See Chapter 2 and for example Jones (1975) for an elaborate survey of the early growth literature.

[15] See for example Romer (1990) and more recently Cameron (1998) and Temple (1999).

[16] Dean (1950), Hirsch (1965), Levitt (1965), Vernon (1966) and Cox (1967), among others. Chapter 2 will elaborate on the life cycle concept.

17 A recent example of linking the product life cycle to skill biases in technical change is Mendez (2001).

18 The maturation of an innovation is in itself a mixed process of unintended knowledge accumulation through for example learning by doing and the intentional efforts to improve the product and underlying production process. Chapter 2 provides more details.

19 Not necessarily all the way back to the original position though. Chapter 4 provides the argument in more detail.

20 This life cycle explanation is very close to what Aghion (2001) refers to as the *major technical change explanation.*

21 Sample periods and age groups differ between countries due to data availability constraints. The original table contained eight additional OECD countries. No large deviations from the general trend were recorded there.

22 See for example Mühlau and Horgan (2001).

23 France and Germany experienced relative wage compression over the 80s. In the Netherlands, Denmark, Italy and Scandinavia relative wages remained stable whereas Belgium, Portugal, Spain and Austria had some divergence. Only the United Kingdom and Ireland witnessed relative wage shifts comparable to those in the US. As Australia, New Zealand and Canada also experienced some divergence the literature distinguishes the Anglo-Saxon and Continental European countries. See Card, Kramarz and Lemieux (1996), OECD (1996), Berman, Bound and Machin (1998), Machin and Van Reenen (1998) and Freeman and Schettkat (2000).

24 See Colecchia and Papaconstantinou (1996) Table 3, for example, for a decomposition of employment shifts in 7 OECD (Australia, Canada, France, Italy, Japan, New Zealand and the United States) countries. None of the computed within industry components falls below 85% in manufacturing. It is worth noting, however, that including services and the public sector reduces the within component considerably for France and Italy (to 58 and 38 percent respectively), and not for the Anglo-Saxon countries and Japan. As these are the only representatives of mainland Europe in the sample this might be a first indication of more moderate demand shifts in Continental European Countries.

25 See Machin and Van Reenen (1998) and Colecchia and Papaconstantinou (1996).

26 This hypothesis is also referred to as the Unified Theory (Blank (1997, p. 14)), the Transatlantic Consensus (Atkinson (1999)) or the Krugman Hypothesis (Acemoglu 2002b, p.60), as it was first formulated in 1994 by Paul Krugman (1994, 1995). The term trade-off hypothesis is used here as it best catches the essence of the argument.

27 See Howell and Hübler (2001), Table 1.

28 Here the causality runs the other way. In the bargain higher unemployment rates depress wage claims. For a given relative supply of workers a higher relative unemployment rate reduces relative wages. Lower relative employment rates thus lower effective supply at lower relative wages. See Chapter 5 for further details.

29 See Blundell and MaCurdy (1999) for a survey.

30 As voluntary unemployment is the complement of participation a minus sign appears.

31 These elasticities are usually obtained by regressing the wage level on a regional unemployment rate in a labour force survey. The variation in the regional unemployment rates is used to estimate the sensitivity of wages to unemployment. Note that the wage is now the dependent variable, so the causality is assumed to run the other way. These results suggest that employment (one minus the unemployment rate) is more sensitive to changes in the wage level than participation. Chapter 5 provides a more elaborate survey of the evidence.

32 See Nickell and Bell (1995), Blank (1997), Howell, Duncan and Harrison (1998), Atkinson (1999), Galbraith, Conceicao and Ferreira (1999), Howell and Hübler (2001), Howell (2002) and Mühlau and Horgan (2001).

33 The unemployment ratio is defined as the ratio of low over high skilled unemployment rates.

[34] The composition of the labour force closely followed that of the working age population as relative participation rates dropped in the US and EU. The OECD (1994a) Table 1.4 shows that the participation ratio rose faster in France than the US for the period 70-90 but by far less in Germany and the UK over the period 80-90. In addition all changes in the ratio are less than 1% per year. Generally speaking participation is around 90% in all countries except France, which is probably also due to statistical definition issues.

[35] In levels Europe overtook the US in the early 80s. In the early 70s levels were about one half of those in the US. By the mid 90s European levels are considerably higher for both skill groups.

[36] A popular hypothesis, put forward by Nickell and Bell (1996), argued that the actual (as opposed to the measured) skill distribution in Western Europe was much more compressed than in the US, in particular below the median. This implies that low skilled in Europe are not that low skilled and can perhaps adjust to new technology with training while in the US unskilled are actually fired, driving down wages in their labour market segment. Although comparisons of literacy and formal education levels clearly support this hypothesis, Howell and Hübler (2001) conclude that the impact is too limited to explain much of the differences. In addition such differences should also have shown up in the estimated elasticities of substitution.

[37] They conclude that, despite higher rates of job creation for both skill levels, the number of low skilled jobs per worker dropped much faster in the Anglo-Saxon countries than in Europe relative to high skilled jobs per worker.

[38] Tinbergen (1975, p.79) first referred to *the race between education and technology* as the driving force behind the distribution of income among skill groups.

[39] As low skilled workers earn a fixed minimum wage all productivity gains reduce unit production costs and increase profits. For high skilled an increase in productivity is partially or entirely lost on wage increases as wages are renegotiated or competition over high skilled workers increases. Obviously this mechanism can only work if employers retain unskilled workers when they have to pay a wage above their marginal productivity. Employment is not on the labour demand curve.

[40] In 1999 the share of high skilled ICT workers in the EU were on average 1.6% against 2.4% in the United States, see OECD (2002a). Mobile phone and Internet penetration also shows Germany and France clearly lag the UK and US by about 4-5 years (although Scandinavian countries clearly lead the mobile phone ranking). See OECD (2003a), Appendix Tables 8-3 and 8-4.

[41] BERD is business R&D expenditure over value added in %.

[42] See Cameron (1998) for a full sectoral breakdown in his Table 5.

[43] Arguably basic knowledge, developed in European Institutes and Universities, has been essential for US business R&D to be successful. Creative thus refers to commercial, not scientific creativity.

[44] The technology balance of payments includes payments for the transfer of techniques (patents, licences etc.), designs (licensing and franchise), services with technical content and industrial R&D.

[45] To keep the focus on the labour market, the issue of education will be left unexplored in this book, which is not to say it is unimportant. The analysis below suggests that educational policy, rather than for example labour market or income policy is a crucial tool in managing inequality in the long run. Introducing education in the analysis is therefore high on the agenda for further research.

[46] See OECD (1998).

[47] Another more sophisticated way of avoiding the financial consequences of policy advice is to argue for taxes instead of subsidies or budget neutral adjustments to the existing tax and subsidy schemes.

[48] Labour taxes include social security contributions by both employees and employers.

[49] See OECD (1995). The US ranks low in tax revenue over GDP at around 30%. The Netherlands, Germany and France all rank high with percentages over 37%. Over the 1978-

1992 period only France (5% points) increased its tax revenue by more than the OECD average increase of 4.3 point. The US had a moderate increase by 0.5 percentage point. Germany, the Netherlands and the UK all increased below average with 1.7, 3.3 and 2.2 percentage points respectively.

[50] Examples of the former are environmental taxes and excise taxes on tobacco and alcohol. If successful such behaviour altering taxes do not yield high revenues as the tax base is eroded.

[51] See for example Moore (1995) for a proposal to replace all taxes by a sales tax in the US. He presents various examples of distortions such a reform would eliminate.

[52] This difference in tax rates explains the fact that in Europe between 20 and 30% of all tax revenue is raised through consumption taxes while in the US it accounts for a mere 4% of the total budget and also goes a long way in explaining the differences in overall tax pressure.

[53] See Norton (2003), Hines (2001), Congressional Budget Office (1996) and Cronin (1999).

[54] Only in the UK did this share drop to a little over 40% during the 80s.

[55] 1978-1991, see OECD (1994b) Table 9.1. These rates are overall marginal tax wedges, including consumption taxes. Table 9.3 in the same publication shows that consumption tax rates remained stable in the US while in the EC rates converged to a slightly rising average. This implies that the tax wedge for personal income taxes and social security contributions fell by over 10% in the US. In the EC it has remained stable or even rose.

[56] With perfectly inelastic relative labour supply the wedge only affects after tax wages. As workers will accept any wage the full burden of the tax is borne by the worker. To the extent that supply is reduced with higher taxes, employers share in the burden as total output and therefore profits fall.

[57] Not only because they pay taxes over a larger tax base, their income, but also because they pay a higher rate.

[58] See OECD (1995).

[59] APW=Average Production Workers Wage.

[60] Apart from the fact that in the US the overall tax burden and therefore tax rates at all income levels are significantly lower than in Europe. This difference has widened slightly over the 80s, as the US kept its tax burden stable while in Europe it rose in most countries. See OECD (1995).

[61] See for example Arjona, Ladaique and Pearson (2001). For a clear explanation of the Gini-coefficient any standard economics textbook will do. See for example Todaro (1997, p. 143).

[62] The UK is more in the European camp when tax progression is considered. By the same token Germany, Italy and France might be classified Anglo-Saxon when their position relative to the UK is considered.

[63] See OECD (2001). Structural unemployment stood at 6.8% in the OECD in 1990. While the US outperformed the average by 1%, in Europe rates lie consistently higher with 9.3 % for France, 6.9% for Germany, 7% for the Netherlands and 8.5% for the UK.

[64] See OECD (1996).

[65] Both substitution and biased innovation may cause a drop in the general demand for labour.

[66] Of course that depends on where that poverty line is drawn. Working two jobs, 70 hours for a little over 400 dollars to support a family of 3, which is no exception among single mothers in the US, puts one below that line by any definition.

[67] See OECD (1996).

[68] See OECD (1994a) and Mühlau and Horgan (2001).

[69] Obviously at higher income levels the replacement rates are lower. Data in OECD (2002b) are presented for incomes up to 200% of the average production worker.

[70] The OECD hosted a conference on this topic in June of 1997.

[71] See Sheenan (2002).

[72] The US government accounted for 50% of total R&D expenditure and spent 1.2% of total GDP on R&D in the early 80s. This percentage rose with business R&D to about 1.4% in

1986 and was then reduced to 1.1 while business R&D continued to grow to 1.6%. In Europe government R&D was about 0.8% of GDP for the entire decade while business R&D rose from 0.8 to 1.0% by 1986 and stayed there well into the 90s. Civil R&D rose from 1.8 in 1981 to 2% of GDP in 1985 and stayed there in the US, implying military R&D rose from 0.6 to 0.8% of GDP. As a share of total R&D it thus increased over the early but fell over the late 80s. See OECD (2000).

[73] The data indicate some 50% up until the mid 80s, then falling quickly to 25% in 1990 and less than 10% in 1999. In Europe the corresponding numbers are 25% in 1981 and falling gradually to 20% in 1985, 15% in 1990 and 10% in 1999.

[74] See Internet Society (2001).

PART I
TECHNICAL CHANGE AND LABOUR DEMAND

I n this part the interaction of technical change and labour demand will be addressed. The American situation as described in Section 1.1 is the empirical touchstone for the model in this part, since its labour market institutions are generally assumed to least interfere with the market clearing process. This assumption will be relaxed in Part II of this book.

Chapter 2 introduces definitions and terminology and positions this thesis in the literature. Those familiar with the economics of technical change are advised to browse it for it merely sets the stage. However, sections 2.1.5 and 2.1.7 could still be of interest as they formally introduce the concept of biased technical change and discuss the product life cycle, respectively. Chapter 3 then presents several key models from the literature. The focus here is on general modelling techniques and the basic structure of endogenous innovation driven growth models. Chapter 4 presents a general model that allows one to illustrate both the induced bias and the product life cycle mechanism in a unified framework. To study the long-run properties and transitional dynamics of this model, the chapter also contains an analysis of the comparative statics in the steady state and some numerical simulation experiments.

The contribution of this part lies in bringing together several related but to date largely isolated strands of literature and formulating hypotheses to explain the apparently persistent skill biases in US technical change. It combines and reinterprets existing models and proposes a new model that explains skill biased technical change.

CHAPTER 2

THE ECONOMICS OF TECHNICAL CHANGE

Economists have always been ambivalent in their attitude towards technical change. On the one hand it is credited for the historically high and apparently sustainable rates of economic growth one observes in large parts of the world over the past few centuries. But on the other technical change is also blamed for important structural shifts in the economy that caused dramatic changes in the income distribution, both between and within countries.

Technical change, however, is a complex process, that comes in a multitude of forms and has important social, historical, scientific and technical dimensions. Economists therefore tended to avoid the issue and it has long been sidestepped in mainstream economics. Recently it is gaining its due attention, but technical change has always been discussed in the periphery.

To address the issues that are raised in this book it is useful to summarise the concepts that have been developed in the literature and allow one to start thinking about technical change in the economic sense of the term. In doing so this chapter firmly embeds the analysis in the literature and traces its intellectual roots. The aim is to reconstruct how economists have reduced the complexities of reality to a set of highly stylised and abstract concepts that have been used in mathematical models such as the ones developed in Chapters 3 and 4.

In discussing the interaction between technology and economy there are two directions of causality that guide this survey of the literature. This chapter first presents the concepts developed to describe the impact of technological change on the economy. Then it traces the concepts necessary to analyse the economics of technical change.

2.1 THE ECONOMIC IMPLICATIONS OF TECHNICAL CHANGE

In this section the aim is to introduce the conceptual framework that has been developed in the literature to analyse the impact of technical change on the economy in general and the aggregate relative demand for skilled labour in particular.

It starts with formulating a workable definition of technology. Based on some widely accepted definitions one may conclude that the driving factor in technical change is the introduction of innovations to the process of production and consumption. Each innovation is by definition unique but to avoid being limited to case studies, some generalisations have to be made. This section brings them together in a simple taxonomy of technical change, introducing a formal representation of technical change in the process.

Then it turns to the impact that innovations might have on the aggregate relative demand for skilled labour. A crucial characteristic in this respect, identified in Chapter 1, is the direction or factor bias of an innovation. If individual innovations are systematically biased towards skilled workers it is obvious that over time labour demand shifts towards more skilled workers in the aggregate. It has also been argued in Chapter 1, however, that the bias of an innovation is likely to change over its life cycle irrespective of its exact individual characteristics. The changes in the aggregate distribution of technologies over their life cycles then provide a second source of aggregate shifts in relative labour demand. This source has received relatively little attention in the literature so far and by taking it into consideration this book introduces it to the theoretical literature on skill-biased technical change.

2.1.1 DEFINING TECHNOLOGY

Definitions of technology in the economic literature are plenty. Schmookler (1966, p. 1) for example defined it as: *the social pool of knowledge of the industrial arts*. Technological progress is then the expansion of this knowledge over time. The expansion of this knowledge base implies as Jones (1975) put it, that more, better and entirely new products can be produced using the same inputs.

Jones' definition seems to adequately capture the consensus among economists that technological change is defined as the result of increments in knowledge, new ideas that are referred to as *inventions*. They allow one to produce the same output using less inputs, more output using the same inputs or a different kind of output altogether through quality improvements or the introduction of entirely new products and processes. For technological change to have an impact on the economy and on labour demand in particular, inventions have to be introduced into the economic system.[1] The commercial introduction of inventions as new products and services or the adoption of new technologies in the main production processes of a firm is referred to as an *innovation*.

At this point the invention becomes relevant to economists and this concept is therefore central to the economics of technical change.[2] As was also clear in the above definition, the literature frequently distinguishes *product* and *process* innovations. Those innovations that allow one to produce more output from a given amount of resources are process innovations; those that allow one to produce a different kind or quality of output are product innovations. Of course this distinction is problematic in classifying actual innovations. As Rosenberg (1982, p.4) observes: *One producer's process innovations are another one's product innovations.* In addition many innovations can be regarded as hybrids.[3] Still this crude taxonomy will prove useful in discussing technical change in later chapters and process and product innovations are discussed in separate sub-sections below.

2.1.2 PROCESS INNOVATIONS

All products are produced using inputs and a process that turns inputs into output. That process can be represented by a *production function*:[4]

$$y_{it} = f_i(\{x_{i0t}, x_{i1t}, ..., x_{imt}\}, t) \tag{2.1}$$

where y_{it}, a number of units of output of type i at time t, can be produced using a set of m inputs indexed by j, x_{ijt}. The knowledge that is relevant for producing product i is described by the function f_i, which is written as a function of time itself to allow for new ideas, *process innovations*, to change the process over time. Usually $f_i'(.)>0$ is assumed in all arguments, including time, to exclude the possibility of technical regress -one can always stick to the old process.

This definition allows one to measure the rate of process innovations at the firm level as the percentage increase in output for a given set of inputs over a given period of time. Since most final output has a market price one can calculate the aggregate rate of process innovation as the rate at which the constant price weighted basket or volume of total output expands keeping the aggregate inputs constant.[5] Using such a measure, generally referred to as Total Factor Productivity (TFP), Solow (1957) estimated that about 90% of the real GDP per worker increase in the US between 1909 and 1914 was due to process innovations; the famous Solow Residual. Table 2.1, taken from Grossman and Helpman (1991b), illustrates that similar high percentages can be found for other industrialised countries and in other periods.

Table 2.1:   TOTAL FACTOR PRODUCTIVITY SHARE IN GDP GROWTH

COUNTRY	1950-73			1973-84		
	GDP Growth	TFP	ATFP	GDP Growth	TFP	ATFP
FRANCE	5.1	78	60	2.2	84	42
GERMANY	5.9	73	61	1.7	92	67
JAPAN	9.4	62	50	3.8	32	11
NETHERLANDS	4.7	71	50	1.6	51	9
UNITED KINGDOM	3.0	71	50	1.1	115	60
UNITES STATES	3.7	50	28	2.3	22	-12

Source: Grossman and Helpman (1991b) computations based on Maddison (1987), Tables 11 and 20.[6]

This residual begged for explanation. As Abramowitz (1956, p. 11) rightfully observed it was *a measure of our ignorance*. Explaining these total factor productivity increases became a core issue in the economics of growth. A survey of that literature, however, is postponed to Section 2.2.

2.1.3 PRODUCT INNOVATIONS

Total factor productivity provides a useful measure of the importance of process innovations. It is a little harder to find a similar measure for product innovations. Product innovations do not affect the existing production functions, yet it is clear that the introduction of new and better products increases consumers' appreciation of consuming total output.

To measure the impact of product innovations one therefore needs the formal representation of consumers' appreciation of consumption, the *utility function*.[7] A measure for product innovations that is conceptually very similar to TFP can then be derived. The utility function specifies how much utility or enjoyment a consumer can produce from a given bundle of inputs, the consumed products. Assume there is a representative consumer whose utility function is given by:

$$u(\{c_{0t}, c_{1t}, ..., c_{nt}\}, t) \tag{2.2}$$

The utility function $u(.)$ specifies how much utility is enjoyed when a bundle $\{c_{0t}, c_{1t},..., c_{nt}\}$ of n different goods is consumed at time t. Generally it is assumed that the goods consumed are normal, in the sense that consuming more of at least one of them increases utility so $u'(.) > 0$ in all elements of the consumption bundle. Analogous to the production function, the utility function captures the knowledge necessary to enjoy the consumption goods.

Time, t, is again a separate argument to allow for product innovations to increase utility without increasing consumed quantities. When new or better products are introduced this improves the consumption technology and the consumer can choose from a wider variety of goods of better quality. The utility function of a representative individual now provides a standard for weighing new, old and improved products against each other.[8] The impact of product innovation can be measured by the percentage increase in utility given the consumption set.[9]

2.1.4 THE RATE OF AGGREGATE TECHNICAL CHANGE

One can consolidate the economy and define a measure of the aggregate rate of technical change.[10] By substituting output for consumption in (2.2) and substituting the production functions in (2.1) for output one can write:

$$U = u(\{f_0(\{x_{00t}, x_{01t}, ..., x_{0mt}\}, t), ..., f_n(\{x_{n0t}, x_{n1t}, ..., x_{nmt}\}, t)\}, t) \quad (2.3)$$

where x_{ijt} is the amount of factor j used to produce product i at time t.[11] By weighing process and product innovations by their contribution to utility, one can define the rate of technical change in the proper economic sense. The increase in utility due to increases in knowledge given the input bundle. By this new definition, all growth in utility that is not due to growth in the amount of resources used to generate the output that generates utility is due to technical change.[12]

Of course this conceptualisation is of little help to empirical growth accounting since aggregate utility is as hard to measure empirically as the changes in the stock of knowledge that constitute aggregate technical change.[13] But unlike knowledge, utility is homogenous and as such it is used as a measure for the rate of technical change in the theoretical models below. The change in utility due to innovation measures the combined effect of individual innovation size and aggregate innovation speed. To know where the economy is heading at that speed a measure of direction is also required. The next section will develop the necessary formal arguments that allow one to establish the inputs that new technology requires or favours.

2.1.5 THE DIRECTION OF TECHNICAL CHANGE

For the purpose of this book it is useful to classify individual innovations and the resulting aggregate technical change according to the direction in which they change factor demand in general and labour demand in particular. The introduction of the robot-arm, for example, reduced the demand for manual labour and increased that for technicians. The conveyer belt on the other hand enabled low skilled intensive mass production to replace the skilled artisan production on demand. A concept that allows one to measure the direction for individual innovations but also for technical change at the aggregate level is *factor bias*. An individual innovation can be biased towards one input or another, increasing or decreasing the demand for that input more or less than for others. The concept has a long history in economic theory and Hicks (1932) was the first to define it:

> *We can classify inventions accordingly as their initial*
> *effects are to increase, leave unchanged or diminish*
> *the ratio of the marginal product of capital to that of*
> *labour. We may call these inventions labour-saving,*
> *neutral and capital saving respectively.*
> - Hicks (1932), p. 121 -

Bias must be distinguished from substitution, which leaves that ratio unchanged.[14] Constructing a measure again starts with a formal definition. Kennedy and Thirwall (1972), who interpret the given initial situation as maintaining a given factor ratio, show that for the two factor, one good case bias can be defined formally as:

$$\frac{d(f_K / f_L)}{dt} * \frac{f_L}{f_K} \quad \left| \begin{array}{l} >0 \ L \text{ saving} \\ =0 \text{ neutral} \\ <0 \ K \text{ saving} \\ \text{for given } K/L \end{array} \right. \tag{2.4}$$

The two production factors are K and L and f_X represents the partial derivative of the production function with respect to factor X. In the more general n goods, m inputs case this yields n times m-1 bias measures per input.[15] By using the consolidated utility function in (2.3) and measuring the marginal products in terms of the ultimate marginal contributions to utility one can reduce this to m-1 bias measures per input measuring the bias of aggregate technical change with respect to that input.

Binswanger (1974) developed a method that reduces this still potentially large number of indicators per input to 1. He argued that in a competitive market equilibrium, where all inputs are paid their marginal value product and total output is paid out to the inputs, a change in relative input prices for a given aggregate initial input vector $X=\{\Sigma_I x_{I0t}, \Sigma_I x_{I1t},..., \Sigma_I x_{Imt}\}$, implies that the input shares in the total output have changed. And because input prices are equal to the marginal product, a shift in input shares given the input vector thus indicates bias. [16] For input j aggregate bias can now be defined as:

$$\left. \frac{dsh_j}{dt} * \frac{1}{sh_j} \right| \begin{array}{l} >0 \text{ input } j \text{ using} \\ =0 \text{ neutral} \\ <0 \text{ input } j \text{ saving} \\ \text{for given } X=\{ \Sigma_I x_{I0t}, \Sigma_I x_{I1t},..., \Sigma_I x_{Imt}\} \end{array} \qquad (2.5)$$

Where, taking utility as the relevant output measure, sh_j is defined as:

$$sh_j \equiv \frac{du(.)}{dX_j} * \frac{X_j}{u(.)} = \sum_{i=0}^{n} \frac{\partial u(F(X,t),t)}{\partial f_i(X,t)} \frac{\partial f_i(X,t)}{dX_j} * \frac{X_j}{u(F(X,t),t)} \qquad (2.6)$$

and $X_j = \Sigma_I x_{ijt}$. There are large empirical problems in separating factor price induced substitution from factor price induced technological bias as both simultaneously shift the relative factor share over time in the same direction. Bias cannot be measured directly as the marginal product cannot be observed, much less its marginal contribution to utility. An empirical measure of bias is therefore by definition indirect and involves making assumptions, such as the existence of competitive markets. Only in cases when bias is strong enough to move both relative demand and relative prices in favour of some factor, can bias be observed. Still, even then it cannot be measured. In theoretical models, however, this is no problem as bias and substitution are clearly defined.

Distinguishing high and low skilled labour, changes in the share of both worker types in the total wage bill can be used to measure the skill bias. Schimmelpfennig (1998) defined skill bias for a two skill level labour supply:[17]

> Technological change is skill biased, if it leads to a fall in unskilled labour's income share after controlling for changes in the skill composition of labour supply.
> - Schimmelpfennig (1998), p. 5 -

Obviously the initial introduction of just one skill-biased innovation cannot cause large aggregate demand shifts. It is by the strength of numbers that individually biased innovations affect the composition of aggregate labour demand. As was argued in Chapter 1 the observed collapse in low skilled labour demand must have been caused by a large wave of individually skill-biased innovations. The idea of a general-purpose technology might explain why such waves could emerge.

2.1.6 GENERAL PURPOSE TECHNOLOGIES

In a seminal contribution to the theory of technical change Breshnahan and Trajtenberg (1995) coined the term general-purpose technology (GPT). An innovation qualifies as a general-purpose technology if *it has the potential for pervasive use in a wide range of sectors in ways that drastically change their modes of operation.*[18] By their very nature such technologies have an economy wide impact. It takes a long time for a general-purpose technology to develop, but once introduced, it can be used in a wide range of production processes and/or has many potential applications in consumption. Hence such a general-purpose technology sparks a cluster of related innovations that is based on the same basic innovation. The bias of the basic innovation might thus carry over to this offspring and cause serious skill bias in the aggregate demand for labour. In the words of Breshnahan and Trajtenberg:

> *The phenomenon involves innovational complementarities, that is, the productivity of R&D in a downstream sector increases as a consequence of innovation in the GPT technology. These complementarities magnify the effects of innovation in the GPT, and help propagate them throughout the economy.*
> - Breshnahan and Trajtenberg (1995), p. 84 -

When authors conclude that aggregate technical change has been skill biased over the past decades, they usually think of the wave of ICT-related innovations that occurred at the end of the 70s and diffused during the 80s and 90s. From the often-observed close correlation between computer use and skill intensity, they conclude that this general-purpose technology must have been skill biased to the extent necessary to explain the observed patterns in low skilled labour market performance. The next sub-section will argue, however, that another source of aggregate bias, related to the dynamics of product and process innovations, may exist, and is especially important when a wave of innovations follows the introduction of a general-purpose technology.

2.1.7 THE DYNAMICS OF TECHNICAL CHANGE

Innovations change the nature of aggregate technology. The rates of innovation measure the speed and size of their impact. The bias of innovations measures the direction in which they change factor demand. The concept of a general-purpose technology explains why innovations may come in waves or clusters. What then is the impact of technical change, caused by a flow of innovations, on the evolution of labour demand?

If innovations were static that impact would be entirely determined by the combination of the speed, size and direction that characterise individual innovations. A general-purpose technology related cluster of skill-biased innovations would shift the economy to a permanently higher relative demand for skilled labour. An innovation is, however, not static. Its introduction into the economic system is a dynamic process in which the direction, speed and size of the innovation change and interact with existing and new technologies. And although this interaction is unique between any two technologies over any period of time, there are some general characteristics of this dynamic process that emerge from a large case study literature.

In that literature researchers have identified a *product life cycle*.[19] That life cycle starts with invention and innovation but upon its first commercial introduction an innovation must *diffuse* through the economy. In the diffusion process there is a stage of *adoption* in which the innovation increases its market share. Then saturation occurs in a stage of *maturity*. Then the continued inflow of new substitutes causes the product or process to gradually *decline* until it is *obsolete*.

There is a large literature on the geographical aspects that was initiated by Vernon (1966) and of which the models by Krugman (1979) and Grossman and Helpman (1989, 1991a), discussed extensively in Chapter 3, are direct descendants. Another strand of literature, for example Acs (1996), focuses on the market structure and firm size over the life cycle of industries. The focus that is most relevant to the purpose of this book, however, is on the evolution of final demand and production technology, as the combination of both explains the life cycle evolution of relative factor demand at the individual technology level.

Table 2.2:   HIRSCH'S PRODUCT LIFE CYCLE

CHARACTERISTICS	CYCLE PHASE		
	Early	Growth	Mature
TECHNOLOGY	Short runs Rapidly changing techniques Dependence on external economies	Mass production gradually introduced Variations in technique frequent	Long runs and stable technology Few innovations of importance
CAPITAL INTENSITY	Low	High, due to obsolescence	High, due to specialised equipment
INDUSTRY STRUCTURE	Entry know-how determined Numerous firms providing specialised services	Growing number of firms Many casualties and mergers Growing vertical integration	Financial resources critical for entry Number of firms declining
CRITICAL HUMAN INPUT	Scientists and Engineers	Management	Unskilled and low-skilled labour
DEMAND STRUCTURE	Sellers' market Performance equally important to price	Growing price elasticities Spread of product information	Buyers' market

Source: Freeman and Soete (1997).

A first attempt to link the life cycle of products to factor demand is Hirsch (1965), who concluded from case studies that a product requires changing amounts and qualities of capital and labour over its life cycle. He also observed and reported the typical evolution of the industry structure, the evolution of final demand and technology in very broad terms. Table 2.2 shows the characteristics of the product life cycle as presented by Hirsch. Note that the first line in Table 2.2 illustrates that there is a close relation between the life cycle of the product and the process that is used to produce it. Moving from one stage to the next in the Hirsch cycle implies changing the production process rather than changing the product itself. In fact the production process is a key determinant of the stage a product is in and process innovation is a precondition for moving a product from one stage to the next. This implies that product and process innovation are dynamically interrelated. This interrelatedness is quite evident when a few examples are considered.

The conveyer belt was by all definitions a process innovation that revolutionised manufacturing in general and the car industry in particular. Its introduction allowed car producers to shift the car from an early stage, where a few high skilled mechanics produced a car on demand, to maturity.[20] Also a relatively new technology like the PC has shown clear signs of a life cycle. Initially used by a few very high skilled programmers the PC is now used by many at work and home. The development of user-friendly interfaces like windows can be regarded as innovations that matured this product.[21]

To test for the existence of the Hirsch cycle in a more general setting, Audretsch (1987) first determined the lifecycle stage of all 4-digit Standard Industrial Classification Industries for the US in 1977, using data on their real sales from 1958 to 1977.[22] The industries are classified as growing, mature or declining industries depending on the sign of the coefficients in a simple regression of real sales on time and time squared.[23] Then some variables that Hirsch suggested would characterise the cycle, research intensity, skill intensity and capital intensity, were used as explanatory variables in a probit regression on each of the stages.

Audretsch' results confirmed the existence of a product life cycle. The skill intensity of employment indeed varied over the cycle as Hirsch had hypothesised. Recently the interest in these aspects of the life cycle has resurfaced in the literature. Goldin and Katz (1998) for example argued that in most manufacturing sectors firms went through the Hirsch cycle. Empirical research, for example Bartel and Lichtenberg (1987) and Xiang (2002), also corroborated Hirsch's finding that high skilled workers are on average more in demand in rapidly changing technological environments. Recent studies by Aw and Batra (1999) and Baldwin and Raffiquzzaman (1999) also show that wage differentials vary over the life cycle as Hirsch had suggested.[24]

As the focus of this book is on the relative demand for skilled labour, the relevance of that aspect in the product life cycle is evident. It implies that progress over the cycle will shift the skill intensity of labour demand. But if this is the case at the product level then, by aggregation, the distribution of total output over the life cycle stages affects aggregate relative labour demand.

As was argued in Chapter 1, the introduction of a general-purpose technology like ICT can now produce an aggregate bias, not necessarily because the individual ICT-related innovations are biased but because they are new. The distribution over the life cycle is driven by innovation both from the outside due to entry and exit and internally as innovation is also required to shift existing technologies over their life cycle. A key difference is that, as the innovations mature and the distribution shifts back, so will aggregate relative labour demand and relative wages.

Aggregate Technology can now be defined as a body of knowledge that consists of the innovations made up to a point, weighed by their penetration rates in consumption and production and distributed over the several life cycle stages. Aggregate technical change may then be skill biased and cause shifts in aggregate relative labour demand for two reasons. First a drop in relative low skilled labour demand may have been caused by a wave of low skilled labour saving or high skilled labour using innovations. Second a wave of product innovations may have caused a shift in the aggregate distribution of jobs towards the early stages and process innovation has yet to move the new products and services over their cycle to restore the balance.

The interesting question that arises at this point is: Why would anyone want to develop, introduce or adopt product and process innovations in the first place and secondly why indeed if the innovations that are adopted are biased towards a factor that continuously increases its relative price. To answer that question one must turn to the economics of technical change.

2.2   THE ECONOMICS OF TECHNICAL CHANGE

The previous section argued that innovation may cause bias in aggregate relative labour demand. The observed positive correlations between skill intensity and technology indicators such as computer use and R&D efforts strongly suggest that explanation. What remains to be addressed is why individual innovations might have been biased and why innovation changed the cycle phase structure in a way that caused aggregate bias.

In Chapter 1 it was argued that technical change is the result of deliberate action on behalf of the innovator. For an economist the question is to what extent this deliberate action is economically motivated. Generally formulated economically motivated behaviour is the result of a rational decision by an agent to commit scarce resources to the pursuit of some gain. Rationality implies that the benefits achieved outweigh the costs to achieve them. Answering the question above as an economist thus requires a closer look at the agents, costs and benefits in the invention, innovation, diffusion and obsolescence stages of the life cycle.

2.2.1   THE ECONOMICS OF INVENTION

Invention is the initial conception of an idea. The agent in invention is therefore an individual or group of individuals that comes up with such an idea. In the literature these inventors have been discussed extensively.

Usher (1954) claimed that the views on the process of invention always find themselves between two extremes.

The *transcendentalist approach* at one extreme attributes the advances made in technology to the individual genius of the inventor. According to this view James Watt actually developed the steam engine from scratch and was not motivated by economic incentives but pursued his own intellectual challenges. In this approach the economy simply absorbs the inventions that are supplied and it was therefore labelled the *supply push* approach. Although useful for gaining a historical perspective the example immediately exposes the weaknesses of this approach. Watt developed his engine based on an earlier design by Newcomen. He was inspired to do so while working on a scaled down teaching model a mining company had commissioned him to build. And upon his invention he and many other engineers worked for many years to perfect the engine and invent new, profitable applications.[25]

At the other extreme is the *mechanistic approach* that claims invention is merely the result of people looking for and finding the solution to problems that daily life confronts them with. In this view technological change merely responds to the signals from the society it develops in. Obviously in capitalist societies economic (price-) signals then play an important if not dominant role and it was therefore labelled *demand pull* approach. In this approach James Watt was a mere instrument of history. He happened to be faced with the problem how to drain water from mining shafts and that problem required a solution. By reducing Watt's invention to a mere mechanistic response to an external historical fact or economic incentive, Watt's genius is fully denied, as if any other could and would have done the same thing in his position.

Scherer's (1982) attempt to establish the relative importance of demand pull and supply push empirically was inconclusive. He confirmed results obtained by demand pull proponents such as Schmookler (1966) but also found significant effects of such proxies as the size and richness of an industry's knowledge base, indicating significant supply push effects.

These results and the steam engine case show that reality is usually to be found somewhere between the extremes. Usher himself put forward an alternative, the *cumulative synthesis approach*. In this approach inventors combine their individual genius with the existing knowledge base in society and apply this package to the economic or intellectual challenge they wish to apply it to. Since individual genius and society's knowledge base develop largely independent of economic considerations, these provide the supply push elements in his approach.[26] The demand-pull elements come from the anticipation of and the testing and revising in economic applications that feeds back into the invention process. Both supply push and demand pull elements thus play a role and for each individual invention in varying degrees. This also implies that in the aggregate the direction and rate of invention are determined both by economic and non-economic factors.

Summarising the above in economic terms clarifies the picture. In the invention stage inventors, individuals or those employed in large R&D laboratories, are the agents whose actions shape new technologies. In the process they face costs, even if crucial inputs such as the existing knowledge base and individual genius are available to them free of charge, providing supply push elements. Labour time foregone, physical inputs and the costly process of trial and error put a price on invention. To the extent that these agents act rationally, weighing these costs against the benefits of their action, invention is an economic activity. The benefits come to some extent in the form of profits.[27] Demand pull elements therefore operate mainly through benefits, whereas supply push elements tend to affect costs. There is room for both in the economics of invention when agents respond rationally and direct their efforts towards projects that they perceive to have a positive balance.

2.2.2 THE ECONOMICS OF INNOVATION

In the innovation stage of the life cycle an invention is commercialised. Invention is thus a necessary condition for innovation, and supply push elements in the invention stage carry over to this stage. Economic incentives and rational decision-making, however, become increasingly important. According to Schumpeter (1934) entrepreneurs who seek to either gain or consolidate monopoly rents are the agents that commercialise inventions. Again the entrepreneur could be an individual starting up a new firm from his garage or an executive at a large electronics company who considers commercialising some invention made in the company's R&D lab. Initially Schumpeter saw these entrepreneurs in much the same way as the inventors described above. They were supposed to commercialise their invention and then expose themselves to the market where a process of natural selection would pick winners and losers. In that view the supply push elements in invention would carry over to innovation one-for-one.

But the emergence of the firm-based R&D laboratories and the strong demand pull for military technology in the mid 30s showed that the allocation of resources in innovation responds strongly to profit incentives. As entrepreneurs introduce an invention commercially they can be expected to be motivated mainly by (anticipated) profits and therefore pre-select the inventions they will commercialise. Unlike the inventors, the entrepreneurs can pre-select, as they may purchase these inventions from inventors and are not bound to any specific invention. This also implies, however, that there is competition over inventions and under certain conditions a market for them can emerge. The costs to the entrepreneur are then equal to the market price of an invention. His benefits are the profits he expects to make.

On this common basic foundation economists have developed a new field in economics, the economics of innovation.[28] In that field both the endogenisation of the rate and the direction of technical change have been attempted. These strands of literature are at the heart of the analysis in following chapters and a short survey of both is offered here.

The early literature on the economics of innovation can be classified in three broad approaches.[29] The first focussed on the microeconomics of innovation in general and centred on the Schumpeterian hypothesis and the relation between market structure and innovation in particular.[30] This approach focussed on the agents and their private costs and benefits, and much less on the macroeconomic implications of their actions.

The second approach followed up on Solow's (1957) work and focussed on explaining aggregate technical progress without much consideration for microeconomic foundations. The focus was on incentives and environmental factors, much less on the behaviour of agents. An early reference taking this approach is Arrow's (1962) article on learning-by-doing. He hypothesised that aggregate production would generate a knowledge stock that increases productivity without agents actually introducing further innovations. Technical change is endogenous but treated as an unintended and costless side effect of production.

The third approach took an evolutionary perspective on innovation. This approach is much more empirical and descriptive in nature.[31] In this approach the rationality of agents under the extreme uncertainties involved is questioned, with very interesting results that are of little interest to this book, as the whole analysis below rests on the assumption of rational behaviour.

The microeconomic and growth theoretic approaches, however, are also of little use when considered in isolation. The former does not allow one to analyse the impact of innovation on and feedback effects of aggregate variables such as labour demand or the aggregate stock of knowledge, the latter lacks a decision theoretic foundation that would explain how bias is the result of rational decision-making.

Fortunately the economics of innovation has progressed and with the contributions of Romer (1986), Lucas (1988) and especially Romer (1990), Grossman and Helpman (1991b) and Aghion and Howitt (1992) 'New Growth Theory', integrating the micro- and macroeconomic perspective, was born. Aghion and Howitt (1998), provide an overview that explicitly links this field of research to the Schumpeterian approach in which the search for monopoly rents provides the incentives for innovative activity. Barro and Sala-I-Martin (1995) give an overview of endogenous growth extensions to the neo-classical class of growth models that have their roots in the Solow growth model. These models typically address the issue of market failure and usually link economic growth to positive externalities (Arrow (1962), Romer (1990), Grossman and Helpman (1991b)) or constant returns to capital, the so-called AK models (Romer (1986, 1987), Lucas (1988) and Rebelo (1991)).[32]

For the purpose of this book a subclass of endogenous growth models, that of the R&D or innovation driven growth models, is particularly relevant.[33] In these models individual innovations are the results of a rational decision making process on behalf of an R&D sector. This sector aims to maximise profit and represents both the inventor and the Schumpeterian entrepreneur. The costs of R&D are expenditures on scarce resources this sector has to compete for. However, the existence of knowledge spillovers at the aggregate level captures the idea that the innovators can benefit from an evolving knowledge base. As such these models consider the microeconomic foundations of aggregate technical change but also capture important feedbacks and supply push elements present in the economic environment in which these innovators operate.

Romer (1990), Grossman and Helpman (1991b) and Aghion and Howitt (1992) were the first to introduce a research and development sector that produces innovations/ideas that are non-rivalrous inputs in the production of final output into a model.[34] The resources allocated to R&D are a decision variable in these models, which endogenises the rate of innovation and explains how it is a result of the combination of preferences, market interaction and individual rational decision-making. Still these models concentrate on a homogenous R&D output by dealing with one type of innovation at a time, precluding the analysis of individually biased innovations or the aggregate distribution of products and processes over life cycle stages.

Acemoglu (1998) and Kiley (1999) explicitly address the issue of individually biased innovations and introduced heterogeneity in R&D output by allowing agents to choose between innovations that are complementary to skilled or unskilled labour. By using similar techniques it is also possible to endogenise the life cycle by distinguishing and endogenising the types of innovations that move the product over the life cycle as in Van Zon and Sanders (2000), and Sanders (2002). Before turning to such models in the next chapter, however, it is useful to provide some additional background. The ideas underlying Acemoglu (1998) and Kiley (1999), and indeed all other work that addresses the issue of endogenous bias, can be traced back to the debate on Hicks' (1932) induced innovations hypothesis, briefly mentioned in Chapter 1 above.

The debate on endogenous biases in technical change was initiated when Hicks (1932) put forward the inducement hypothesis:

> *A change in the relative prices of the factors of production is itself a spur to innovation, and to inventions of a particular kind – directed at economizing the use of a factor that has become relatively expensive.*
> - Hicks (1932), pp. 124-125 -

Here too there exists a micro-, a macro and a historically oriented literature. David (1975) provides a comprehensive review of the debate from the economic historians' perspective. There are many interesting accounts in this literature but again no useful reference is made to decision theoretical foundations. Thirtle and Ruttan (1987) give an extensive summary of the debate on induced innovation both from the microeconomic and growth-theoretical perspective.

The microeconomic debate focussed on the issue of factor substitution versus factor bias, addressed briefly in the previous section. Based on a substitution argument Salter (1960) refuted Hicks' original claim, that factor price changes would induce innovations that are biased towards saving the relatively more expensive factor. He argued that due to factor substitution all factors are always equally expensive to a firm (at the margin since they all are paid their marginal products). Hence the incentive to bias the allocation of R&D resources towards saving the more expensive factor would disappear. Salter, however, defined his production function to include all feasible production techniques that *can* be developed from the existing knowledge base. He then called the choice between these techniques factor substitution and thereby defined away all possible bias in technical change.

Fellner (1961, 1962, 1966) introduced market power and expectations into the Salter framework and Ahmad (1966) redefined Salter's isoquant as an innovations possibility curve (IPC), an envelope of all the alternative isoquants a firm might expect to develop given its available R&D resources. Both were able to rehabilitate the induced innovation hypothesis. The latter model also allowed the supply push elements to affect technical change since an exogenous shift in the IPC would reflect the autonomous progress in scientific knowledge.[35]

In this debate the agents are typically assumed to be firms considering whether or not to develop or adopt a particular innovation. They are constrained by the alternative production technologies available to them and driven by profits. With their focus on firms both the proponents and opponents of the induced bias hypothesis stress the demand pull factors in innovation although both reach diametrically opposed conclusions. The concentration on firm behaviour also shifts the focus away from innovation and towards adoption and diffusion, discussed below.

The macroeconomic growth theoretical approach, on the other hand, has focussed on the issue of explaining the empirical constancy of factor shares without having to assume purely labour augmenting technical change.[36] Kennedy (1964) proposed an innovation possibilities frontier (IPF) for the aggregate economy. It describes the rate of labour augmentation that can be generated by technical change as a function of the rate of capital augmentation. Underlying this curve is the assumption that R&D resources are scarce and have to be allocated to augmenting either factor and represents the analogue of a production possibilities frontier in R&D.

When the aim is to maximise unit cost reductions at given relative factor prices, this curve yields an optimal allocation of R&D resources and hence a bias may result endogenously. Kennedy (1966) also showed that, if technical change only occurs in final goods production, the stable rates of technical change are necessarily Hicks neutral in the long run. If technical change also affects the production of capital goods, a long-run stable growth path only exists if technical change is purely labour augmenting.

Drandakis and Phelps (1966) and Samuelson (1966) subsequently integrated the Kennedy model in the standard neo-classical growth model by Solow (1957). Von Weizäcker (1966) extended the model by explicitly modelling the decision regarding the total amount of resources (labour only) to be allocated to R&D, which allows for the determination of the optimal rate of technical change. Still, as before, the macroeconomic approach does not address the decision theoretical foundations of innovation and analyses technical change at the aggregate level only. For an analysis of product life cycle effects it is required that these micro foundations are addressed.

A main further criticism that can be put forward on both approaches is that the IPF, like the IPC are both simply assumed to exist, to exhibit the required properties and to be known to the decision-makers in the economy.[37] Especially the required long-run stability is an undesirable feature of the IPF since the rate of capital or labour augmentation is not likely to be boundless. If labour augmentation is limited than a purely labour augmenting exogenous drift in the IPF is required to re-establish the stable long-run growth equilibrium, which brings us back to square one. The assumption of purely labour augmenting technical change is merely replaced by the assumption of a labour augmenting drift in the IPF. The innovation possibilities frontier lacks the sound microeconomic foundation that endogenous growth models do provide.

The debate on endogenous biases in technical change has not been concluded and little attention was devoted to it until recently. By combining a micro-approach to innovation with a macro-approach to technical change, R&D driven growth models allow for the analysis of endogenous bias. Among the few recent theoretical contributions are the above-mentioned models by Kiley (1999) and Acemoglu (1998, 2002a), which will be discussed in more detail in Chapter 3. Before turning to their work, however, this chapter first shortly discusses the possible impacts of economic considerations over the diffusion and obsolescence stages of the life cycle.

2.2.3 THE ECONOMICS OF DIFFUSION AND OBSOLESCENCE

Upon being introduced commercially an innovation will (usually) diffuse. The speed at and extent to which it diffuses as well as the time it takes for substitutes to compete the innovation out of the market are all variables that affect the impact of that innovation on aggregate labour demand.

Empirical evidence shows that there are large differences in the speed and extent to which new innovations diffuse.[38] Casual observation reveals that some innovations have been around for ages whereas others had hardly seen the light of day when the next innovation wiped them out.[39] Still the descriptive literature on diffusion finds a remarkable empirical regularity in the diffusion of new products and processes. Diffusion, measured by the market share of a new technology over time typically follows an S-shape. This pattern was also present in the diffusion pattern of PCs in the US shown in Chapter 1. The S-shaped pattern of diffusion is well described by so-called contagion models. These models argue that adoption follows information, which spreads through a population like a contagious disease.[40] The first contributions, made by Griliches (1957) and Mansfield (1961) apply the epidemic approach to the diffusion of new process innovations. Such models, however, lack decision theoretical foundations entirely. Agents adopt whenever they are infected, and are assumed to be automatons, not rational decision makers. Saturation levels and adoption speed are observed or assumed rather than explained.

This empirically robust pattern justifies the above-discussed R&D driven growth models in simply sidestepping the diffusion stage. They conveniently assume that events between innovation and obsolescence are similar and predictable for all innovations. All relevant information is available and can be discounted to the time of innovation. Introducing endogenous aggregate profit erosion or hazard rates can thus capture diffusion.[41]

It was argued above, however, that subsequent innovation in the diffusion stage plays a key role in moving innovations over their cycle. Events in the diffusion stage, in particular the introduction of maturing process innovations, drive the dynamics in the distribution of aggregate output over the life cycle. Fortunately progress on a decision theoretical foundation has been made particularly for an important category of subsequent process innovations - new capital equipment. The adoption of such innovations requires large investments on behalf of firms, so benefits and costs are large and firms must behave rationally if they want to remain in business. The economics behind the adoption of new capital equipment have therefore been studied extensively and are consequently better understood than for other types of innovation.

For example David (1969) and Davies (1979) investigated possible links between diffusion speed and economic environment by regressing the probability that a firm adopts a new technology on firm characteristics. Both find that a firm adopts when the cost reduction allowed by the new technology outweighs the costs of adoption. Obviously that cost reduction depends on factor and output prices as well as on the technical characteristics of the new process considered.

In models proposed by Stoneman (1981), Tsur, Sternberg and Hochman (1990) and Kim, Hayes and Hallam (1992) the effects of expectations and learning on adoption costs are taken into account. These models are shown to go a long way in explaining observed patterns of intra-firm diffusion and stress the importance of information gathering and knowledge accumulation. To explain international diffusion Grossman and Helpman (1991a), mentioned above, also used the idea that anticipated operational cost reductions drive the innovative effort required to move a product over its cycle stages. The required effort is reduced as knowledge accumulates.

Now consider the economics of obsolescence. The phasing out of an obsolete product or process usually follows an inverse S-shape. This is again attributed to the evolution of demand, not the supply of the technology itself. Since obsolescence is the result of adopting substitutes, this pattern can be explained as the mirror image of diffusion.

At this point it should be noted that both diffusion and scrapping models assume that the agent is a firm that is motivated by expected cost reductions and constrained by the availability of the technology and required knowledge to operate it. Once that constraint is lifted he can adopt the new technology at a cost.[42] This makes their decision comparable to that of the entrepreneurs in R&D driven growth models. The model in Chapter 4 will illustrate this by assuming that the transition of a new product to a next life cycle stage requires an additional, costly process innovation.

2.3 CONCLUSION

In this chapter concepts, definitions and ideas from various strands of literature on technical change have been presented. First aggregate technology was defined as the stock of knowledge that allows us to generate utility from a bundle of outputs produced with a given bundle of inputs. Then it was argued that the evolution of aggregate technology is determined by the introduction, diffusion and exit of a flow of new technologies that may or may not be clustered around a general-purpose technology. The bias of (a cluster of) individual technologies, the speed at and extent to which individually biased innovations diffuse, and the distribution of the economy over the life cycle have been identified as potentially complementary sources of bias in aggregate technical change, resulting in shifting relative aggregate input demands.

It was also argued that the individual bias and life cycle distribution are at least partly the result of economic decision-making and therefore affected by economic variables such as relative factor prices. Since these prices are likely to respond to demand shifts, this implies that the economic effects of technical change feed back into the processes of invention, innovation and diffusion.

The analysis in this chapter was kept informal to keep the focus on tracing the origins of ideas and concepts in the literature. To evaluate the exact implications of the hypotheses, it is useful to formulate them in more precise mathematical models. The next chapter will discuss the tools needed to do so by presenting relevant models from the literature.

NOTES

[1] A first subtlety that is easily overlooked is the difference between *technical* and *technological* change. Kennedy and Thirwall (1972) define the former as the impact on the economy of the latter, implying all technical change is preceded by technological change. Not all technological change results in technical change.

[2] In fact in most of the literature the distinction is not made.

[3] The introduction of personal computers for example could easily be classified both as a product or process innovation. The characteristics of a product innovation then apply to the personal computer to the extent that it is a product innovation. Admittedly this is a tautological argument but useful in defending this and the following generalisations.

[4] Any micro-economic textbook presents the conditions for such a production function to exist. See for example Mas-Colell, Whinston and Greene (1995).

[5] Formally this measure would be given by:

$$g_{process} = \frac{1}{\sum_{i=0}^{n} \overline{p}_i f_i(\overline{X}_R, t)} * \left(\sum_{i=0}^{n} \overline{p}_i \frac{df_i(\overline{X}_R, t)}{dt} \right)$$

where vector X_{it} represents $\{x_{i0t}, x_{i1t}, \dots, x_{imt}\}$ and there are n types of output that can be traded at prices p_i in the base year. The bar over p and X indicates constant prices and input quantities, respectively.

[6] TFP growth equals GDP growth minus the imputed contributions of labour accumulation, residential and non-residential capital accumulation. Augmented TFP (ATFP) growth equals GDP growth minus the imputed contributions of labour accumulation, residential and non-residential capital accumulation and imputed contributions of increases in labour and capital quality.

[7] Again any micro-economic textbook will provide the conditions for such a function to exist.

[8] Formally utility is an ordinal concept that has no cardinal interpretation. Micro economists would therefore probably object to this abuse of the utility concept. It is common practice, however, to give utility a cardinal interpretation. For example by assuming a representative consumer, where one implicitly weighs the utility of individual consumers and by assuming diminishing marginal utility, which implicitly compares utility intra-personally.

[9] One obtains:

$$g_{product} = \frac{1}{u(\overline{C}_t, t)} * \frac{du(\overline{C}_t, t)}{dt}$$

which can be interpreted as the rate of product innovation. Again the consumption set was written as a vector. Empirically the above measure is not so easily implemented. The problem is to choose a price to weigh the new products and even if that problem were solved, the impact of quality improvements on existing products goes unnoticed. A large literature exists on the topic. For an excellent overview of the issues see, for example, Trajtenberg (1990).

[10] This implies assuming that all output is consumed at the aggregate level. This is effectively a closed economy assumption as international trade would allow for consumption and production to differ.

[11] Of course this amount will be 0 for some j in producing product i.

[12] Formally:

$$g = \frac{1}{u(F(\overline{X}_R, t), t)} \frac{\partial u(F(\overline{X}_R, t), t)}{\partial t} = \frac{1}{u(F(\overline{X}_R, t), t)} \left(\sum_{i=0}^{n} \frac{\partial u(F(\overline{X}_R, t), t)}{\partial f_i(\overline{X}_R, t)} * \frac{\partial f_i(\overline{X}_R, t)}{\partial t} + \frac{\partial u(\overline{C}_t, t)}{\partial t} \right)$$

where $F(X, t)$ is a vector of production functions and the last term between brackets is equal to the rate of product innovation defined above. The impact of process innovation on utility is captured by the first term, which is very close to the aggregate rate of process innovation defined in Note 5.

13 Which is not to say that empirical economists do not try to measure utility, basically by making adjustments for quality improvements and product innovation in price indices. Adelman and Griliches (19961) is a early contribution to this literature. More recent applications are found in Shapiro and Wilcox (1996), Breshnahan and Gordon (1997), Moulton and Moses (1997) and Houseman (1999).

14 This so-called Hicks-Robinson classification has provoked quite a debate in the literature. Various authors have proposed alternative formulations of the same concept. Kennedy and Thirwall (1972) stay closest to Hicks original definition in their formal definition and is used here. The reader is referred to Thirtle and Ruttan (1987) for an excellent overview of the issues and additional references.

15 In the m input case there are m $(m-1)/2$ pairs per production process.

16 He derives this result the other way around. Assuming there is a dual minimum cost function to every production function, Binswanger (1974) shows that given prices any shift in factor shares indicates bias.

17 Schimmelpfennig also considered Harrod- and Solow-neutral technical change. These concepts, though important in their own right, are of little use when the focus is on the impact of technology on the aggregate income distribution and the composition of labour demand. See Barro and Sala-I-Martin (1995) for a short summary and Chang (1970) or Thirtle and Ruttan (1987) for more detailed explanations.

18 Helpman (1998), p. 3.

19 For references see Note 15 in Chapter 1.

20 Obviously a host of other, less conspicuous innovations to process and product were required to make the conveyer belt such a success. Examples are the standardisation of parts and all innovations required to guarantee the reliable production of such parts.

21 The PC and ICT technologies in general have the property that they can be regarded as product or process innovations as they have affected production as much as consumption. The development of a user interface can thus be regarded as a product innovation maturing a process and the other way around. The key issue here is that a new innovation may change the characteristics of an existing one, as was he case for the conveyer belt.

22 At the 4-digit level this classification is very close to the product level one would ideally use.

23 If sales rise at an increasing rate (both coefficients positive) the industry is in growth, if sales decrease it is in decline and if both coefficients are insignificant the industry is mature.

24 They analyse the wage differential between blue- and white-collar workers.

25 See Suplee (2000).

26 Popper (1959) and Kuhn (1962) for example provide a theory for the dynamics in science that is largely if not entirely independent of economic considerations.

27 Personal gratification, satisfaction of curiosity and intellectual status and the pursuit of an academic career are other, less quantifiable aspects of the benefits. It should also be noted that perceived future benefits are what motivates inventors. Their expectations may well be way off but this does not change the rationality of their behaviour.

28 This literature does not distinguish between the innovation, diffusion or invention stage for simplicity. The usual assumption is that inventions are immediately commercialised and that the adopting population is fully informed and homogenous. The latter implies that all adopt when one adopts and diffusion is immediate. The former implies that the innovating agent is inventor-entrepreneur and weighs entrepreneurial benefits against invention costs.

29 Schneider and Ziesemer (1995).

30 See for example Kamien and Schwartz (1982). Schumpeter posed the hypothesis that monopoly rents are the incentive for innovation and hence a testable implication would be that monopolistic sectors are more innovative than competitive ones.

31 Dosi et al. (1988) collects many contributions in this approach.

32 Jones (1999) and Jones and Manuelli (1999) contain useful updated overviews that place different accents.

[33] Other classes of endogenous growth models follow, for example, Lucas (1988) and focus on the endogenous accumulation of human capital or Jones (1999) where the focus is on explaining the stability of growth. These approaches are less suitable in analysing the implications of product life cycles in innovation, as they do not allow for labour demand to be distributed over individual products and technologies.

[34] See Jones (1999). Their work will be discussed in greater detail in Chapter 3.

[35] Ahmad (1966) assumed that this shift would be Hicks neutral, however, this assumption could easily be dropped to allow for exogenous biases as well.

[36] This is one of the famous Kaldorian stylised facts of growth. In Jones (1975) among many others it is shown that sustainable growth with fixed income shares requires technical change to be Harrod-neutral in the aggregate production function. Harrod (1939) defined neutrality as technical change that for a given interest rate leaves the capital share in output unaffected. His concept is equivalent to Hicks' for a Cobb-Douglas production function. For all others Harrod neutrality implies that technical change is purely labour augmenting in Hicks' definition.

[37] Hacche (1979) discusses the relationships between IPC and IPF in detail.

[38] See for example David (1975) and Mokyr (1999).

[39] Examples are sailing boats and steam powered automobiles, respectively. Of course the essence of the life cycle hypothesis is that innovations that have been around for ages will change, sometimes dramatically, over time due to further technical change.

[40] Meijers (1994) gives a brief summary of the literature in this field and refers to Stoneman (1983, 1991) and Gomulka (1990) for more elaborate and detailed surveys.

[41] See Chapter 3.

[42] This cost covers the removal of old and installation of the new equipment. The price of the new machine also includes (part of) the development costs incurred by the innovator.

CHAPTER 3:

MODELLING ENDOGENOUS TECHNICAL CHANGE

In this chapter the aim is to bridge the gap between the descriptive analysis in the previous chapter and the formal mathematical one in the next chapter. To do so it is useful to consider some basic models in the endogenous innovation literature. In addition to providing the required modelling tools and their underlying intuition, this approach is intended to give due credit to the work of others upon which the model in Chapter 4 was built.

The first section shortly presents the basic structure of a model by Grossman and Helpman (1991b). It illustrates how product innovation can be modelled. The aim is to trace the roots, identify basic principles and provide the necessary intuition and analytical tools for the Acemoglu (2002a) model, presented in detail in Section 2. His model allows for individually biased innovations and offers the market size explanation, mentioned in Chapter 1.

Section 3 then adds insights from product life cycle models by presenting the innovation driven life cycle model by Grossman and Helpman (1989, 1991a). Their insights make it possible to introduce the life cycle explanation for the observed shifts in relative labour demand and feature prominently in the model in Chapter 4.

To avoid being swamped by mathematical technicalities, the main text in this chapter will present the models in an intuitive way. All models presented are also summarised in formal synopsis tables at the end of every section to facilitate comparison and summarise the main ingredients of these models. Derivations, proofs and all but the most obvious mathematics are deferred to the appendices.[1]

3.1   THE INGREDIENTS OF A MODEL WITH ENDOGENOUS INNOVATION

This section will focus on a model by Grossman and Helpman (1991b), illustrating the endogenisation of product innovations. It will relate this model in endnotes to models by Romer (1990) and Aghion and Howitt (1992), shortly pointing out the similarities and differences when the aim is to model process innovation.[2] All these authors regard the generation of ideas or innovations, which are non-rivalrous and therefore generate positive externalities, as crucial to explain long-run (steady state) economic growth. In addition they all:

> *...treat commercial research as an ordinary economic activity that requires the input of resources and responds to profit opportunities. Returns to R&D come in the form of monopoly rents in imperfectly competitive product markets.*
> - Grossman and Helpman (1991b), p.43 -

Thus introducing the basic channels for interaction between labour demand and technical change.

3.1.1 A MODEL OF ENDOGENOUS PRODUCT INNOVATION

The Grossman and Helpman (1991b) book is among the first and most significant contributions to the field of endogenous growth theory in general and innovation driven growth models in particular.[3] Being among the first in their kind, their model provides a useful starting point for the more precise formal arguments that follow. As was argued in Chapter 2, a model of product innovation requires the specification of consumer preferences in a utility function. This formal representation should reflect consumers' valuation of products relative to other products. In addition, as R&D requires resources that have to be invested in advance, the utility function must also reflect consumers' preferences over time, since savings are required to finance innovative activity.

A first key property of the utility function, which is commonly assumed in growth models, is therefore time separability. The idea is to separate the decision on how to spend a given budget on the available consumption bundle *at any point in time* from the decision what budget to consume *over time*. This property thus implies that it is possible to separate the *intra-* and *intertemporal* decision. Although consumers can borrow and lend to shift consumption over time, they are constrained to the extent that the present value of their lifetime consumption cannot exceed that of their lifetime earnings. Intuitively, utility is maximised when consumers spend and save over time in such a way that the marginal utility of spending a dollar on consumption today is equal to the discounted marginal utility of spending the return on risk free asset, $(1+r)$ dollars, on consumption tomorrow.[4] In Cell 1 of the formal synopsis table below the consumers' problem in Grossman and Helpman (1991b) is represented formally.

Table 3.1: **FORMAL SYNOPSIS OF GROSSMAN AND HELPMAN**
(1991B)

AGENT(S)		PROBLEM(S) SUBJECT TO CONSTRAINT(S) ⇒RESULTS
CONSUMERS	1	$\max\limits_{E(t)} : \int\limits_{t}^{\infty} e^{-\rho(\tau-t)} \log(E(\tau)/P(\tau))d\tau$
		s.t $Y(t)+rA(t)=E(t)+dA(t)/dt$
		$\Rightarrow \dfrac{\dot{E}(t)}{E(t)} = r - \rho$

On the left the problem is presented as choosing the budget $E(t)$ to be spent on a consumption index with a unit price of $P(t)$ to maximise a time separable utility function subject to the lifetime budget constraint. The budget constraint limits the expenditure on consumption and the accumulation of assets $A(t)$ to total income, the sum of labour income $Y(t)$ and the interest r earned on assets owned at time t. Appendix 3A derives the result that consumers will save to ensure:

$$\frac{\dot{E}}{E} = r - \rho \qquad (3.1)$$

Equation (3.1) implies that if the return on assets exceeds the subjective discount rate, ρ, consumers are willing to postpone consumption such that in the future they may consume more. Equation (3.1) conveniently implies that, when the budget is normalised to one in every period, the equilibrium interest rate must equal the discount rate. Given these preferences, assets that yield a higher rate of return will be in infinite demand, whereas the consumer will not purchase those with a lower rate of return. This in turn implies that all investment, including R&D, must yield a rate of return equal to the exogenously given discount rate in equilibrium. Most if not all innovation driven growth models will implicitly or explicitly assume a version of the above Ramsey (1928) optimal savings rule to describe consumers' intertemporal consumption decisions.[5] It describes how much consumers wish to save and spend on consumption in each period.

Grossman and Helpman (1991b) then proceed with the derivation of the (intratemporal) demand curves. To maximise their utility, consumers must spend the budget they decided to spend at every point in time such that they maximise direct utility. The consumers' appreciation for product innovations is embedded in the specification of direct utility.

Table 3.1:   FORMAL SYNOPSIS OF GROSSMAN AND HELPMAN
(Cont'd)   (1991B)

AGENT(S)		PROBLEM(S) SUBJECT TO CONSTRAINT(S) ⇒RESULTS
CONSUMERS	2	$\max_{c(i)} : U(.) = \left(\int_0^n c(i)^\alpha di \right)^{\frac{1}{\alpha}}$ s.t. $\int_0^n p(i)c(i)di \le E$ $\Rightarrow c^D(i) = \left(\frac{p(i)}{P} \right)^{\frac{1}{\alpha-1}} \frac{E}{P}$ $\Rightarrow P \equiv \left(\int_0^n p(i)^{\frac{\alpha}{\alpha-1}} di \right)^{\frac{\alpha-1}{\alpha}}$

The intratemporal problem is formally represented in Cell 2 of the synopsis table above. Intuitively a consumer maximises utility by setting the marginal utility of spending a dollar on one product equal to the marginal utility of spending that dollar on any of the other products available. Appendix 3A derives the formal results for an n varieties direct utility function. Note at this point that demand for any individual variety i is proportional to the budget and obviously the effect of price increases is to reduce demand. But note also that due to increases in n direct utility (E/P) increases whereas c^D_i falls. This makes the model a *variety expansion* model.[6] Consumers will reduce their demand for existing varieties when a new product enters the market.

Now consider the second group of agents in the model, producers, who are assumed to maximise their profits. They do so by setting a price and/or choosing a quantity to produce such that their marginal revenue equals marginal costs. In Appendix 3A the Amoroso-Robinson condition for setting profit maximising prices is formally derived and it is shown that that price is a mark-up over marginal costs.[7]

$$p_i = \frac{\sigma_i}{1+\sigma_i} mc_i \qquad \text{with } \sigma_i \equiv \frac{dc^D_i(p_i)}{dp_i} \frac{p_i}{c^D_i(p_i)} < 0 \qquad (3.2)$$

where σ_i is defined as the (negative) price elasticity of demand for good i. Corresponding profits are given by:

$$\pi_i = \frac{-1}{1+\sigma_i} mc_i c^D_i(p_i) \ge 0 \qquad (3.3)$$

It can be verified that under perfect competition, with producers facing a price elasticity of (minus) infinity, prices would fall to marginal costs and profits would fall to 0. In innovation driven growth models, however, market power is assumed as positive profits are required to provide an incentive to innovators below. In Grossman and Helpman every producer is therefore assumed to be a monopolist in his own market. They face the downward-sloping iso-elastic demand curve for variety i in Cell 2 alone. In that case it is easily verified that $\sigma_i = 1/(\alpha-1)<-1$ is the price elasticity of demand for all products i and the mark-up of prices over marginal costs is $1/\alpha>1$.[8] Grossman and Helpman then assume a simple one-for-one production technology with labour, L, as the sole input, such that marginal costs equal wages, w.[9]

Table 3.1:   **FORMAL SYNOPSIS OF GROSSMAN AND HELPMAN**
(Cont'd)   (1991B)

AGENT(S)		PROBLEM(S) SUBJECT TO CONSTRAINT(S)	$\Rightarrow$RESULTS
PRODUCERS	3	$\max_{p(i)} : \pi_c(i) = c(i)p(i) - tc(i)$ $\Rightarrow p(i) = \dfrac{1}{\alpha}mc(i)$	s.t. $c(i) = c^D(i)$
	4	$\min_{l(i)} : wl(i)$ $\Rightarrow l^D(i) = \alpha E / wn$	s.t. $c^D(i) = l(i)$ $\Rightarrow L^D = \alpha E / w$
	5	$\pi_c(i) = (1-\alpha)E/n \; \forall i$ $\Rightarrow \dfrac{\dot{\pi}_c(i)}{\pi_c(i)} = -\dfrac{\dot{n}}{n}$	

All monopolists therefore set their price at w/α. With prices equal and symmetry in the utility function, the quantity demanded of each variety is equal and aggregate labour demand is equal to the aggregate quantities consumed. One obtains $L^D=E/p=\alpha E/w$.[10] Profits are then given by:

$$\pi_i = -\frac{1}{\sigma}\frac{E}{n} = \frac{1-\alpha}{n}E \qquad (3.4)$$

These results are summarised in Cells 3 to 5 of Table 3.1, where a dot over a variable signifies the time derivative.

The ownership claims to these profits are assets that consumers can buy. The price of such an asset, assumed equal to the consumers' willingness to pay, will be equal to the discounted present value of all future profit flows. In general the return on an asset equals the cash flow, here the instant profit flow, plus the change in the value of the asset, $\dot{v}_i(t)$, divided by the current price of the asset, $v_i(t)$. For consumers to be willing to hold such assets, this total return must, as was derived above, equal the consumers' discount rate.[11] Grossman and Helpman present the resulting capital market arbitrage condition as:

$$(\rho =)r = \frac{\pi_i + \dot{v}_i}{v_i} \tag{3.5}$$

where time arguments have been dropped to save on notation. Since all assets are assumed to be perfect substitutes they must all yield the common rate of return and since, in a rational expectations model with perfect foresight, an asset's value is equal to the discounted flow of future cash flows, the above arbitrage condition is always fulfilled. But v is not only the value of an existing firm at any point in time. It is also the value of the marginal new firm at that point in time and hence the maximum amount an entrepreneur is willing to invest in R&D.

In the variety expansion model in Grossman and Helpman (1991b) the R&D sector can produce innovations that allow an entrepreneur to set up a the $n+1$th firm. Hence the number of firms, n, increases over time according to the following *innovation function*:

$$\dot{n} = a L^{R\&D} n \tag{3.6}$$

Despite the fact that (3.6) is a relatively simple equation, the intuition behind it is important to stress at this stage. Parameter a is merely a productivity parameter that allows one to measure R&D labour inputs, $L^{R\&D}$, in the same units as for production. The presence of n on the right hand side, however, requires some elaboration. It represents the externality effect of knowledge accumulation. The behaviour of the R&D sector is summarised in Cells 6 and 7 of the formal synopsis table:

Table 3.1:   **FORMAL SYNOPSIS OF GROSSMAN AND HELPMAN**
(Cont'd)   (1991B)

AGENT(S)		PROBLEM(S) SUBJECT TO CONSTRAINT(S) ⇒ RESULTS
R&D	6	Price taking in R&D $\Rightarrow v(i) = \dfrac{\pi_c(i) + \dot{v}(i)}{r} = \dfrac{\pi_c + \dot{v}}{r}$ $\forall i$
	7	$\max\limits_{L_{R\&D}} : \pi_{R\&D} = \dot{n}(L_{R\&D}) * v - w L_{R\&D}$ s.t. $\dot{n}(L_{R\&D}) = a L_{R\&D} n$ $\Rightarrow w = anv$

n is introduced in Cell 7 as a proxy for the accumulated knowledge available to all R&D firms at no costs.[12] By introducing a new variety, an individual entrepreneur generates and appropriates the value of one firm, v, but by increasing n he also increases the productivity of R&D labour in producing future innovations. This externality is the driving force of this endogenous growth model, enabling steady state positive growth rates and introducing increasing returns at the aggregate level. With the R&D sector fully specified, all basic elements of a product innovation driven growth model are now present

A simple labour market clearing condition, $L^{R\&D}+L^D=L^*$, is sufficient to close the model and allows one to write down an equation for the evolution of the number of varieties in equilibrium as:[13]

$$\frac{\dot{n}}{n} = aL^{R\&D} = a(L^* - L^D) = a\left(L^* - \frac{\alpha E}{avn}\right) = aL^* - \frac{\alpha E}{vn} \qquad (3.7)$$

Together with (3.5) this yields a system of two differential equations in two unknowns, v and n.[14] That system of equations can be solved for the steady state growth rate, a constant given by:

$$g = \dot{n}/n = (1-\alpha)aL^* - \alpha\rho \qquad (3.8)$$

The formal synopsis of the full model is presented in Table 3.1. One can verify in Cell 2 that the normalised and therefore constant expenditure generates increasing utility due to the drop in P as n increases. Hence, by the assumed proportionality between knowledge and the number of existing varieties, the utility value of normalised consumption expenditure can grow at a positive rate in equilibrium. This is the case for sufficiently inelastic demand; low α, a sufficiently productive R&D sector; low a, a large enough supply of labour; L^*, and sufficiently patient consumers; low ρ, see Equation (3.8). Of course this result does not depend on the normalisation chosen. If the price of a util, P, had been normalised to 1, then the consumption budget (and wages) would grow over time at rate g.[15] In the variety expansion model presented here, the only form of innovation is final output variety expansion and one should realise that only new entrants will issue stock to finance R&D activity. The incumbent firms do not have the means or the incentive (see Equation (3.4)) to innovate in this model, but a capital market must exist in order to allow entrepreneurs to use savings for the investment in product innovation.[16]

Table 3.1:   FORMAL SYNOPSIS OF GROSSMAN AND HELPMAN
(Full)   (1991B)

AGENT(S)		PROBLEM(S) SUBJECT TO CONSTRAINT(S) $\Rightarrow$ RESULTS
CONSUMERS	1	$\max\limits_{E(t)} : \int_{t}^{\infty} e^{-\rho(\tau-t)} \log(E(\tau)/P(\tau)) d\tau$ s.t. $Y(t) + rA(t) + E(t) + dA(t)/dt$ $\Rightarrow \dfrac{\dot{E}(t)}{E(t)} = r - \rho$
	2	$\max\limits_{c(i)} : U(.) = \left(\int_{0}^{n} c(i)^{\alpha} di \right)^{\frac{1}{\alpha}}$ s.t. $\int_{0}^{n} p(i)c(i)di \leq E$ $\Rightarrow c^{D}(i) = \left(\dfrac{p(i)}{P} \right)^{\frac{1}{\alpha-1}} \dfrac{E}{P}$ $\Rightarrow P \equiv \left(\int_{0}^{n} p(i)^{\frac{\alpha}{\alpha-1}} di \right)^{\frac{\alpha-1}{\alpha}}$
PRODUCERS	3	$\max\limits_{p(i)} : \pi_{c}(i) = c(i)p(i) - tc(i)$ s.t. $c(i) = c^{D}(i)$ $\Rightarrow p(i) = \dfrac{1}{\alpha} mc(i)$
	4	$\min\limits_{l(i)} : wl(i)$ s.t. $c^{D}(i) = l(i)$ $\Rightarrow l^{D}(i) = \alpha E / wn$ $\Rightarrow L^{D} = \alpha E / w$
	5	$\pi_{c}(i) = (1-\alpha)E/n \; \forall i$ $\Rightarrow \dfrac{\dot{\pi}_{c}(i)}{\pi_{c}(i)} = -\dfrac{\dot{n}}{n}$
R&D	6	Price taking in R&D $\Rightarrow v(i) = \dfrac{\pi_{c}(i) + \dot{v}(i)}{r} = \dfrac{\pi_{c} + \dot{v}}{r}$ $\forall i$
	7	$\max\limits_{L_{R\&D}} : \pi_{R\&D} = \dot{n}(L_{R\&D}) * v - wL_{R\&D}$ s.t. $\dot{n}(L_{R\&D}) = aL_{R\&D}n$ $\Rightarrow w = anv$
EQUILIBRIUM CONDITIONS		
LABOUR MARKET	8	$L^{*} = L_{R\&D}{}^{D} + L^{D}$ $\Rightarrow \dfrac{\dot{n}}{n} = aL^{*} - \dfrac{\alpha E}{nv}, \; \dfrac{\dot{v}}{v} = \rho - \dfrac{(1-\alpha)E}{nv}$
ASSET MARKET	9	$d\dfrac{nv}{Y} / dt = 0$ $\Rightarrow \dfrac{\dot{n}}{n} = -\dfrac{\dot{v}}{v}$ such that $nv/Y = nv$ is constant
STEADY STATE	10	$\Rightarrow \; g = (1-\alpha)aL^{*} - \alpha\rho$

Grossman and Helpman show that positive long-run equilibrium growth can be maintained even if knowledge-spillovers are less than proportional in Equation (3.6). Also GDP growth, when it includes the value added of the R&D sector, adequately measures the rate of technical change.[17]

A similar set-up and in fact identical results can be derived from a quality ladder version of this model as is illustrated in Appendix 3B and Grossman and Helpman (1991b) Chapter 4. Romer (1990) and Aghion and Howitt (1992) introduce process innovation as an expanding variety and a quality ladder in intermediate goods, respectively. Technically and conceptually they therefore differ very little from the two Grossman and Helpman models.[18]

Aghion and Howitt chose a process innovation interpretation because they focus on the welfare implications of the two externalities that exist in the quality ladder model.[19] Aghion and Howitt reintroduce the term *creative destruction* for the negative spillover effect to stress the linkages to the Schumpetarian tradition. Their model is also set up in more general terms than Grossman and Helpman's, as Appendix 3C illustrates. In their model Aghion and Howitt show that two 'wrongs', a positive externality due to the quality ladder and a negative one due to creative destruction of rents, do not necessarily make a 'right' and socially optimal growth may differ from private equilibrium.

Romer (1990) introduces process innovation by considering a two-stage three-factor production function in which capital is a CES-aggregate of intermediate products at the lowest level.[20] In this model the key result is that knowledge spillovers are required to maintain long-run positive growth rates as was illustrated above. All endogenous growth models share this property. The differences are in the way these spillovers are modelled and interpreted.

3.1.2 CONCLUDING REMARKS

Comparison of the structure of Tables 3.1 and 3B.1-3D.1 in the appendices clearly illustrates how the models discussed fit the general structure in Table 3.2. Although many have made generalisations and extensions in later models, this general structure still constitutes the core of R&D-driven growth models in general and of the model to be presented below in particular.

In the Grossman and Helpman (1991b), Romer (1990) and Aghion and Howitt (1992) models innovations respond to profit levels and as such labour market developments caused by technological shocks were allowed to feed back into technical change. In all models an exogenous productivity shock in R&D would for example initially increase R&D labour demand and increase the innovation rate such that production labour demand also rises. Then, due to competition between R&D and production, wages rise. This erodes profitability, reduces the value of innovations and in the long-run equilibrium the increase in demand for R&D is at least partially reversed.

Table 3.2:   STRUCTURE OF INNOVATION DRIVEN GROWTH MODELS

AGENTS		PROBLEM	CONSTRAINT	RESULT
CONSUMERS	1	Choose savings/ consumption to maximise intertemporal utility	Intertemporal Budget Constraint $Y+rK=E+\Delta K$	Savings and Consumption $S(r)(=\Delta K)$ $E(r)=Y+rK-S(r)$
	2	Choose consumption volumes to maximise intratemporal utility	Intratemporal Budget Constraint $pC=E$	Demand Function $C^D(p,E)$
PRODUCERS[21]	3	Set prices to maximise profits	Demand Functions $C^D(p,E)$	Supply Schedule $C^S(p)$
	4	Choose inputs to minimise costs	Production Function $C^S(X,L)$	Input Demand Functions $X^D(p_X)$, $L^D(w)$
INTERMEDIATE PRODUCERS[22]	5	Set prices to maximise profits	Demand Functions $X^D(p_X)$	Supply schedule $X^S(p_X)$
	6	Choose inputs to minimise costs	Production Function $X^S(K,L)$	Input Demand Functions $K_X^D(r)$, $L_X^D(w)$
R&D	7	Set prices to maximise profits	Demand Function	Price Taking $V_{C,x}=f(\pi_{C,x})$
	8	Choose inputs to minimise costs	Innovation Function $R(K,L)=$ Innovations	Input Demand Functions $K^{R\&D}(r)$, $L^{R\&D}(w)$
EQUILIBRIUM CONDITIONS				
INTRA-TEMPORAL	9	All markets clear intratemporally $K^{R\&D}(r)+K_X^D(r)+K^D(r)=K(t)$, $L^{R\&D}(w)+L_X^D(w)+L^D(w)=L^*$, $X^D(p_X)=X^S(p_X)$ and $C^D(p,E)=C^S(p)$		w^*, p^*, p_X^*, r^*
INTER-TEMPORAL	10	Savings finance R&D intertemporally $S(r^*)=R_{C,x}(K^*,L^*)V_{C,x}$		g^*, K^*

Technological developments caused by labour market shocks also feed back into the labour market. As Jones (1995) pointed out, a labour supply shock, for example, would cause lower wages, generate higher rates of innovation and consequently higher long-run wages and growth rates.[23]

Jones (1995) criticised the above models for this property since it seems in sharp contrast to the empirical evidence on demographics, R&D employment and growth.[24] Despite this critique these models do identify the key elements for a model that hopes to identify labour technology interaction mechanisms and are a useful first step in explaining induced biases, as the next section will show.[25]

The models discussed so far have no or at best trivial implications for the relative position of low skilled labour, admittedly because they did not aim to address that issue. Those models that distinguish two types of labour, Romer (1990) and Aghion and Howitt (1992), have introduced manual labour in such a way that a fixed share of total income is spent on a fixed amount of labour. Technical change takes the form of or can be reduced to total factor augmenting innovation, leaving the relative positions of high and low skilled labour unaffected. To extend the models in that direction, the innovations that generate technical change should somehow be made skill-specific. This implies that, in addition to having (at least) two types of labour, one has (at least) two types of innovations in one model. Combining two types of innovation in one model, however, requires one to rethink some issues.

A first issue is patent protection. The variety expansion models by Romer (1990) and Grossman and Helpman (1991b) and many more assume that the patent system provides perfect and indefinite protection to the innovator. This assumption sanctions the monopolistic market structure in final or intermediate output markets and the flow of monopoly rents generated thus lasts indefinitely. It declines over time, however, due to the introduction of ever more varieties that compete for scarce inputs in production.

The perfect patent protection assumption is dropped without blinking an eye when quality improvements are considered. To replace the rent erosion due to increased competition in input markets the possibility of being replaced is introduced and reduces the value of an innovation. To deal with the possibility that many entrepreneurs try to improve the same product at the same time, both Grossman and Helpman (1991b) and Aghion and Howitt (1992) introduce a stochastic lottery type of innovation function in which only one entrepreneur can win and the losers have wasted their effort.[26]

If one would like to combine different types of innovation in one model, there is a choice to be made. Assuming lifelong patent protection implies that no producers can ever come in and steal a patent holder's business. This has implications when combining product and process innovations. If patents are protecting the product design, a new process, that produces that product cheaper using a wider variety of or higher quality of inputs, is only valuable if the patent on the product is owned or purchased first.

The assumption of indefinite patent protection for final and intermediate products thus implies that the value of quality improvements or product specific process innovations is limited to the *additional* discounted flow of rents that accrue to the incumbent producer. The cost reductions generating such additional flows of rent were already identified as a key driving force in the diffusion of new capital equipment in Chapter 2. This requires a minor but important change in the modelling of the R&D sector decision.

A second issue that could be raised here is that of R&D inputs. The models by Grossman and Helpman (1991b) assume labour to be homogenous and the only input in innovation and production. This assumption obviously will not stand in a model with multiple skill levels. The assumption is generally made, however, to stress the idea that labour has an alternative use in final or intermediate production, such that the R&D sector must compete for its employment. That element of competition in factor markets disappears when R&D is performed using a specialised factor such as in Aghion and Howitt (1992) or final output.[27]

It will come as no surprise that empirically the key input in R&D is high skilled labour.[28] It is also evident that these workers can be employed in current production and the R&D sector must compete for them with other sectors in the economy. The Romer (1990) model is slightly more sophisticated than the Grossman and Helpman (1991) models in the sense that it does distinguish between human capital and manual labour. In the aggregate final output production the two types of labour are substitutes but Romer (1990) assumes a substitution elasticity of 1. The model presented below will be more general in that respect.

The next section proceeds with two model specifications by Acemoglu (2002a) that formally illustrate the market size explanation in a model with high and low skilled labour and two skill specific variety expansion types of skill specific process innovation.

3.2   MODELLING ENDOGENOUS BIAS IN INNOVATION

Acemoglu's models (1998, 2002a) are best known among the few recent attempts in the literature to link endogenous growth theory to the issue of biased technical change.[29] Acemoglu considers aggregate skill biases in technical change to be the result of (a wave of) innovations that are individually biased towards or, as he calls it, *complementary* to high skilled labour. To develop and adopt such innovations is relatively profitable when high skilled wages are low. This biased innovation then generates a shift in demand that, under normal circumstances, generates rising relative wages and the bias in innovation would go back and forth, always shifting towards complementing the relatively cheaper factor.[30] This would be consistent with Hicks' original formulation of the induced bias hypothesis; as was argued in Chapter 1, however, it is inconsistent with empirical facts.

Figure 3.1:   THE MARKET SIZE EFFECT

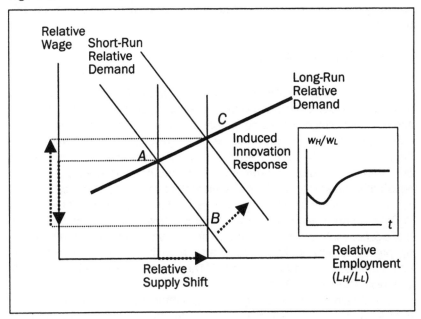

Acemoglu introduced skill type specific innovations in various guises to explain the paradoxical simultaneous decrease in relative wages and demand for low skilled. In his models an exogenous supply shock causes a shift in innovation towards complementing high skilled labour as in the older induced bias models. Through knowledge spillovers, however, the shock now has a lasting positive effect on the R&D productivity for that type of innovation. As this productivity increase translates into a higher rate of skill complementary innovation, relative demand for skilled labour shifts up. Under various specifications and restrictions Acemoglu shows that a situation can emerge where the induced bias is so strong that relative wages have to rise above their pre-shock levels to re-establish long-run equilibrium.

Figure 3.1, taken from Acemoglu (1998), p. 1057 and repeated from Chapter 1, illustrates how, following the relative supply shock, relative wages drop initially, but as technology responds, move up to their long-run equilibrium level at *C*, which may lie above *A*. Acemoglu (2002a) labelled this the *strong induced bias hypothesis*. In Chapter 1 and below it is also referred to as the *strong market size effect*.

A more formal treatment of the 2002 variety expansion model will show how Acemoglu's work relates to the general class of innovation driven growth models presented above and the life cycle models presented below.

3.2.1 A MODEL OF ENDOGENOUS BIAS

Acemoglu (2002a) illustrates the strong market size effect in a variety expansion model. Synopsis Table 3.3 presents Cells 1-7 in this model.[31] Acemoglu introduces consumers, final output producers and intermediate output producers, who face the decisions discussed extensively above. Consumers in Cells 1 and 2 are trivial as they consume the homogenous final output and their intertemporal time preferences merely provide a constant interest rate at which the innovators can borrow later on.

Homogenous final output, *Y*, is produced by a competitive sector in Cells 3 and 4 according to a CES production function, combining two homogenous intermediate inputs, Y_H and Y_L, produced in an earlier stage, by high and low skilled labour and a skill specific range of sub-intermediates, $x_{H,L}$, in Cells 5 and 6. These sub-intermediates expand in variety in Acemoglu (2002a).[32]

Finally, in Cell 7 two (groups of) monopolistic producers, who can choose a price, $\chi_{H,L}$, such that their profits provide an incentive to innovate, produce these sub-intermediates. Compared to the general structure presented above, he thus distinguishes one additional step in the production chain. By doing so, high and low skilled labour are still substitutes in final output production but innovation can be made skill specific.

As is customary in innovation driven growth models, a separate R&D sector 'produces' the innovations for each range of skill specific sub-intermediates. Following the variety expansion model presented above, Acemoglu (2002a) assumes deterministic innovation functions, indefinite patent protection and expanding monopolistic competition.[33] He also assumes the competition for resources between production and innovation away for convenience.

Table 3.3:   FORMAL SYNOPSIS OF ACEMOGLU[34]
(2002A) Basic Structure

AGENT(S) RESULTS		PROBLEM(S) SUBJECT TO CONSTRAINT(S) $\Rightarrow$
CONSUMERS[35]	1	$\max_{E(t)} : \int_{t}^{\infty} e^{-\rho(\tau-t)} \dfrac{U(E(\tau))^{1-\theta} - 1}{1-\theta} d\tau$ s.t. $Y(t) + rA(t) = E(t) + dA(t)/dt$ $\Rightarrow \dfrac{\dot{E}(t)}{E(t)} = (r-\rho)/\theta$
	2	$\max_{c} : U(E) = C$ s.t. $pC \le E$ $\Rightarrow C = E/p$
FINAL OUTPUT PRODUCER	3	Perfect Competition $\Rightarrow p = mc \equiv 1$
	4	$\max_{Y_H, Y_L} : \pi_Y = Y(Y_H, Y_L) - p_H Y_H - p_L Y_L$ s.t. $Y(Y_H, Y_L) = \left(b_H Y_H^{\alpha} + b_L Y_L^{\alpha}\right)^{\frac{1}{\alpha}}$ $\Rightarrow \dfrac{p_H}{p_L} = \dfrac{b_H}{b_L}\left(\dfrac{Y_H}{Y_L}\right)^{\alpha-1} \Rightarrow p = \left(b_H p_H^{\frac{\alpha}{\alpha-1}} + b_L p_L^{\frac{\alpha}{\alpha-1}}\right)^{\frac{\alpha-1}{\alpha}}$
INTERMEDIATE PRODUCER	5	Perfect Competition $\Rightarrow \dfrac{p_H}{p_L} = \dfrac{mc_H}{mc_L}$
	6	$\max_{L_H, x_H} \pi_{Y_H} = p_H Y_H - w_H L_H - X_H x_H$ s.t. $Y_H = A_H(x_H, t) L_H^{\beta}$ $\max_{L_L, x_L} : \pi_{Y_L} = p_L Y_L - w_L L_L - X_L x_L$ s.t. $Y_L = A_L(x_L, t) L_L^{\beta}$ $\Rightarrow \dfrac{w_H}{w_L} = \dfrac{b_H}{b_L}\left(\dfrac{A_H(x_H, t)}{A_L(x_L, t)}\right)^{\alpha}\left(\dfrac{L_H}{L_L}\right)^{\alpha\beta-1}$ $\Rightarrow \dfrac{X_H}{X_L} = \dfrac{A_H'(x_H^D, t)}{A_L'(x_L^D, t)} \dfrac{b_H}{b_L}\left(\dfrac{A_H(x_H^D, t) L_H^{\beta}}{A_L(x_L^D, t) L_L^{\beta}}\right)^{\alpha-1}$
SUB-INTERMEDIATE PRODUCER	7	$\max_{x_H} : \pi_H = X_H x_H - tc_{x_H}$ s.t. $x_H = x_H^D(X_H)$ $\max_{x_H} : \pi_L = X_L x_L - tc_{x_L}$ s.t. $x_L = x_L^D(X_L)$ $\Rightarrow X_H = \dfrac{\sigma_H}{\sigma_H + 1} mc_{x_H}$ $\Rightarrow X_L = \dfrac{\sigma_L}{\sigma_L + 1} mc_{x_L}$

The model can be interpreted as a combination of elements from the models discussed above. The main novelty in Acemoglu's work is that there are now two types of innovations. One increases the productivity of high and one that of low skilled labour. This allows him to link the *relative* labour market position of low skilled to technical change and analyse the feedbacks that emerge.

To model this skill specificity, innovation takes the form of increases in n_H and n_L, the number of sub-intermediate goods in both sectors (Cell 6 in Table 3.3). The value of a new design in both sectors is given by the present value of the monopoly rents a new sub-intermediate producer can expect to receive. Acemoglu (2002a) identifies and analyses two distinct innovation function specifications. He refers to these specifications as the 'lab equipment' specification and the 'knowledge based' specification. In the former new varieties are produced using units of final output as the input. In the latter an exogenous supply of scientists is allocated over low and high skilled complementary variety expansion.[36] The resources required to innovate differ between these specifications but they do share the property that two innovative activities compete for the same pool of R&D resources. The lab equipment specification is summarised in Table 3.4.

Table 3.4:   FORMAL SYNOPSIS OF ACEMOGLU
(2002A) Lab Equipment

AGENT(S)		PROBLEM(S) SUBJECT TO CONSTRAINT(S) $\Rightarrow$ RESULTS S indexes Sector/Skill
INTERMEDIATE PRODUCER	6	$\min_{S,x_s(i,j)} : tc_{Y_s}(i) = p_s Y_s(i) - w_s L_s(i) - \int_0^{n_s} x_s(j) x_s(i,j) dj$ s.t. $Y_s(i) = A_s(i) L_s(i)^\beta$ $\Rightarrow L_s(i)^D = \beta \dfrac{p_s Y_s(i)}{w_s} \qquad \Rightarrow w_s = \beta \dfrac{p_s Y_s}{L_s^*}$ $A_s(i) = \dfrac{1}{1-\beta} \int_0^{n_s} x_s(i,j)^{1-\beta} dj$ $\Rightarrow x_s^D(i,j) = \left(\dfrac{p_s}{X_s(j)}\right)^{\frac{1}{\beta}} L_s(i)$ $\int L_s^D(i) di = L_s^D$ and $\int x_s(i,j) di = X_s^D(j)$ $\Rightarrow X_s^D(j) = \left(\dfrac{p_s}{X_s(j)}\right)^{\frac{1}{\beta}} L_s^D$

Table 3.4:   **FORMAL SYNOPSIS OF ACEMOGLU**
(Cont'd)   (2002A) Lab Equipment

AGENT(S)		PROBLEM(S) SUBJECT TO CONSTRAINT(S) ⇒ RESULTS S indexes Sector/Skill
SUB-INTERMEDIATE PRODUCER	7	$\max\limits_{X_s(j)} : \pi_s(j) = (X_s(j) - \psi)X_s(j)$ s.t. $X_s(j) = X_s^D(j)$ $\Rightarrow X_s(j) = \dfrac{\psi}{1-\beta}$
	8	$\min\limits_{l_s(j)} : tc_s(j) = \psi X_s(j)$ s.t. $X_s^D(j) = (1-\beta)l_s(j)$ $\Rightarrow \psi = (1-\beta)$
	9	$\pi_{X_s}(j) = \beta p_s^{\frac{1}{\beta}} L_s^D$ $\Rightarrow \dfrac{\pi_{X_H}}{\pi_{X_L}} = \left(\dfrac{n_H}{n_L}\right)^{\frac{\alpha-1}{1-\alpha+\alpha\beta}} \left(\dfrac{b_H}{b_L}\right)^{\frac{1}{1-\alpha+\alpha\beta}} \left(\dfrac{L_H^D}{L_L^D}\right)^{\frac{\alpha\beta}{1-\alpha+\alpha\beta}}$
R&D	10	Price taking in R&D $\Rightarrow v_s(j) = \dfrac{\pi_{X_s}(j) + \dot{v}_s(j)}{r}$
	11A	$\max\limits_{R_s} : \dot{n}_s v_s(j) - tc_s^{R\&D}$ s.t. $\dot{n}_s = a_s R_s$ $\Rightarrow v_s(j) = 1/a_s$ $\Rightarrow \dfrac{\dot{v}_s(j)}{v_s(j)} = 0$ $tc_s^{R\&D} = R_s$ $\Rightarrow \dfrac{n_H}{n_L} = \left(\dfrac{a_H}{a_L}\right)^{\frac{1-\alpha+\alpha\beta}{1-\alpha}} \left(\dfrac{b_H}{b_L}\right)^{\frac{1}{1-\alpha}} \left(\dfrac{L_H}{L_L}\right)^{\frac{\alpha\beta}{1-\alpha}}$ $\Rightarrow r = \beta\left(b_H \left(a_H L_H^*\right)^{\frac{\alpha\beta}{1-\alpha}} + b_L \left(a_L L_L^*\right)^{\frac{\alpha\beta}{1-\alpha}}\right)^{\frac{1-\alpha}{\alpha\beta}}$

EQUILIBRIUM CONDITIONS

LABOUR MARKETS	12A	$L_H^D = L_H^*$ and $L_L^D = L_L^*$
ASSET MARKETS	13A	$d\dfrac{nv}{Y} = 0$ such that $\dfrac{nv}{Y} = \dfrac{n_H/a_H + n_L/a_L}{Y}$ is constant $\Rightarrow \dfrac{\dot{n}_H}{n_H} = \dfrac{\dot{n}_L}{n_L} = \dfrac{\dot{Y}}{Y} = \dfrac{r-\rho}{\theta}$
STEADY STATE	14A	$\Rightarrow g = \dfrac{\beta\left(b_H \left(a_H L_H^*\right)^{\frac{\alpha\beta}{1-\alpha}} + b_L \left(a_L L_L^*\right)^{\frac{\alpha\beta}{1-\alpha}}\right)^{\frac{1-\alpha}{\alpha\beta}} - \rho}{\theta}$

In this specification a steady state in which relative prices and wages are constant implies that the innovation rate in both sectors is equal. Consumption, output and R&D effort then grow in proportion to that rate such that growth can be sustained.[37] As is shown in Appendix 3E, the long-run elasticity of substitution between high and low skilled labour is given by $(1-\alpha)/(\alpha\beta-1+\alpha)$ under this specification, which is positive for $\beta>(1-\alpha)/\alpha$.[38]

Table 3.5:   FORMAL SYNOPSIS OF ACEMOGLU
(2002A) Knowledge Based

AGENT(S)		PROBLEM(S) SUBJECT TO CONSTRAINT(S) $\Rightarrow$ RESULTS S indexes Sector/Skill
	10	Price taking in R&D $\Rightarrow v_s = \dfrac{\pi_{x_s}(j) + \dot{v}_s(j)}{r}$
R&D	11B	$\max\limits_{R_s} : \dot{n}_s v_s - tc_s^{R\&D}$ s.t. $\dot{n}_s = a_s n_s^{\frac{1+\delta}{2}} n_{-s}^{\frac{1-\delta}{2}} R_s$ $\Rightarrow v_s = \dfrac{p_R}{a_s}\left(\dfrac{n_s}{n_{-s}}\right)^{\frac{1+\delta}{2}} n_{-s}$ $\Rightarrow \dfrac{\dot{v}_s}{v_s} = \dfrac{\dot{p}_R}{p_R} + \dfrac{\dot{n}_{-s}}{n_{-s}}$ $tc_s^{R\&D} = p_R R_s$ $R^* = R_H + R_L$ $\Rightarrow R_H = \dfrac{R^*}{1 + \dfrac{a_H}{a_L}\left(\dfrac{n_H}{n_L}\right)^{\delta-1}}$
EQUILIBRIUM CONDITIONS		
LABOUR MARKETS	12B	$L_H^D = L_H^*$ and $L_L^D = L_L^*$
ASSET MARKETS	13B	$d\dfrac{nv}{Y} = 0$ such that $\dfrac{nv}{Y} = \dfrac{n_H v_H + n_L v_L}{Y}$ is constant $\Rightarrow \dfrac{\dot{Y}}{Y} = \dfrac{\dot{n}_s}{n_s} = \dfrac{\dot{n}_H}{n_H} + \dfrac{\dot{n}_L}{n_L} + \dfrac{\dot{p}_R}{p_R}$, $\Rightarrow \dfrac{\dot{v}_s}{v_s} = 0$ $\Rightarrow \dfrac{n_H}{n_L}^{SS} = \left(\left(\dfrac{a_H}{a_L}\right)^{1-\alpha+\alpha\beta}\left(\dfrac{b_H}{b_L}\right)\left(\dfrac{L_H}{L_L}\right)^{\alpha\beta}\right)^{\frac{1}{(1+\delta)(1-\alpha+\alpha\beta)-\alpha\beta}}$
STEADY STATE	14B	$\Rightarrow g = \dfrac{a_H R^*}{\left(\dfrac{n_H}{n_L}\right)^{SS\,\frac{1-\delta}{2}} + \dfrac{a_H}{a_L}\left(\dfrac{n_H}{n_L}\right)^{SS\,\frac{\delta-1}{2}}}$

The knowledge-based specification, summarised in Table 3.5, is more interesting, because the externality is explicitly identified as a knowledge spillover that generates growth. As will be shown below, it also relaxes the restriction on the parameters a bit. In this specification an exogenous supply of scientists, R^*, uses a stock of knowledge that has been accumulated over the past to invent new varieties. Like Grossman and Helpman (1991b), Acemoglu (2002a) assumes that the knowledge that has been accumulated is proportional to the number of varieties that have been invented, n_H and n_L. In this specification Acemoglu allows for cross-sectoral knowledge spillovers.

The parameter $(1-\delta)/2$ in Cell 11[B] determines the degree of cross-sectoral knowledge spillover.[39] Again a balanced growth path requires both ranges of intermediates to expand at the same rate, such that the ratio n_H/n_L is constant. This time, however, long-run positive growth is possible even if there are diminishing returns to the number of scientists.[40] Also the strong market size effect is more likely to occur than in the lab equipment model. The parameter restriction that has to hold for the long-run relative demand to be upward sloping is now $\beta > (1-\delta)(1-\alpha)/\alpha$.[41] As the right-hand side is now lower, this condition is met for a larger range of β.

For the model to have a stable steady state, however, an additional condition now has to be met. Intuitively the reason is that, when cross-sectoral knowledge spillovers are small, a lock-in in one type of innovation can emerge, such that relative wages tend to 0 or infinity in the long run. In the extreme case of no such spillovers, $\delta=1$, the knowledge accumulated by innovations of a given type only increase the productivity of scientists in that field and only one type of R&D is undertaken if high and low skilled workers are substitutes, $\alpha\beta/(1-\alpha)>1$, $\sigma_{SR}<-1$. It turns out that this situation will not occur when $1+\alpha\beta/(1-\alpha)<1/\delta$.[42] So one obtains that the strong market size will emerge iff:

$$1-\delta < \frac{\alpha\beta}{1-\alpha} < \frac{1-\delta}{\delta} \tag{3.9}$$

Hence the existence of the strong market size effect depends on the interaction of demand and production parameters that enter the decision to innovate through profitability and knowledge spillover parameters that affect the costs of R&D. Acemoglu concludes that a low cross-sectoral knowledge spillover combined with a high derived short-run elasticity of substitution makes the strong market size effect more likely.

3.2.2 CONCLUDING REMARKS

In the Acemoglu (2002a) model the Hicksian induced biases hypothesis is taken to its extreme to explain the observed labour market trends in the US. And the key predictions of his model are indeed consistent with the observed facts. Relative wages are predicted to drop first but then rise in response to a high skilled supply increase as observed in the mid 70s. In the 90s relative wages indeed seem to stabilise at the new, higher level. However, some questions remain. The strong market size effect requires high elasticities of substitution to generate skill bias. The empirical evidence is inconclusive in this respect. Freeman (1986) concludes that the elasticity is larger than 1 and 1.4 is often suggested, but only few find estimates above 2.[43] This range implies that the strong market size effect does not occur in the lab equipment specification and depends on the knowledge spillover specification in the knowledge-based model. It will be shown below that the more general innovation functions make the strong market size effect less, not more likely.

Finally, current output producers do not compete for R&D resources, implying that the growth rate is fully determined by an exogenously given stock of scientists.[44] These issues will be taken up in the next chapter. A final point to be made here is that in the knowledge-based specification the strong market size effect requires restrictions on the knowledge spillover parameter for which Acemoglu offers no empirical or theoretical intuition. He remarks that empirical evidence is not available and there are no a priori theoretical constraints. The former is beyond dispute but in the remainder of this chapter it will be argued that some a priori intuition can be developed when the product life cycle is considered.

3.3   MODELLING THE PRODUCT LIFE CYCLE

In this section two models from the literature are shortly discussed. They illustrate how product life cycles can be represented in models of innovation driven growth. The models considered, Krugman (1979) and Grossman and Helpman (1991a), address a seemingly very different topic than skill bias; the impact of product life cycles on international specialisation and trade patterns. Still these models provide the intuition to pin down the knowledge spillover parameters in Acemoglu's knowledge-based innovation functions. As before the mathematical details of these models are presented in the appendices, Appendices 3F and 3G.

3.3.1 PRODUCT LIFE CYCLE MODELS

As was shown in Chapter 2 the idea of a product life cycle has been formulated early on in the economic literature. Krugman (1979) noted, however, that the actual modelling of this empirically robust phenomenon was taken up relatively slowly.

> *One might have expected that phenomena, which are of recognized importance and at the same time display clear empirical regularities, would have attracted the attention of theorists. But there have been few attempts to introduce technological change into the theory of international trade.*
> - Krugman (1979), p. 254 -

And he presented a model in which the life cycle of products plays a prominent role in explaining the international pattern of specialisation and distribution of income. In Van Zon, Sanders and Muysken (2001) it was shown that this model provides an excellent basic framework for introducing product life cycles in a closed economy as well. The basic idea in Krugman (1979) is that the North invents new products and has the exclusive capacity to produce them for some time.[45] Then these new products are imitated in the South and they start producing them as well. Both 'countries' are identical in all other respects. He assumes that there is no labour mobility and free trade between the North and South.

Having the background in innovation driven growth models that was developed in previous sections, it is easy to see that the exogenous invention and imitation parameters in the Krugman model can be endogenised in an innovation driven growth model.[46] Grossman and Helpman (1991a) took up this issue. They merely applied the endogenous innovations framework developed in Grossman and Helpman (1991b) above to the Krugman (1979) model. By introducing R&D sectors that use labour to generate new designs (North) or actively acquire and imitate the existing Northern designs (South), they present an endogenous innovation driven product life cycle model.[47]

In line with the endogenous innovation models discussed above, they introduce monopolistic competition and entrepreneurs who innovate or reverse engineer to obtain the resulting monopoly rents. As before, the entrepreneurs borrow from consumers to finance the required R&D expenditures. Deviating from custom in variety expansion models, however, patent protection is not assumed to be perfect. Rents that flow to a successful Northern innovator are not permanent. In this model Northern innovators run the risk of being replaced in the world market by a low cost producer from the South. In the quality ladder models mentioned above, there was a similar risk of being replaced by a local competitor introducing a higher quality of the same variety. The risk of replacement in this model is dealt with in the same way: the flow of profits in the North is discounted at a higher rate to compensate for the replacement risk. Obviously this risk depends positively on the reverse engineering efforts in the South.

With monopolistic competition firms in the North set monopoly prices. As was derived above prices are thus a fixed mark-up over marginal costs. Grossman and Helpman assume the latter to equal wages in both countries. Because Bertrand competition drives the profits to zero if a second Northern producer imitates, no Northern entrepreneurs will do so, as they would be unable to recover the strictly positive reverse engineering costs.[48] Hence for every variety there is at most one Northern producer. For the same reason there will also be at most one Southern firm imitating it. Thus two possible equilibria exist in a single product market: an uncontested Northern monopoly or a duopoly with one Northern and one Southern producer. If a Southern competitor steps in, however, he has lower marginal costs due to the fact that wages are lower in the South.[49] Hence he can and will undercut the Northern competitor's marginal costs and take the entire world market for that product. However, it depends on the wage gap between North and South whether he can charge his monopoly price and still undercut his competitor. The maximum price a Southern imitator can charge is the Northern firm's marginal costs. Therefore Southern imitators' profits decrease rapidly when the wage gap is closed. This implies that, when all varieties have been imitated and wages are equal, the incentive to imitate a variety is zero as was the case for the Northern entrepreneurs.

This feature overcomes a rather peculiar feature of the knowledge spillover structure assumed in the Grossman and Helpman model. They assume that the rate of imitation is produced using labour as an input according to:

$$\dot{n}_S = a_S L_S^{R\&D} n_S \qquad (3.10)$$

Note that the knowledge spillover in this innovation function is strictly proportional to previously imitated products, n_S, whereas Krugman (1979) implicitly assumed an international knowledge spillover as imitation was an exogenously fixed percentage a_S of the existing *new* products, n_N, implying:

$$\dot{n}_S = a_S n_N (= n - n_S) \tag{3.11}$$

As opposed to Krugman (1979) it is therefore in principle possible in the Grossman and Helpman (1991a) model to imitate non-existing varieties; n_S can grow even if n_N=0. Because of the above argument though, that will not happen in the equilibrium. Grossman and Helpman then show that there is unique and stable steady state equilibrium in their model. As in the Krugman model, the share of the North in the total number of varieties is constant and both n_S and n_N grow at the same rate.

Table 3.6:   FORMAL SYNOPSIS OF GROSSMAN AND HELPMAN (1991A)

AGENT(S)		PROBLEM(S) SUBJECT TO CONSTRAINT(S) $\Rightarrow$ RESULTS C indexes Countries North and South
CONSUMERS	1	$\max\limits_{E(t)}: \int_t^\infty e^{-\rho(\tau-t)} \log(E(\tau)/P(\tau)) d\tau$ s.t. $Y(t)+rA(t)=E(t)+dA(t)/dt$ $\Rightarrow \dfrac{\dot{E}(t)}{E(t)} = r - \rho$
PRODUCERS	2	$\max\limits_{c(i)}: U(.) = \left(\int_0^n c(i)^\alpha di \right)^{\frac{1}{\alpha}}$ s.t. $\int_0^n p(i)c(i)di \leq E$ $\Rightarrow c^o(i) = \left(\dfrac{p(i)}{P} \right)^{\frac{1}{\alpha-1}} \dfrac{E}{P}, \Rightarrow P \equiv \left(\int_0^n p(i)^{\frac{\alpha}{\alpha-1}} di \right)^{\frac{\alpha-1}{\alpha}}$
PRODUCERS	3	In North Monopolist $\max\limits_{p(i)}: \pi(i) = c(i)p(i) - tc_N(i)$ s.t. $c(i) = c^o(i)$ $\Rightarrow p_N(i) = \dfrac{1}{\alpha} mc_N(i)$ In South Bertrand-Competition $\max\limits_{p(i)}: \pi(i) = c(i)p(i) - tc_N(i)$ s.t. $c(i) = c^o(i), p_N(i)^{MIN} = mc_N(i)$ $\Rightarrow p_S(i) = \min\left[\dfrac{1}{\alpha} mc_N(i), mc_N(i) \right]$

Table 3.6: **FORMAL SYNOPSIS OF GROSSMAN AND HELPMAN**
(Cont'd)   (1991A)

AGENT(S)		PROBLEM(S) SUBJECT TO CONSTRAINT(S) $\Rightarrow$ RESULTS
		C indexes Countries North and South

AGENT(S)		
PRODUCERS	4	$\min\limits_{l(i)} : wl(i)$ s.t. $c^D(i) = bl(i)$ $\Rightarrow p_N(i) = \dfrac{w_N}{\alpha b}$ $\Rightarrow L_N^{\ D} = \dfrac{n_N}{b}\left(\dfrac{w_N}{\alpha b P}\right)^{\frac{1}{\alpha-1}}\dfrac{E}{P}$ $\min\limits_{l(i)} : wl(i)$ s.t. $c^D(i) = bl(i)$ $\Rightarrow p_s(i) = \min\left[\dfrac{w_s}{\alpha b}, \dfrac{w_N}{b}\right]$ $\Rightarrow L_s^{\ D} = \dfrac{n_s}{b}\left(\dfrac{\min[w_s/\alpha, w_N]}{bP}\right)^{\frac{1}{\alpha-1}}\dfrac{E}{P}$
	5	$\pi_N(i) = \dfrac{(1-\alpha)E}{n_N}\left(1 + \dfrac{n_s}{n_N}\left(\max\left[\dfrac{w_N}{w_s}, \dfrac{1}{\alpha}\right]\right)^{\frac{\alpha}{1-\alpha}}\right)^{-1}$ $\Rightarrow \dfrac{\dot{\pi}_N}{\pi_N} = \dfrac{\dot{E}}{E} - \dfrac{\dot{n}_N}{n_N}$ $\pi_s(i) = \dfrac{(1-\alpha)E}{n_s}\left(1 + \dfrac{n_N}{n_s}\left(\min\left[\dfrac{w_s}{w_N}, \alpha\right]\right)^{\frac{\alpha}{1-\alpha}}\right)^{-1}$ $\Rightarrow \dfrac{\dot{\pi}_s}{\pi_s} = \dfrac{\dot{E}}{E} - \dfrac{\dot{n}_s}{n_s}$
R&D	6	Price taking in R&D $\Rightarrow v_N = \dfrac{\pi_N + \dot{v}_N}{r + \dot{n}_s/n_N}$ and $v_s = \dfrac{\pi_s + \dot{v}_s}{r}$
	7	$\max\limits_{L_N^{R\&D}} : \pi_N^{\ R\&D} = \dot{n}(L_N^{\ R\&D}) * v_N - w_N L_N^{\ R\&D}$ s.t. $\dot{n}(L_N^{\ R\&D}) = a_N L_N^{\ R\&D} n$ $\Rightarrow w_N = a_N v_N n$ $\max\limits_{L_s^{R\&D}} : \pi_s^{\ R\&D} = \dot{n}_s(L_s^{\ R\&D}) * v_s - w_s L_s^{\ R\&D}$ s.t. $\dot{n}_s(L_s^{\ R\&D}) = a_s L_s^{\ R\&D} n_s$ $\Rightarrow w_s = a_s v_s n_s$

Table 3.6:   **FORMAL SYNOPSIS OF GROSSMAN AND HELPMAN**
(Cont'd)   (1991A)

		EQUILIBRIUM CONDITIONS
LABOUR MARKETS	8	$L_c^* = L_c^{R\&D} + L_c^D$ $$\Rightarrow \frac{\dot{n}}{n} = a_N(L_N^* - L_N^D), \frac{\dot{n}_s}{n_s} = a_s(L_s^* - L_s^D)$$ Normalising $w_N = n$ $\Rightarrow \frac{\dot{V_N}}{V_N} = 0, \frac{\dot{V_S}}{V_S} = 0$
ASSET MARKETS	9	$d\dfrac{nv}{Y} = 0$ such that $\int v(i)di / Y = \dfrac{n_N v_N + n_s v_s}{Y}$ is constant $$\Rightarrow \frac{\dot{Y}}{Y} = \frac{\dot{E}}{E} = \frac{\dot{n}}{n} = \frac{\dot{n}_s}{n_s} = \frac{\dot{n}_N}{n_N}$$
STEADY STATE	10	$\Rightarrow g = (1-\alpha)a_s L_s^* - \alpha\rho$

Appendix 3G and Table 3.6 present the Grossman and Helpman (1991a) model formally and in full detail. The equilibrium innovation rate determines relative wages as in the Krugman model. Due to the feedbacks of wages on innovation and imitation, however, the response to shocks is very different. An increase in Northern labour supply, for example, simply lowered the Northern wage and had no impact on technology in Krugman (1979). In Grossman and Helpman (1991a), however, the same shock increases the rate of innovation in the North as Northern R&D employment increases. Consequently the steady state demand for labour in the North rises and relative wages may increase in favour of the North.[50] The Grossman and Helpman (1991a) terms of trade effect is very similar to the Acemoglian (1998) market size effect discussed above.

In fact, Grossman and Helpman also argue that in their model it may be strong enough to offset the initial downward relative wage pressure. As Grossman and Helpman essentially assume a zero cross-sectoral (international) knowledge spillover the result once more depends entirely on the elasticity of substitution between Northern and Southern workers in aggregate world output.

3.3.2 CONCLUDING REMARKS

By replacing 'Northern' by 'high skilled', 'Southern' by 'low skilled' and interpreting 'imitation' as a process innovation that enables low skilled workers to produce a product, these models provide quite an adequate description of a stylised endogenous innovation driven product life cycle.[51] The translation, however, is not one on one. Whereas Krugman (1979) lacks the endogenous innovation element, the Grossman and Helpman (1991a) specification suggests that there is no link between introducing a product and introducing the innovation that moves it to the next stage in the cycle. There are therefore some issues that have to be addressed if one wants to interpret these models in a closed economy context.

First of all in the Grossman and Helpman (1991a) model, the R&D resources can be used for final output production and R&D, but are not mobile between the types of innovation. Southern workers earn Southern wages and the Southern R&D sector competes for them with the Southern production sector. In a closed economy context, however, it is more realistic to assume that low skilled workers earn low skilled wages and low skilled complementary R&D competes for *high* skilled workers with high skilled complementary R&D and new output producers.[52] This implies high skilled labour has three alternatives whereas low skilled labour can only be employed in mature goods production.

The second issue is patent protection. Without patent protection there are no monopoly rents in the closed economy and with it imitation is prohibited. When imitation is interpreted as moving a product into a mature stage, then patent protection can only be assumed if, as was argued above, process innovators capture only additional rents.[53]

The final issue to be addressed is the knowledge spillover structure. In the models by Krugman (1979) and Grossman and Helpman (1991a) this has not received much attention and the relevant parameters have been set at mathematically convenient values. Grossman and Helpman (1991a) use $\delta=1$, Krugman (1979) only implicitly suggests an extremely asymmetric positive spillover from past product innovation to present imitation/process innovation. Taking the life cycle seriously implies that more general and asymmetric spillover structures should be considered. The next chapter will present a model that does so and introduces Acemoglu's arbitrage between types of R&D into an appropriately reinterpreted innovation driven product life cycle framework with arbitrage between production and R&D as in Grossman and Helpman (1991a).

3.4 CONCLUSION

In this chapter several models have been presented. The explicit aim was to introduce the mathematical tools necessary to build a model that can endogenise the market size and the life cycle explanation for aggregate biases in technical change offered in Chapter 1. It can be concluded that such a model must distinguish at least two production sectors using high and low skilled labour respectively and two R&D sectors that generate the technical change in them. The Grossman and Helpman (1991a) life cycle model illustrated that the introduction of intertemporal and international knowledge spillovers in R&D allows one to combine the life cycle and endogenous growth. Acemoglu (2002a) illustrated that sector specificity of innovation is required to allow for endogenous bias at the individual innovation level.

Still these models are inadequate to illustrate the full story outlined in Chapter 1. The Grossman and Helpman (1991a) model requires several adjustments to apply to a closed economy with a high and low skilled sector, whereas the Acemoglu (2002a) model provides no empirically or intuitively well-founded specification of the innovation functions and has no life cycle structure. It would also be interesting to see if the Acemoglu (2002a) model yields different results when the trade-off between innovation and production is introduced and R&D must compete for its resources with (one of) the final goods sectors. The next chapter will present a model that incorporates all these elements. It allows one to analyse the strong market size explanation and the life cycle explanation jointly and separately in a unified framework.

NOTES

[1] The appendices are not included in the printed version of this book but can be downloaded in .pdf and word-format at www.marksanders.nl.

[2] The appendices to this chapter contain the no-frills formal derivation of the models referred to. Each appendix concludes with a synopsis table of the mathematical structure as the one developed for Grossman and Helpman (1991b) in this section. Those familiar with innovation driven growth models can quickly browse these tables for reference and proceed with the model by Acemoglu (2002a) that bears more direct relevance for the analysis in Chapter 4.

[3] In it they position this then new field of research in the older neoclassical tradition and influential early models by Arrow (1962) and Shell (1967) and also consider a host of extensions to their basic framework. This sub-section is based primarily on their Chapter 3 as that chapter contains the most relevant model for the purpose of this book. The model in their Chapter 4, in which a slightly different interpretation of product innovation is given, is presented in Appendix 3B.

[4] See Appendix 3A for the formal proof. Basic textbooks such as Barro and Sala-I-Martin (1995) and Obstfeld and Rogoff (1996) are much more elaborate on the issue of intertemporal utility maximisation.

[5] An often-applied shortcut is to assume a constant exogenous interest rate. The above optimisation programme can be thought of underlying this assumption. Appendix 3A presents a slightly more general case that yields a similar relation between consumption growth, interest rates and the parameters of the utility function.

[6] As opposed to the *quality ladder* model presented in Chapter 4 of Grossman and Helpman (1991b) and Appendix 3B, where quality improvements increase the direct utility of consuming a *given* number of varieties.

[7] If demand is iso-elastic this is a general result.

[8] Note that it is assumed that many products are in the market, such that one individual price, p_i, does not affect the cost-minimising price of a util, P. See Appendix 3A.

[9] Obviously such a production technology precludes any analysis of process innovations but it simplifies the model a great deal. More complicated production structures are considered below.

[10] Note that by the assumption that the utility function is symmetric and all producers use the same production technology, profits, prices, produced quantities and required inputs are identical for all producers, so one can drop the index i.

[11] Grossman and Helpman assume a unitary elasticity of intertemporal substitution and a normalised/constant consumption budget to derive this result. See Appendix 3A.

[12] Grossman and Helpman (1991b) show that without such a spillover the variety expansion model will not generate a positive steady state growth rate. In other words, in the end innovation will stop without it.

[13] See Appendix 3A.

[14] The fact that in the steady state the value of total assets is constant (relative to the consumption budget) is used. See Appendix 3A.

[15] See for example Appendix 3C and Romer (1990).

[16] By introducing new varieties incumbents would be eroding the profits on their existing varieties. However small this erosion, they can never outbid the entrants for funds. Of course the authors abstract here from a host of reasons why incumbents might actually be at an advantage in introducing new products. A vast literature on imperfect information and the Schumpetarian hypothesis deals with the implications of such admittedly more realistic assumptions. Still to the extent that future profits drive the demand for R&D the innovation driven growth models capture the elements of innovation this book will focus upon.

[17] See Grossman and Helpman (1991b) Chapter 3 for further details.

[18] As Grossman and Helpman (1991b) point out in their book the instant utility specifications can easily be interpreted as intermediate production functions. To see the analogy one only has to consider that the mathematical structure of the utility function could also describe how homogenous final output is produced using a range of different intermediate goods, a heterogeneous input. Doing that for variety expansion basically yields a specification like Romer (1990) whereas Aghion and Howitt (1992) present a model with quality ladders in intermediate products. The main difference between these models and the models above comes from the fact that labour is now combined with the intermediates to produce final output instead of being the single primary factor in the model. See the derivations and synopsis tables presented in the Appendices 3C and D.

[19] As was shown in Appendix 3B, in a quality ladder model there is the positive knowledge spillover from inherited quality but the future replacement of firms by innovators reduces the ex ante value of innovation and creates a negative externality.

[20] Cell 4 in the synopsis table of Appendix 3D shows that this capital aggregate is combined with 'human capital', H, and 'labour', L, at the highest level to produce a homogenous output. In Romer (1990) R&D competes with final output production for human capital, H, not labour, L.

---

21 Imperfect competition assumed when innovation is interpreted as product innovation through quality improvements or variety expansion in final goods. Otherwise the usual assumption is perfect competition and price taking. Step 3 is then trivial. Prices are fixed at minimum marginal costs.

22 Imperfect competition is introduced here when innovation is interpreted process innovation through quality improvements or variety expansion in intermediates. Otherwise intermediates are trivial and disregarded.

23 In the Romer (1990) model that effect requires a positive shock to H, not L.

24 His critique is mainly aimed at the models' property that a high population growth rate would imply a high and actually increasing GDP growth rate. As population growth rates are typically negatively correlated to economic growth rates this is strongly contradicted in the data.

25 Jones (2004) surveys the literature that emerged following his critique. Most models that succeeded in addressing his points used more complicated innovation functions but borrow heavily from the early work presented above and mainly use the tools developed there. More importantly none of these newer models deviates a lot from the general structure presented in Table 3.2.

26 It can be seen in the Tables 3.1 and 3B.1-3.D1 that the role of profit erosion:

$$\dot{v}(L^{**})$$

in the VE model is taken over by the creative destruction of rent flows at a flow rate:

$$-\Pr(L^{**})$$

in the QL models. Depending on the normalisation chosen, v is either constant or grows at the common growth rate in QL models so in these models one has:

$$\dot{v}(L^{**}_{0,}) \, .$$

27 Although of course the use of final output as an intermediate input in the innovation function can be interpreted as using a two-stage innovation function where the first stage is identical to production. This assumption implies innovation competes with consumers for intermediate inputs.

28 See for example Cameron (1998).

29 Another early paper was Kiley (1999), who pursued a similar modelling strategy as Acemoglu (2002a). As was mentioned in Chapter 2 these models build on the older induced bias models developed in the 60s. See Chapter 2 for more references.

30 Note how close this is to normal substitution. In Acemoglu, however, an act of innovation is required to make the switch towards higher skilled. Innovation also causes a permanent change in the shape of the production possibilities frontier.

31 Acemoglu (1998) introduces it into a quality ladder model. Both models are process innovation models and have Cells 1 to 6 in Table 3.2 in common. Table 3.3 below presents these common steps in the familiar formal synopsis table.

32 And exhibit a quality ladder in Acemoglu (1998).

33 Also in line with the models discussed above, Acemoglu's (1998) quality ladder model assumes probabilistic innovation functions, no patent protection and full displacement of the incumbent monopolists.

34 This structure is identical for the Acemoglu (1998) quality ladder model. See Appendix 3E.

35 In Acemoglu (1998) the marginal utility of consumption is assumed constant and the interest rate equals ρ, the rate of time preference, as in Aghion and Howitt (1992). In Acemoglu (2002a) the slightly more general CIES specification of Romer (1990) is used. This, however, is trivial for the results.

36 In the former the R&D sector buys resources at a given price until marginal product equals marginal costs. In the latter, the R&D sector employs a given amount of resources that earns a wage that is equal to the marginal product at that employment level. The specifications are not that different in that respect.

[37] The spillover that is essential for any endogenous growth model is here provided by growth itself. More output reduces the price of output and hence the costs of R&D. Constant returns then ensures the innovative effort grows with output. Introducing diminishing returns to lab equipment would imply that non-zero steady state growth is not possible. Note also that the constant returns specification implies that out of equilibrium all R&D investment is spent entirely on one or the other type of innovations until the balanced growth path is reached.

[38] As this condition is identical to the one obtained in Acemoglu (1998), this result illustrates once more that variety expansion and quality ladders can yield equivalent reduced form results.

[39] Acemoglu actually only considers cases where $\delta > 0$ and cross-sectoral spillovers are smaller than intrasectoral ones. In Sanders (2002) a slightly more general version with the possibility of asymmetric spillovers, i.e. using different δ's in the two equations is considered. The next chapter will present an even more general spillover structure.

[40] Even though Acemoglu (2002a) does not consider this generalisation. It will be argued in Chapter 4 that this is crucially important for the market size effect.

[41] See Appendix 3E.

[42] This condition implies that the steady state relative range n_H/n_L is positive in relative labour supply, which is necessary for the model to converge to a steady state. See Acemoglu (2002a) and Appendix 3E for details.

[43] In Chapter 4 the empirical evidence and the conditions for the strong market size effect are discussed in more detail.

[44] Of course the *bias* in technical change, Acemoglu's main focus, is fully endogenised since the allocation of the R&D resources over the two innovation types is endogenous.

[45] Krugman does not assume that one firm holds this exclusive capacity. Perfect competition is assumed in the North and South. Innovation is exogenous in this model. See Appendix 3F for a full formal derivation of the Krugman model.

[46] Actually Krugman's imitation rate is quasi-endogenous since he assumes a fixed percentage of all new goods is imitated. See Equation (3.11) below.

[47] In Grossman and Helpman (1991c) a model is presented that illustrates how the product life cycle operates in a quality ladder model. This model, however, needlessly complicates matters and, since the model in Chapter 4 will feature variety expansion, it is less relevant.

[48] Under Bertrand competition a duopolist sets his price optimally given his opponents price. His opponent does the same and they end up undercutting each other until price equals marginal costs and profits are zero. Any microeconomics textbook contains the details and proof. See for example Mas-Colell, Whinston and Green (1995).

[49] In an equilibrium with international specialisation this must be the case as was already shown by Krugman (1979).

[50] This is formally derived in Appendix 3G.

[51] In fact the underlying idea behind the international product life cycle is that products move from the skilled labour abundant North to the unskilled labour abundant South, precisely because the production becomes less demanding.

[52] In Grossman and Helpman (1991a) this would be equivalent to assuming international labour mobility for Northern workers only and assuming that imitation requires Northern workers' effort. As will be shown in the next chapter, that minor adjustment will reduce the possibility of a strong market size effect in their model.

[53] A similar result follows from assuming that process innovators can keep their innovation secret and engage in Bertrand competition. In that case no patent protection is required.

CHAPTER 4:
TECHNICAL CHANGE AND LABOUR DEMAND

T he models presented above studied life cycle dynamics and endogenous individual biases separately. In this chapter a model that is general enough to incorporate both the market size effect and the life cycle effect is developed. The market size effect turns out to be very sensitive to the exact specification of the model. The life cycle explanation on the other hand is quite robust. In light of this result it can be concluded that the life cycle explanation is an interesting alternative explanation for the drop in relative demand for low skilled workers.

Section 1 presents a general model that allows for several specifications, varying from an adapted Grossman and Helpman (1991a)-like endogenous life cycle model to an Acemoglian (2002) model of endogenous individual biases.[1] The model is built up along the lines of a standard final output variety expansion model as described above and to stress the linkages with these models it too is presented in a formal synopsis table. The mathematical details are presented in the appendices to this chapter.[2]

Section 2 analyses the comparative statics in the steady state equilibrium. From this analysis it is concluded that the strong market size effect is an interesting but not a very general steady state result. In particular the introduction of diminishing returns in R&D, often advocated to deal with the Jones' critique, mentioned in Chapter 2, proves devastating to the strong market size effect.

To evaluate the complementary life cycle hypothesis proposed in Chapter 1, however, comparative statics analysis alone is inadequate. The life cycle explanation attributes (a part) of the shift in US demand to a *temporary* acceleration in high skilled complementary ICT-related product innovation. By definition such a shock does not affect the steady state and will therefore not show up in comparative statics analysis.

Section 3 therefore turns to transitional dynamics in the model. The absence of an analytical solution to the general model makes it too complex for more traditional, analytical transitional dynamics. Therefore real time numerical simulations are presented to bring out the response that such a temporary shock implies. Numerical simulation generates hypothetical time series that illustrate both the transitional dynamics and steady state equilibrium effects of exogenous shocks in an intuitively appealing way. However, there is also the disadvantage of specificity.

The specificity problem is all the more pressing as the presentation and discussion of numerical simulation results is quite extensive and one has to be selective on what specifications to present.

Therefore some time is spent justifing the values chosen for parameters in the model. Then Section 3 presents a baseline simulation for two versions of eight different specifications. These simulations show that the model has a stable steady state equilibrium that can be calibrated in such a way that they reproduce the situation in the US in the mid-1970s. By introducing an exogenous shock to relative labour supply, the strong market size effect is illustrated in some specifications.

In Section 4 the simulations combine the exogenous labour supply shock with a calibrated R&D productivity shock that represents the introduction of a new general-purpose technology. Such a shock can yield the desired relative wage shift in all specifications. In this section the aim is to establish the empirical plausibility of the life cycle hypothesis by reproducing the stylised facts without getting lost in inevitable data problems and econometric details.

In addition to providing a possible explanation for the US experience, the general model also provides a summary of recent models of endogenous biases in technical change. It allows one to study several linkages between technical change and the demand for labour and as such it sets the stage for the analysis of labour market institutions and their (lack of) interaction with technology in the next part.

4.1   A GENERAL MODEL

The model presented here is an endogenous variety expansion model that follows pretty much the same steps as outlined in the previous chapter. This can be verified in the formal synopsis in Table 4.1.

In Cell 1, consumers save and consume in a by now standard fashion. Maximisation of the love of variety direct utility function in Cell 2 generates the required iso-elastic demand curves for goods that are symmetric in all aspects except the production method. In Cell 3 the monopolistic producers set prices as a mark-up over marginal costs to maximise profits. In Cell 4 diminishing returns in production imply that marginal costs are a function of wages and employment when costs are minimised. While Krugman (1979) and Grossman and Helpman (1991a) assumed constant returns, this generalisation brings the model in line with the Acemoglu (1998, 2002a) models presented above. For convenience a variable X_S was defined to represent the total expenditure on goods of type $S=\{H, L\}$. Note that this variable depends positively on total expenditure, the relative number of varieties per type and the productivity of labour in both sectors but negatively on relative wages.

Table 4.1: FORMAL SYNOPSIS OF THE GENERAL MODEL

AGENT(S)		PROBLEM(S) SUBJECT TO CONSTRAINT(S) ⇒RESULTS S indexes Sector/Skill	
CONSUMER(S)	1	$\max\limits_{E(t)} : \int_t^\infty e^{-\rho(\tau-t)} \log U(E(\tau))d\tau$ s.t. $Y(t)+rA(t)=E(t)+dA(t)/dt$ $\Rightarrow \dfrac{\dot{E}(t)}{E(t)} = r - \rho$	
	2	$\max\limits_{c(i)} : U(.) = \left(\int_0^n c(i)^\alpha di\right)^{\frac{1}{\alpha}}$ s.t. $\int_0^n p(i)c(i)di \le E$ $\Rightarrow c^D(i) = \left(\dfrac{p(i)}{P}\right)^{\frac{1}{\alpha-1}} \dfrac{E}{P}$ $\Rightarrow P \equiv \left(\int_0^n p(i)^{\frac{\alpha}{\alpha-1}} di\right)^{\frac{\alpha-1}{\alpha}}$	
PRODUCER(S)	3	$\max\limits_{p_s(i)} : \pi_{s_c}(i) = c_s(i)p_s(i) - tc_s(i)$ s.t. $c_s(i) = c_s^D(i)$ $\Rightarrow p_s(i) = \dfrac{1}{\alpha} mc_s(i)$	
	4	$\min\limits_{l_s(i)} : w_s l_s(i)$ s.t. $c_s^D(i) = b_s l_s(i)^\beta$ $\Rightarrow l_s^D(i) = \dfrac{\alpha\beta}{n_s w_s} X_s\ ^3$ $\Rightarrow L_s^D = \dfrac{\alpha\beta}{w_s} X_s$	
	5	$\pi_{s_c}(i) = (1-\alpha\beta)X_s / n_s$ $\forall i \in n_s$ $\Rightarrow \dfrac{\dot{\pi}_s(i)}{\pi_s(i)} = -\dfrac{\dot{n}_s}{n_s}$ iff $\dfrac{\dot{X}_s}{X_s} = 0$	

Note also that when these relative variables are constant total expenditure on goods of type S is also constant when total expenditure is normalised to 1. In Cell 5 this implies that profits fall at the growth rate of the relevant variety range. From Cell 4 one can derive relative labour demand in function of relative wages. It is given by:

$$\frac{L_H}{L_L} = \frac{n_H}{n_L} \left(\frac{b_H}{b_L}\right)^{\frac{\alpha}{1-\alpha\beta}} \left(\frac{w_H}{w_L}\right)^{\frac{-1}{1-\alpha\beta}} \tag{4.1}$$

For given relative employment levels, for example when exogenous inelastic labour supplies are assumed, (4.1) can be rewritten to trace out a concave upward sloping curve in n_H/n_L-w_H/w_L space.

Figure 4.1: GRAPHICAL CONSTRUCTION OF THE *PMA* CURVE

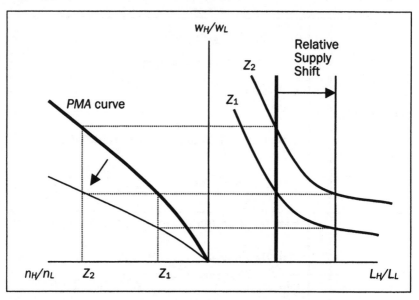

This curve represents the labour market equilibrium in the short run and therefore also in the steady state. Below it will be referred to as the product market arbitrage or *PMA* curve as it equates the relative marginal product of labour in production to the relative wage. This curve is constructed graphically in Figure 4.1.

In the right panel the labour market is depicted. An exogenous relative supply is equated to a relative demand that is conditional on n_H/n_L. Two relative demand curves have been drawn and were labelled Z_1 and Z_2. By plotting the equilibrium wage with these curves against the corresponding values for n_H/n_L one obtains the *PMA* curve in the left panel. Intuitively this curve is upward sloping as the employment level per variety is negatively related to the relative number of varieties per range and therefore positively to the relative marginal value product.[4]

The figure also illustrates the impact of an increase in relative labour supply. For every n_H/n_L the relative wage now drops. Consequently an increase in relative supply, L_H/L_L, will cause the *PMA* curve to rotate down and to the right as is illustrated in the left panel.[5]

So far the model has closely followed the standard models of Chapter 3. There is a lot more to tell about the R&D cells (Table 4.1 is continued below). As before, in Cell 6 it is assumed that innovations are priced competitively and therefore an innovation is valued at the discounted profit flow it will generate. In the absence of a product life cycle, the value of an innovation is equal to the discounted profit flow, as usual.

Table 4.1: **FORMAL SYNOPSIS OF THE GENERAL MODEL**
(cont'd)

AGENT(S)		PROBLEM(S) SUBJECT TO CONSTRAINT(S) $\Rightarrow$ RESULTS S indexes Sector/Skill	
		Price taking in R&D	
		Product Life Cycle	No Product Life Cycle
R&D	6	$$v_H = \frac{\pi_H(i) + \dot{v}_H(i)}{r} = \frac{\pi_H + \dot{v}_H}{r}$$ $$v_L = \frac{\pi_L + \dot{v}_L}{r} - \lambda\frac{\pi_H + \dot{v}_H}{r}$$	$$v_S = \frac{\pi_S + \dot{v}_S}{r}$$
	7	**Product Life Cycle** $$\max_{R_s} : \pi_R^{R\&D} = \dot{n}(R_R)v_H - w_R R_R$$ $$\max_{R_D} : \pi_D^{R\&D} = \dot{n}_L(R_D)v_L - w_R R_D$$ $$\text{s.t.} \begin{array}{l} \dot{n}(R_R) = a_R n^\varphi n_H^{(1-\varphi)x} n_L^{(1-\varphi)(1-x)} R_R^{\gamma} \\ \dot{n}_L(R_D) = a_D n^\psi n_H^{(1-\psi)\zeta} n_L^{(1-\psi)(1-\zeta)} R_D^{\gamma} \\ \dot{n}_H = \dot{n} - \dot{n}_L \end{array}$$ $$\Rightarrow \begin{array}{l} w_R = \gamma a_R n^\varphi n_H^{(1-\varphi)x} n_L^{(1-\varphi)(1-x)} R_R^{\gamma-1} v_H \\ w_R = \gamma a_D n^\psi n_H^{(1-\psi)\zeta} n_L^{(1-\psi)(1-\zeta)} R_D^{\gamma-1} v_L \end{array}$$ **No Product Life Cycle** $$\max_{R_s} : \pi_S^{R\&D} = \dot{n}_S(R_S)v_S - w_R R_S$$ $$\text{s.t.} \begin{array}{l} \dot{n}_H(R_R) = a_R n^\varphi n_H^{(1-\varphi)x} n_L^{(1-\varphi)(1-x)} R_R^{\gamma} \\ \dot{n}_L(R_D) = a_D n^\psi n_H^{(1-\psi)\zeta} n_L^{(1-\psi)(1-\zeta)} R_D^{\gamma} \\ \dot{n} = \dot{n}_H + \dot{n}_L \end{array}$$ $$\Rightarrow \begin{array}{l} w_R = \gamma a_R n^\varphi n_H^{(1-\varphi)x} n_L^{(1-\varphi)(1-x)} R_R^{\gamma-1} v_H \\ w_R = \gamma a_D n^\psi n_H^{(1-\psi)\zeta} n_L^{(1-\psi)(1-\zeta)} R_D^{\gamma-1} v_L \end{array}$$	

In a closed economy product life cycle model, however, patent protection implies that the incumbent producers of new products cannot be competed out of the market. Even if the entrant has a process that allows him to produce at lower cost with low skilled labour. As has been discussed in Chapter 3, this implies that only the discounted *additional* profit flow is the return to the entrant, as he must compensate the incumbent or sell his process innovation to him at his maximum willingness to pay. In Cell 6 a switch variable, $\lambda=\{0,1\}$, has been introduced to enable the product life cycle. In Cell 7 the innovation functions are introduced. The most obvious extension to the models in Chapter 3 is the very general Cobb-Douglas knowledge spillover structure that was assumed.

With this general structure Grossman and Helpman's (1991a) life cycle, the knowledge-based specification in Acemoglu (2002a) and an infinite number of other structures can be analysed. A subtler but also important generalisation is the innovation output elasticity of R&D resources, γ. It will be shown below that this turns out to be quite a significant parameter for the strong market size effect. At any rate this extension is required when numerical simulation is considered.[6]

Finally it is important to note that in a product life cycle model, $\lambda=1$, one R&D sector expands the total range of varieties, whereas the other R&D sector moves them from the first to the second stage. In the non-life cycle models both ranges are expanded independently and merely add up to the total range. Note that the life cycle operator, λ, can also be used to switch between specifications in the general innovation functions:

$$\dot{n} = n^{\varphi} n_H^{(1-\varphi)\chi} n_L^{(1-\varphi)(1-\chi)} a_R R_R^{\gamma} + (1-\lambda)\dot{n}_L \qquad 0 < \gamma \leq 1$$

$$\dot{n}_L = n^{\psi} n_H^{(1-\psi)\zeta} n_L^{(1-\psi)(1-\zeta)} a_D R_D^{\gamma} \qquad\qquad 0 \leq \varphi \leq 1$$

$$n_H \equiv n - n_L \qquad\qquad \text{where} \quad 0 \leq \chi \leq 1 \qquad (4.2)$$

$$\dot{n}_H = \dot{n} - \dot{n}_L \qquad\qquad\qquad\qquad\qquad 0 \leq \psi \leq 1$$

$$\qquad\qquad\qquad\qquad\qquad\qquad\qquad\qquad 0 \leq \zeta \leq 1$$

Setting $\lambda=0$, $\zeta=(1-\delta)/2$, $\gamma=1$, $\chi=(1+\delta)/2$, $\varphi=0$, $\psi=0$, yields the Acemoglian (2002a) structure. Setting $\lambda=1$, $\zeta=0$, $\gamma=1$, $\chi=0$, $\varphi=1$, $\psi=0$ yields Grossman and Helpman's (1991a) specification.[7] With λ equals 0 one has a standard two-sector innovation driven growth model, where, by the lack of strong intuitions on spillover parameter values, it is natural to assume knowledge spillovers to be symmetric. In Equation (4.2) one can distinguish *intrasectoral*, *cross-sectoral* and *joint* knowledge spillovers. When knowledge is represented by the number of innovations made in each sector the intrasectoral knowledge spillovers in the Acemoglian case are represented by $(1-\psi)(1-\zeta)$ and $(1-\varphi)\chi$. The cross-sectoral knowledge spillovers by $(1-\psi)\zeta$ and $(1-\varphi)(1-\chi)$, and the joint knowledge spillovers by φ and ψ. For these types of models one would therefore typically assume:

$$\varphi = \psi$$
$$\zeta = (1 - \chi) \tag{4.3}$$

Obviously parameter λ equals 1 in any life cycle model but the existence of a life cycle also provides a stronger intuition on the knowledge spillover parameters. On the one hand it is intuitively plausible that process R&D benefits more from product R&D than the reverse. Knowledge about the product is useful and usually even required to design or improve the process to produce the product.

Product R&D, on the other hand, benefits more from the general level of knowledge that has accumulated. Experience in developing new products is more useful in developing the next innovation. Experience in process R&D is by its nature more applied and product specific to the existing varieties. Hence in a product life cycle model one would assume:[8]

$$\varphi > 0.5 > \psi$$
$$(1 - \psi)\zeta > (1 - \varphi)\chi \tag{4.4}$$

The specification of Equation (4.2) also determines to a large extent the possibilities for the market size effect to emerge. To see this, one should consider the steady state in this model. As Figure 4.1 already illustrated a steady state equilibrium requires a stable relative number of varieties in both ranges, n_H/n_L that must lie on the *PMA* curve.

In addition to the *PMA* a second relationship between relative wages and n_H/n_L can be derived from the information in Cells 7 and 8 in Table 4.1. Cell 7 allows one to derive the relative effort in both types of R&D. The steady state condition in line 2 of Cell 8 can be combined with the innovation functions to derive the relative effort for which the ranges all grow at the same rate. Setting these equal yields an expression for the relative value of innovations in the steady state, which, by substituting for profits, is a function of relative wages and the relative size of the variety ranges only.[9] This relationship can be labelled the research and development arbitrage curve or *RDA* curve as it traces out the combinations of relative wages and n_H/n_L for which the R&D sector has no incentive to reallocate means and both goods ranges grow at the same rate.

Table 4.1:   FORMAL SYNOPSIS OF THE GENERAL MODEL
(cont'd)

		EQUILIBRIUM CONDITIONS
LABOUR MARKET	8	Equilibrium with Competition $w_R = w_H$ $R_R + R_D + L_H^D = L_H^*$ $L_L^D = L_L^*$ Equilibrium without Competition $R_R + R_D = R^*$ $L_H^D = L_H^* - R^*$ $L_L^D = L_L^*$
		$\Rightarrow \dfrac{\dot{n}}{n} = \dfrac{\dot{n}_H}{n_H} = \dfrac{\dot{n}_L}{n_L}$ $\Rightarrow \dfrac{\dot{v}_H}{v_H} = \rho - \dfrac{(1-\alpha\beta)E_H}{v_H n_H}, \ \dfrac{\dot{v}_L}{v_L} = \rho - \dfrac{(1-\alpha\beta)E_L}{v_L n_L}$
ASSET MARKET	9	$d\dfrac{nv}{Y} = 0$ such that $\dfrac{n_H v_H + n_L v_L}{Y}$ is constant $\Rightarrow \dfrac{\dot{n}}{n} = -\dfrac{\dot{v}_H}{v_H} = -\dfrac{\dot{v}_L}{v_L}$
STEADY STATE	10	$\Rightarrow$ generally no closed form solution for g

For the general case it is given by:[10]

$$\frac{w_H}{w_L} = \left(\frac{b_H}{b_L}\right)^{\frac{1}{\beta}} \left[\lambda + \left(\frac{n_H}{n_L}\right)^{\frac{(1-\varphi)\chi - (1-\psi)\zeta}{\gamma}} \left(1 + \frac{n_H}{n_L}\right)^{\frac{\varphi-\psi}{\gamma}} \left(\lambda + \frac{n_H}{n_L}\right)^{\frac{\gamma-1}{\gamma}} \left(\frac{a_R}{a_D}\right)^{\frac{1}{\gamma}}\right]^{\frac{1-\alpha\beta}{\alpha\beta}} \quad (4.5)$$

Relative wages enter through relative profits, which affect the relative value of innovations. The relative ranges enter through the knowledge spillover assumed in the innovation function. Figure 4.2 shows the three basic shapes that the *RDA* curve can take on around the steady state, convex downward sloping, concave upward sloping and finally convex upward sloping.

Figure 4.2:   THE SHAPES OF THE *RDA* CURVE

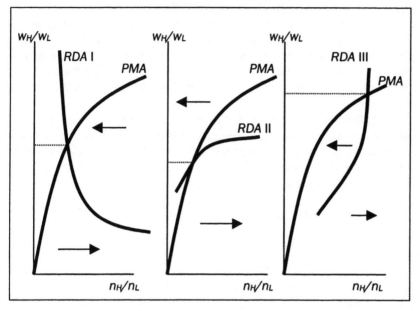

With strong intrasectoral knowledge spillovers the curve is upward sloping. Higher relative wages are required in equilibrium to reduce the incentive to invest R&D resources in the sector with the larger knowledge base. If knowledge spillovers are largely cross-sectoral, however, it could be that lower relative wages are required to offset the incentive to invest R&D resources in the smaller sector.

The arrows indicate the direction in which n_H/n_L will change when one starts in a point off the *RDA* curve. Below the *RDA* curve n_H/n_L will grow. The intuition is quite straightforward. In that situation relative wages are, given the available knowledge stocks, too low. Consequently relative profits are too high and this provokes too much investment in high skilled complementary innovation, causing n_H/n_L to rise. Hence the equilibrium is only stable if the *RDA* curve intersects the *PMA* curve from above and it can be verified that the *RDA* III curve yields unstable equilibria.[11] Hence only in the second case (*RDA* II) will relative wages rise in response to a relative employment shift.[12] As Acemoglu (2002a) has pointed out, the short-run elasticity of substitution, $\sigma_{SR}=-1/(1-\alpha\beta)$ plays a big role in determining the shape of the *RDA* curve.

But Equation (4.5) indicates that it is also determined to a large extent by the innovation functions chosen in Equation (4.2). Appendix 4C and the next section analyse the specifications of the R&D sector and the resulting properties of the *RDA* curve further.

Now shortly consider the final cells in synopsis Table 4.1. In Cell 8 the allocation of high skilled labour over R&D and final output production is still to be determined. As can be seen in Cell 8, the general model can be set up such that R&D competes for high skilled labour. This implies that the wages paid in R&D must equal those in production in equilibrium.[13]

The existence of the market size effect and the life cycle implications of introducing a new general-purpose technology, however, can be fully described by the characteristics of the *RDA-PMA* interaction. As there is no analytical solution in the general model, Cell 9 contains no equilibrium growth rate in parameters and exogenous variables only.

Figure 4.3:   **STEADY STATE EQUILIBRIUM**

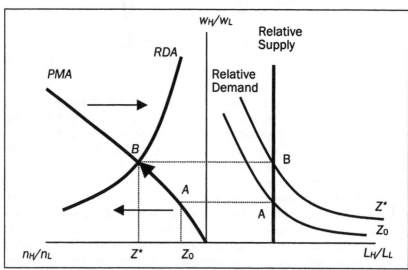

Combining Figures 4.1 and 4.2 yields the complete model in Figure 4.3. Starting from *A* in the right panel, on the *PMA* the position relative to the *RDA* curve implies that n_H/n_L will grow. As n_H/n_L increases, the relative labour demand curve in the right panel shifts out and relative wages increase. In the left panel the economy moves up along the *PMA* curve. This process stops and the model is in steady state equilibrium when the intersection of *PMA* and *RDA* is reached at points *B*.

4.2   COMPARATIVE STATICS IN THE STEADY STATE

In this section a comparative statics analysis of the model identifies under what specifications the strong market size effect occurs. Since the strong market size effect is a steady state property of the model, one can analyse under what conditions it will prevail by analysing how the steady state relative wage responds to a positive shock in relative supply. For some specifications one can calculate the long-run elasticity of substitution directly. Generally its sign depends on the shape of the *RDA* curve, the combination of relative wages and n_H/n_L for which there is no incentive to reallocate R&D resources.

Subsection 4.2.1 starts by analysing the more generalised knowledge spillover structure proposed in Equation (4.2). In this particular sub-class of specifications, the long-run elasticity can still be derived analytically. Then the generalisations made above are analysed one by one to investigate their impact on the sign of the long-run elasticity by numerically analysing the shape of the *RDA*. Table 4.2 gives a schematic overview of this section.

Table 4.2:   GENERALISATIONS CONSIDERED

PROPERTIES	4.2.1	4.2.2	4.2.3
DIMINISHING RETURNS TO LABOUR IN R&D	$\gamma<1$	$\gamma<1$	$\gamma<1$
PRODUCT LIFE CYCLE STRUCTURE	$\lambda=0$	$\lambda=1$	$\lambda=1$
COMPETITION OVER HIGH SKILLED LABOUR BETWEEN R&D AND PRODUCTION	No	No	Yes

In subsection 4.2.1 diminishing returns to scale in R&D are considered. Then the product life cycle is introduced. As the analytical solution is lost at this point, subsection 4.2.2 relies on graphical analysis. Using that technique the impact of endogenising the allocation of high skilled labour can also be considered.

4.2.1   THE IMPLICATIONS OF DIMINISHING RETURNS TO SCALE IN R&D

The *RDA*, Equation (4.5), gives us the relative wage in function of n_H/n_L. If one assumes $L_H=L_H{}^*$ and $\lambda=0$ as in Acemoglu, one can use Equation

(4.1), the *PMA*, to solve for z and substitute into Equation (4.5), the *RDA*, to obtain the relative wage in function of relative supply and the relative wage itself. Dividing both sides by the relative wage and taking the total derivative one obtains the growth rate of the relative wage as a function of the growth rate of relative supply and the level of relative supply and relative wages. Using (4.5) again to substitute for relative wages one then obtains the long-run elasticity as a function of exogenous labour supplies, parameters and n_H/n_L alone. This procedure, however, can only be applied when λ is equal to 0 and high skilled labour only produces final output. For the general model under those restrictions the percentage change in steady state relative wages in response to a percentage change in relative supply is given by:[14]

$$\frac{1}{\sigma_{LR}} = \frac{(\sigma_{SR}-1)\gamma}{(1-\varphi)\chi - (1-\psi)\zeta + \gamma - 1 + (\varphi - \psi)\dfrac{n_H/n_L}{1+n_H/n_L}} - \sigma_{SR} \qquad (4.6)$$

The market size effect exists and the long-run elasticity will now be positive whenever:

$$\frac{\gamma}{(1-\varphi)\chi - (1-\psi)\zeta + \gamma - 1 + (\varphi - \psi)\dfrac{n_H/n_L}{1+n_H/n_L}} > \frac{\sigma_{SR}}{\sigma_{SR}-1} \qquad (4.7)$$

The right-hand side of this inequality is positive and larger than 1.[15] Because the denominator on the left-hand side can be positive under the general parameter restrictions, there are many combinations of the knowledge spillover parameters that satisfy the inequality in Equation (4.7). By choosing $\gamma=1$, $\zeta=(1-\delta)/2$, $\chi=(1+\delta)/2$, $\varphi=0$, $\psi=0$, Acemoglu (2002a) reduces the parameter space to a strictly symmetric ($\chi=1-\zeta$) one-parameter knowledge spillover structure where own spillover effects are always larger than cross-sectoral spillovers ($\chi>0.5$) and he gets:[16]

$$1/(1-\delta) < \sigma_{SR} \qquad (4.8)$$

As was mentioned above the empirical evidence seems to suggest $1<\sigma_{SR}<2$ and the strong market size effect appears as long as δ is not too large. As Acemoglu (2002a) indicated, condition (4.7) fails in this model when the elasticity of substitution is too close to 1. Still he concluded that, since there is no a priori intuition about the value of δ, the market size effect is a plausible explanation for the deterioration in relative wages and employment for the low skilled in the United States over the 80s. One should realise, however, that the implied long-run elasticity goes to infinity or minus infinity as δ approaches $(\sigma_{SR}-1)/\sigma_{SR}$, making it very large and sensitive to small perturbations in the parameters space.

In addition, looking at Equation (4.7), it should be noted that the impact of the knowledge spillover structure is much more complex and important than Acemoglu's (2002a) analysis suggests. In Equation (4.7) the first and second terms in the denominator on the left-hand side are linked to the spillover terms of high skilled complementary innovation on the generation of high and low skilled complementary innovations respectively. In the Acemoglu (2002a) model, where the intermediate machines are intentionally biased towards one or the other type of labour, it might be natural to assume the former to be larger than the latter. In the product life cycle models, Krugman (1979), Grossman and Helpman (1991a) and Sanders (2002), however, it is more natural to assume the opposite, as maturation is likely to benefit much more from the knowledge accumulated in generating the initial product than the other way around. Coming up with a new product will generally benefit little if at all from knowledge accumulated while developing processes for existing products.

The fifth term in the denominator reflects the spillover effect of the expansion of the total range of goods on product range expansion (φ) and process development (ψ). Acemoglu (2002a) conveniently sets these parameters to 0 such that the condition does not depend on the value of z. In the life cycle models seen so far these parameters were 1 and 0 respectively. In the general case, however, the strong market size effect depends on the relative size of the variety ranges as long as these parameters differ from each other - a situation the product life cycle makes intuitively plausible.

Finally, in Equation (4.6) it is easily checked that the derivative of the long-run elasticity with respect to y is positive, so decreasing y decreases the long-run elasticity.[17] Beyond $y=1-(1-\varphi)\chi+(1-\psi)\zeta-(\varphi-\psi)z/(1+z)$, however, the denominator in the first term will drop below 0 and so does the long-run elasticity. The strong market size effect therefore crucially depends on the degree of diminishing returns to scale in R&D - a point that was not recognised in Acemoglu (2002a). The empirical evidence on the degree of diminishing returns to scale in R&D is mixed and will be discussed more extensively below. However it seems unlikely that R&D is characterised by constant returns to scale.

4.2.2 THE IMPLICATIONS OF INTRODUCING THE PRODUCT LIFE CYCLE

To introduce the product life cycle extension the switch parameter λ is set to 1. Now the value of low skilled complementary process innovations must be reduced by the compensation for the patent holder of the corresponding product. It also rearranges the knowledge spillover structure in the innovation functions, such that processes can only be developed for existing products and only product innovation expands the total available variety range. Consider Equation (4.5) under this restriction:

$$\frac{w_H}{w_L} = \left(\frac{b_H}{b_L}\right)^{\frac{1}{\beta}} \left(1 + \left(\frac{n_H}{n_L}\right)^{\frac{(1-\varphi)\chi-(1-\psi)\zeta}{\gamma}} \left(1 + \frac{n_H}{n_L}\right)^{\frac{\varphi-\psi+\gamma-1}{\gamma}} \left(\frac{a_R}{a_D}\right)^{\frac{1}{\gamma}} \right)^{\frac{1-\alpha\beta}{\alpha\beta}} \tag{4.9}$$

It is shown in Appendix 4C that this *RDA* curve now has two possible shapes as in Figure 4.4.

Figure 4.4:   STEADY-STATE WAGE RESPONSE TO A SUPPLY SHOCK

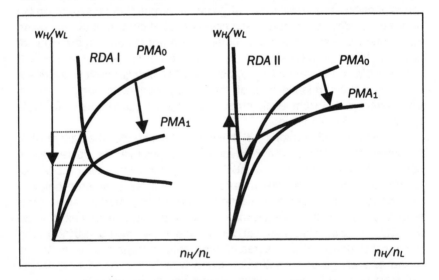

A necessary condition for the *RDA* curve to be of type II and the model to generate a strong market size effect is derived in Appendix 4C.

It is given by:[18]

$$(1 - \psi)(1 - \zeta) - (1 - \varphi)(1 - \chi) > 1 - \gamma \qquad (4.10)$$

As can be verified in Equation (4.10), the presence of strong diminishing returns will reduce the scope for the strong market size effect, as was the case without the product life cycle extension. In addition Equation (4.10) tells us that intrasectoral knowledge spillover must be relatively strong in product innovation (high φ and $(1-\psi)(1-\zeta)$), as was the case before. As the product life cycle intuitively imposes a strong cross-sectoral knowledge spillover towards process innovation, however, the strong market size effect is less likely to occur when the product life cycle extension is considered.

4.2.3 Endogenising the Allocation of High Skilled Labour

When the allocation of high skilled labour between R&D and manufacturing is endogenous, the shift in the *PMA* curve in response to a given relative supply shock is no longer given. The downward shift may be less pronounced when additional high skilled workers move into R&D. However, as an increase in R&D employment will always reduce the marginal productivity in R&D and thereby reduce wages paid in that sector, at least some of the additional high skilled workers will move into manufacturing. As long as some do, the long-run shift in the *PMA* curve will be downward. The size of the shift no longer depends on the size of the exogenous shock alone. It also depends on the relative elasticity of demand in research, development and manufacturing. But as the *RDA* curve is not affected by changes in relative employment levels in manufacturing, the model will or will not generate the market size effect under the same conditions that were derived above. This rather intuitively derived result will be corroborated in the numerical simulation experiments presented below.

4.3   Baseline Simulations of the Market Size Effect

When the model is numerically solved, the steady state relative wage response to a shock in relative supply can simply be calculated. For a numerical solution to make sense, however, parameters and exogenous variables have to be set at reasonable values. As the remainder of this thesis will rely heavily on numerical analyses of the model, it is useful to first set and justify the numerical values for exogenous variables and parameters, used in that analysis.

Exogenous variables typically pose little problems, as they can generally be observed in the data. All relevant data for the US was presented in Section 1.1 and will shortly be recapitulated. Parameters on the other hand come in three sorts. First there are *estimated* parameters on which a lot of empirical research has been conducted. A short overview of the empirical results will do to set realistic and justifiable values for these parameters and determine the appropriate range for sensitivity tests. The remainder can be split in what one might label *specification* and *calibration* parameters. Examples of the former are the knowledge spillover parameters in the innovation functions, as they differ between a life cycle model and a symmetric model. As this section will test several specifications, each specification has its own vector of specification parameters.

Having set estimated and specification parameters and using the exogenous variables, the remainder of the parameters can be calibrated such that endogenous variables in the model replicate observed data as well. This implies that each specification has its own calibration parameter values. Admittedly this reduces the model to a tautology for the period that is used for calibration but not for the response to subsequent exogenous shocks. The model predictions can be compared to developments in endogenous variables in the model. At the very least a fully calibrated model still illustrates that the structure of the model is consistent with the data.

After setting the numerical values, a sub-section will present the baseline simulations of the model for 16 specifications. Some do and some do not have the market size effect. In addition it must be concluded from the analysis that some of the specifications tested here can even replicate the relative wage shock observed in the US from the strong market size effect alone. The analysis will also show, however, that the size and direction of the relative wage change is sensitive to specification and parameter changes.

In the next section the general-purpose technology related temporary positive shock to relative R&D productivity is introduced. This shock can be calibrated to generate wage patterns that are comparable to US relative wage behaviour over the 80s. As such these simulations do not prove that this mechanism underlies that wage behaviour, but it illustrates that the possibility requires serious consideration.

4.3.1   PARAMETERS AND EXOGENOUS VARIABLES

Since the whole recent debate on endogenous biases is centred around the labour market shifts in the US over the 80s and 90s it is natural to start from the US data presented in Section 1.1 to set the exogenous variables for the baseline run. In Figure 1.1 it can be verified that the relative supply of low skilled workers decreased continuously from about 3.6 to 1.4 over 30 years. Normalising total labour supply, $L_L{}^*+L_H{}^*$, to 1000 these numbers imply that $L_H{}^*$ should be set to about 225 (1000/(1+3.6)) for the early 70s and increased to about 400 (1000/(1+1.4)) over some 30 years. By implication $L_L{}^*$ then falls from an initial 775 to 600 over that period.

Data in the OECD (2000) Major Science and Technology Indicators show that about 0.6% of the total labour force was employed in R&D in the US in 1975.[19] However, the they also argue that this number is an underestimation of total effort in innovation activity and double that number would be more appropriate. Since labour constitutes the major input in R&D set R^*, the exogenous supply of R&D resources equal to 0.012*1000=12.[20]

As was mentioned, the general model has three types of parameters for which there are no direct observations available; *estimated*, *specification* and *calibration* parameters. Below the parameters are set in this order.

The estimated parameters, on which empirical research is available, are α, β, γ and ρ. As was shown above, the first two parameters can, by consolidating the model, be linked directly to the elasticity of substitution between high and low skilled labour in production; see Equation (4.1).

Freeman (1986) surveys the empirical literature in this field and concludes that this elasticity most likely lies somewhere between 1 and 2 although values of 8 and above have been reported.[21] Typically, however, these elasticities are estimated as the inverse of the coefficient in a regression of the natural log or percentage change of relative wages on the natural log or percentage change in relative supply. Taking the first difference in natural log of Equation (4.1) immediately shows that these estimates are hard to link directly to $\alpha\beta$ when technology is biased endogenously:

$$d\log\frac{L_H}{L_L} = -\frac{1}{1-\alpha\beta}d\log\left(\frac{w_H}{w_L}\right) + d\log\frac{n_H}{n_L} + v_t \qquad (4.11)$$

Because the second term is omitted, the estimates are biased in these regressions when time series data are used as technical change is correlated with wages in the model above.[22] The problem is that movements along the production possibilities frontier due to substitution cannot be separated from simultaneous movements of the frontier itself due to technical change. In the models presented here the elasticity increases for the long run as technical change responds to the supply shift.[23] This implies that the elasticities obtained using time series are biased upwards and provide at best an upper bound for the short-run elasticity of substitution, $1/(1-\alpha\beta)$, in the model.

Cross-section results are suspect for another reason. Because the wage and relative supply are determined simultaneously, especially when observations are used on well-integrated labour markets such as the US states, the estimated elasticities are also biased. Across countries these problems are less pronounced but there the classification of skill levels usually poses a problem. Tinbergen (1974) addressed this issue explicitly and showed that the bias is upwards as well. In his own analysis he finds elasticities between 0.4 and 2.1, implying $\alpha\beta$ should lie between minus 1.5 and 0.5.

However, in the model $\alpha\beta$ is only indirectly linked to the elasticity of substitution. In fact the α is linked to the elasticity of demand for final output and β parameterises the diminishing returns in production. By the monopolistic competition assumed in the model both are therefore also linked to the profitability of final output production. The model predicts that producers appropriate a share of $(1-\alpha\beta)$ of all expenditure on their product as rents. This property precludes the use of negative values for $\alpha\beta$ in the simulations. Furthermore in equilibrium these rents are used to pay the investors that financed R&D. This would suggest that $\alpha\beta$ should be as large as 0.8, the labour share in income. Considering the fact that monopoly power is not absolute in reality, the actual profit share provides a lower bound for $(1-\alpha\beta)$ at 0.2, implying an upper bound at $\alpha\beta=0.8$. The implied elasticity of substitution would then be as high as 5. In the simulations $\alpha\beta=0.48$ (0.6*0.8) will be used, taking what Acemoglu (2002a) considers the highest possible realistic estimate. One should bear in mind, however, that lower values for $\alpha\beta$ are more realistic when considering the evidence on substitution elasticities.

Nadiri (1993) discusses at length the available empirical evidence on the second estimated parameter, γ, in the innovation functions. The relationship between R&D inputs and outputs has been the subject of many empirical studies. Griliches (1979, 1984) dedicated most of his work to it and Mansfield (1980, 1984) and Jaffe (1986, 1988) also feature prominently in this literature. The estimates for γ, the output elasticity of R&D inputs, in this literature range from 0.2 to 1. Nadiri (1993) argues that it is more likely that this parameter is close to 1 in the late 70s. The lowest estimates are typically obtained in time series analysis on small firms using plain domestic patent counts as R&D output measure. Correcting patent counts for quality differences as in Pakes and Simpson (1989) and Schankerman (1998), discounting R&D expenditures with appropriate (higher) deflators and using cross-section data and large firms all push the estimates up.

However, the output elasticity of R&D when inputs are measured in dollars and output in patents is quite far from the output elasticity of high skilled labour in the innovations function as specified above. Using a dataset based on the communal innovation survey (CIS) for the Netherlands held in 1996, an elasticity of between 0.4 and 0.5 can be estimated in a regression of the log of the number of innovations reported in the 2-digit sector on 1-digit sector dummies and the log of R&D labour employed in FTE in that 2-digit sector.[24] These values correspond very well to results obtained by Acs and Audretsch (1988) for the US and Jacobs, Nahuis and Tang (2002) for the Netherlands, who, both in more elaborate studies, also report values between 0.3 and 0.5.[25] Given the wide range and importance of this parameter, established above, γ will be treated as a specification parameter in the numerical analysis below, with $\gamma=0.4$ (low) and 0.9 (high).[26]

Finally there is ρ, the subjective discount rate. Usually a value of 2-7% is used in the literature.[27] Empirical estimates are rare and vary a lot but indicate that rates of up to 15% are not implausible.[28] As was shown in the previous chapter, this parameter is the return consumers require on the assets in the model to postpone consumption. This is the real rate of return on risk free assets. Using such low rates, however, implies that the value of an innovation is about 10-20 times the current profit flow, provoking a large R&D investment in the model when R&D resources are endogenous.[29] There are two reasons why it is justified to set a higher ρ.

First the risk in R&D projects is much higher than on the assets usually considered in the literature. For this additional risk a consumer requires compensation. Estimates of private returns to R&D investments, which range from 10 to as much as 92% (see Nadiri (1993) Table 1a) therefore provide a better estimate.

Second the success rate of R&D investments in the model is 100% by construction. Lower success rates would reduce the return on R&D investments proportionally and hence a 50% success rate could be represented in the model by doubling the discount rate.[30] When R&D effort is endogenous and ρ is calibrated to obtain an employment share of 1.2%, the resulting values lie between 0.8 and 1.83.[31] Adjusting these for a less than 50% success rate puts them within the 10-92% range mentioned above. As this parameter does not affect the results qualitatively, it is set to the calibrated values in simulations below.

Switch parameter λ, the knowledge spillover parameters, φ, ψ, ζ and χ and the competition over high skilled labour operator (not parameterised although this can easily be done) are the specification parameters in this model.[32] In subsection 4.2.1 the Acemoglian case with $\lambda=0$ was analysed. To check the robustness of the market size effect in that symmetric model, it is useful to also simulate a non-PLC version of the model that satisfies the conditions for a symmetric endogenous bias model in Equation (4.3) but violates the implicit assumptions imposed on the innovation functions in Acemoglu (2002a).[33] With $\lambda=1$ and the spillover parameters set in accordance with the conditions in Equation (4.4) the model can be interpreted as a life cycle model. Here too it is useful to simulate two versions. One ties the model in with the existing product life cycle models of Krugman (1979) and Grossman and Helpman (1991a). As it turns out, that specification has a type I *RDA* curve that rules out the market size effect for all values of γ and σ_{SR}. Therefore a final specification, in which the knowledge spillover structure satisfies the conditions in Equations (4.4) and (4.10) such that a market size effect may emerge, is also simulated.

Table 4.3:   SPECIFICATION PARAMETERS

SPECIFICATION PARAMETERS	SPECIFICATIONS							
	No PLC				PLC			
	EXTREME		MODERATE		EXTREME		MODERATE	
	1	2	3	4	5	6	7	8
λ	0	0	0	0	1	1	1	1
φ	0	0	0.25	0.25	1	1	0.8	0.8
ψ	0	0	0.25	0.25	0	0	0.3	0.3
χ	0.6	0.6	0.75	0.75	0	0	0.8	0.8
ζ	0.4	0.4	0.25	0.25	1	1	0.3	0.3
γ	0.4	0.9	0.4	0.9	0.4	0.9	0.4	0.9

When simulating these four specifications for one high (0.9) and one low (0.4) value for γ, one obtains eight specifications, presented in Table 4.3, of which the endogenous and exogenous allocation of high skilled labour over manufacturing and R&D yield two different versions.[34]

Note that specifications 1-4 are symmetric Acemoglian models with $\delta=0.2$ and 0.5 determining the degree of intra- and cross-sectoral knowledge spillover respectively. Models 3 and 4 add a joint knowledge spillover. Models 5-8 are consistent with the product life cycle, where 5-6 are close to the Grossman and Helpman (1991a) specification presented above.[35] For future reference the models from the literature, 1, 2, 5 and 6, are labelled extreme whereas moderate refers to versions where the built-in assumptions in these existing models are relaxed.

The remaining group of parameters, b_H, b_L, a_R and a_D cannot be considered specification parameters, as they do not change the nature of the model. Direct empirical evidence on their values, however, is also lacking. The value of these parameters can only be linked to empirical evidence indirectly. By rewriting the innovation functions in terms of growth rates of the respective ranges of goods one sees that a unit of labour that produces b_H units of high skilled labour using output can also be used to 'produce' additional growth in a range of goods. It is not unreasonable to assume that the contribution to such an aggregate growth rate is rather small.

Typically the aggregate economic growth rates are around 3% in developed countries and therefore a_D and a_R can be calibrated such that when 1.2% of the labour force is employed in R&D it produces a growth rate of 3% in the steady state. As there is no theoretical or empirical reason to assume that these parameters differ between the two R&D sectors, they are assumed equal.[36]

Having normalised total labour supply to 1000, the exact level of the labour augmenting productivity parameters b_L and b_H also has no particular meaning so one can normalise $b_L=1$.[37] The value of b_H relative to that, however, is of importance and Equation (4.1) shows that one can calibrate it, using relative wages in the mid-70s as a benchmark. Having pinned down all other parameters and setting relative, L_H/L_L, employment at 1/3, b_H is calibrated to yield a long-run equilibrium relative wage of about 1.4 in all specifications. This is the observed wage ratio around 1975 in Figure 1.1. Sensitivity analysis showed that, as might be expected, steady state relative wages respond very strongly to this parameter, whereas other equilibrium variables are less responsive.

Finally ρ, the discount rate as was mentioned above, was calibrated, such that the share of R&D in total employment is about realistic at 1.2% in the base run steady state when the allocation of labour over production and R&D is endogenous.[38] The calibration of the model thus involves solving it numerically for four variables, z, ρ, a_R, and b_H given three additional restrictions.[39]

The parameters and exogenous variables are summarised in Table 4.4 below. In the third column the range over which these variables and parameters have been simulated is given. Appendix 4D presents the actual calibrated numerical values for the calibration parameters.

Table 4.4:   EXOGENOUS VARIABLES AND PARAMETERS

VARIABLE	VALUE	DATA SOURCE	SENSITIVITY TEST RANGE
$L_H{}^*$	225-400	Normalised 1000/(1+L/H)	Normalised
$L_L{}^*$	775-600	Normalised 1000/(1+H/L)	Normalised
R^*	12	OECD (2000) MSTI-database	1.2%*1000 =12
ESTIMATED PARAMETERS	VALUE	RELEVANT RANGE IN LITERATURE	SENSITIVITY TEST RANGE
$\alpha\beta$	0.48	-1.5-0.8	0.1-0.8
γ	0.4 and 0.9	0.3-1	0.3-0.9
CALIBRATED PARAMETERS	VALUE	RELEVANT RANGE IN LITERATURE	SENSITIVITY TEST RANGE
ρ	Calibrated to get $R_R+R_D=0.012(L_H{}^*+L_L{}^*)$	0.02-0.92	+/-50%
a_R	Calibrated to get $G_{nL}=G_{nH}=G_n=0.03$	NA	See Section 4.4
a_D	a_R	NA	See Section 4.4
b_H	Calibrated to get $w_H/w_L=1.4$	NA	+/-50%
b_L	1	Normalised	Normalised

4.3.2   THE MARKET SIZE EFFECT

Section 1.1 proposed the strong market size effect as a possible explanation for the rise in relative labour demand, observed in the US over the 80s. For this hypothesis to have merit, the models specified above should be able to produce the key prediction. Long-run relative wages must rise in response to a relative supply increase. The hypothesis is robust to parameter and specification changes if all models generate a similar response to the same shock. A straightforward way of quantifying the market size effect is to simulate the model and calculate long-run elasticities by dividing the observed percentage change in relative wages or variety ranges by an exogenously introduced percent change in relative supply.

The experiment that was conducted, presented in Table 4.5, allowed the model to settle in its calibrated steady state at a relative wage of 1.4 and then, starting in period 50 over an interval of 30 periods increased the supply of high skilled at a constant growth rate from 225 to 400.[40] The positive elasticities on relative goods ranges, n_H/n_L, indicate the existence of the weak Hicksian induced bias effect in all specifications. This is a precondition for the strong market size effect and a robust result in all specifications.

Table 4.5:   LONG-RUN ELASTICITIES OF RELATIVE SUPPLY

#	SPECIFICATIONS			γ	INDUCED INNOVATION $d(n_H/n_L)/(n_H/n_L)$ over $d(L_H/L_L)/(L_H/L_L)$	MARKET SIZE EFFECT $d(w_H/w_L)/(w_H/w_L)$ over $d(L_H/L_L)/(L_H/L_L)$
1	No COMPETITION	No PLC	EXTREME	0.4	+0.24	- 0.19
2				0.9	+1.57	+0.11
3			MODERATE	0.4	+0.36	- 0.17
4				0.9	+7.36	+0.91
5		PLC	EXTREME	0.4	+0.22	- 0.21
6				0.9	+0.51	- 0.12
7			MODERATE	0.4	+0.77	- 0.06
8				0.9	+1.73	+0.14
1	COMPETITION	No PLC	EXTREME	0.4	+0.24	- 0.20
2				0.9	+1.48	+0.11
3			MODERATE	0.4	+0.36	- 0.16
4				0.9	+6.92	+0.84
5		PLC	EXTREME	0.4	+0.21	- 0.20
6				0.9	+0.56	- 0.17
7			MODERATE	0.4	+0.75	- 0.06
8				0.9	+1.50	+0.12

The strong market size effect, however, is a far less robust result. It is no surprise that Model 2, the extreme, no PLC, high γ model that is closest to Acemoglu's (2002a) specification, yields a strong market size effect. Having set the knowledge spillover parameters and the short-run elasticity of substitution such that the conditions for an upward sloping concave *RDA* curve are met, it would indeed be a surprise if it did not occur. What is more, the inverse long-run elasticity of substitution of about 0.11 implies a new steady state relative wage is about 1.6, the level around which relative wages seem to stabilise in the late 90s. Model 2 therefore replicates the movements in the data in both direction and size.

But as the table shows, this result is far from robust to specification and parameter variations. Model 4 illustrates that a slight change in the knowledge spillover parameters has huge effects on the size of the elasticity. Models 1 and 3 illustrate the devastating effect of assuming diminishing returns to scale in R&D. Model 6 illustrates that introducing a product life cycle the way Krugman (1979) and Grossman and Helpman (1991a) suggested, eliminates the market size effect as well, but Model 8 illustrates that the product life cycle model can generate the strong market size effect and observed wage patterns as well.

A final comment on Table 4.5 is that competition over high skilled labour between R&D and production hardly makes a difference for the results. This, however, need not be a surprise as the discount rate in the competition models was calibrated to yield the exogenously imposed employment level in R&D relative to total employment. As total employment remained at 1000, total R&D employment equalled 12 in the pre- and post-shock steady states.[41] It should also be noted that strong diminishing returns generate much more stable results. The elasticities lie between minus 0.06 and minus 0.2 whereas the models with high values for y have elasticities ranging between minus 0.17 and plus 0.91. This jumpiness also shows up when a sensitivity test is performed on other parameters.[42]

From this it can be concluded that the strong market size effect is not very robust and its size is very sensitive to variations in parameters for which no solid estimates are available. Hence although capable of explaining the relative wage shifts observed in the US over the 70s and 80s, it requires a leap of faith to attribute the observed labour market shifts to the strong market size effect alone. By the same token, however, the lack of robustness can also be regarded a strength of the hypothesis. Small differences in the parameters and specification of the model can cause widely different relative demand shifts in response to similar supply shocks. In light of the international evidence presented in Section 1.2, this flexibility might actually be desirable. As the model does not yet contain the parameters most likely to differ between the US and Europe, this possibility will be discussed in the next part. First a final section presents numerical simulations to evaluate the second hypothesis proposed in Chapter 1.

4.4   THE INTRODUCTION OF A GENERAL PURPOSE TECHNOLOGY

In the previous section it was shown that the market size effect is not robust to parameter and specification changes. In addition to the market size effect, Chapter 1 suggested the combination of a product life cycle (PLC) and the introduction of a new general-purpose technology as a potential explanation for relative demand shifts. Such a shock can be analysed in the context of the general model by simulating its response to a temporary increase in the productivity of high skilled complementary product innovation. The idea is that upon the discovery of a new general-purpose technology there is not an exogenous wave of new products and services (e.g. an exogenous jump in n_H/n_L) but rather a shift in the allocation of R&D resources towards 'mining' the new possibilities. The opening up of such opportunities can best be simulated in the model by temporarily reducing the cost of making a product innovation.[43]

In the simulations presented below the parameter a_R is therefore increased in period 65 by a factor that was calibrated to ensure that relative wages rise to the observed 1.6 in period 80 in the model.[44] Table 4.6 presents the multiplication factors that were found. From these values it can be concluded that some specifications require quite a productivity shock indeed to offset the downward pressure on relative wages. High values for y and endogenous labour allocation reduce that factor considerably.[45] The moderate product life cycle specifications generate observed wage behaviour for a temporary 70-90% increase of the productivity level when diminishing returns are strong in R&D.

Table 4.6: CALIBRATED GENERAL PURPOSE TECHNOLOGY SHOCK[46]

#	SPECIFICATION		y	Figure	a_R/a_D No Competition	Competition
1	No PLC	EXTREME	0.4	4D.1	2.90	2.40
2			0.9	4D.2	1.15	1.05
3		MODERATE	0.4	4D.3	2.75	2.25
4			0.9	4D.4	1.05[47]	0.95[47]
5	PLC	EXTREME	0.4	4.5	2.85	2.40
6			0.9	4.6	1.80	1.40[48]
7		MODERATE	0.4	4.7	1.90	1.70
8			0.9	4.8	1.10	1.00

For high values of y the required productivity shock drops to between minus 5 to plus 15% for the models that also exhibit the strong market size effect. Although empirical research provides little guidance in this respect, it is not unreasonable to assume that the introduction of ICT technology has increased the productivity of research efforts in product innovation by more than 15% relative to product maturing process innovations. The simulation of a general-purpose technology shock can only be justified in the context of a product life cycle model. Figures 4.5-8 present the simulated relative wages with short comments. The results obtained in the symmetric models are less relevant in this experiment. Because the introduction of a general-purpose technology affects both types of innovation equally in a symmetric model, the asymmetric shock would represent a biased general-purpose technology. For completeness and to provide a sensitivity test for a_R the results have been presented in Appendix 4E.

Figure 4.5:   A CALIBRATED GENERAL PURPOSE TECHNOLOGY SHOCK
Extreme Product Life Cycle, ζ=1, φ=1, χ=0, ψ=0, λ=1
Strong Diminishing Returns, γ=0.4

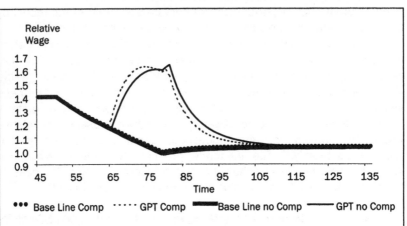

In Figure 4.5 the extreme product life cycle version of the model is simulated with (white) and without (black) competition over high skilled labour between R&D and production. A first observation is that the baseline model has no market size effect. Following the shock to relative supply in period 50-80, the model stabilises at a lower relative wage. However, there is a weak market size effect as induced biases in innovation increase the relative wage from period 80 onwards. The thin lines present the models with supply shock and GPT introduction. Note that the endogenous allocation model is much quicker to adjust as the productivity increase increases product innovation directly but also indirectly as more labour is drawn into product R&D. As the figures below show, smoother series and faster adjustment are a general attribute of competition in the model, even if the competition and no-competition versions converge towards the same steady state.

As is mentioned in the comments given in Figure 4.8 below, the simulations look unrealistically erratic. This is the result of the fact that relative supply and productivity shocks were introduced rather bluntly.[49] The next chapter will be more sophisticated in this respect without altering the main results.

The main conclusion from the simulations is that a productivity shock in the R&D sector generates a temporary positive relative wage shock that is reversed partially or entirely in the long run. That result is robust to various specification changes.

Figure 4.6:   **A CALIBRATED GENERAL PURPOSE TECHNOLOGY SHOCK**
Extreme Product Life Cycle, $\zeta=1$, $\varphi=1$, $\chi=0$, $\psi=0$, $\lambda=1$
Weak Diminishing Returns, $\gamma=0.9$

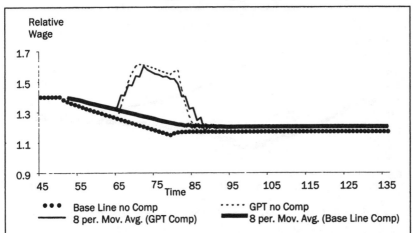

In Figure 4.6 the extreme product life cycle models of Figure 4.5 are presented with a high value for γ. The most important feature in this simulation is the absence of the strong market size effect. As was shown above, this model does not feature the strong market size effect despite the absence of strong diminishing returns. All the other specifications analysed do and so this specification stresses the importance of the knowledge spillover structure. The endogenous high skilled labour allocation version experiences numerical problems. Following the employment shock the number of varieties grows very rapidly as diminishing returns do not put a brake on the inflow of labour into R&D. Strong cross-sectoral knowledge spillovers in combination with labour re-allocation then produces an oscillation, not depicted in the figure. Instead a moving average was plotted to get some feeling for the properties of this model. Such smoothing can be justified as future rent flows are unlikely to be this erratic

The size of the required productivity shock differs with the degree of diminishing returns but the sign of the effect is always robust. From the analysis of the model, the moderate PLC specification of the model therefore emerges as the preferred specification for further investigation. It is preferred over the symmetric models as it contains the intuitively appealing and empirically important product life cycle. Within the class of product life cycle models it is preferred over the extreme specifications, as its knowledge spillover structure does not prevent the emergence of the strong market size effect by construction.

Figure 4.7:   **A CALIBRATED GENERAL PURPOSE TECHNOLOGY SHOCK**
Moderate Product Life Cycle, ζ=0.3, φ=0.8, χ=0.8, ψ=0.3, λ=1
Strong Diminishing Returns, γ=0.4

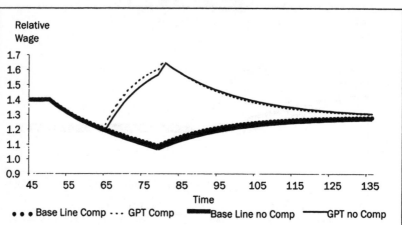

In this figure the moderate product life cycle specification for strong diminishing returns is presented. As can be verified the knowledge spillover structure strongly limits the fall in steady state relative wages from the initial relative supply increase. However, in the steady state still a relative wage drop results. The sharp breaks at period 80, particularly well illustrated in this version of the model, are the result of the abrupt stabilization of relative supply and, in the GPT experiments, the abrupt drop in the relative productivity level that occurs at that period. Comparison to the extreme PLC version in Figure 4.5 suggests that this model has not yet reached a new steady state by period 80, implying its adjustment time is longer and the size of the relative wage effects of a relative productivity shock in R&D are much larger. Hence small relative productivity shocks cause large and long lasting deviations from the baseline evolution of wages and supply.

Recent evidence, notably the evidence collected by Anderson (2001), seems to suggest that over the 90s the situation improved for the low skilled. Their wages seem to have stopped falling relative to the high skilled wages and employment is gradually improving. This makes the low γ version of the moderate PLC specification the preferred model, as it predicts such an improvement after an initial deterioration of low skilled labour market perspectives. It should be noted, however, that that specification does not preclude strong market size effects and leaves the matter to be resolved empirically.

Figure 4.8:   A CALIBRATED GENERAL PURPOSE TECHNOLOGY SHOCK
Moderate Product Life Cycle, ζ=0.3, φ=0.8, χ=0.8, ψ=0.3, λ=1
Weak Diminishing Returns, γ=0.9

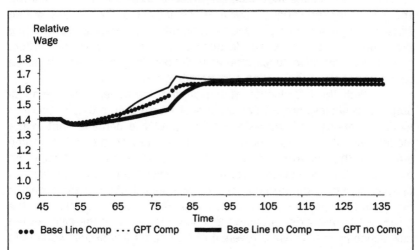

In the final product life cycle specification, the moderate one with weak diminishing returns, the model does exhibit the strong market size effect. And, like in Model 2, the market size effect is strong enough to explain the relative wage shift over the 80s as a steady state phenomenon. Relatively small relative productivity shocks are sufficient to bring about the significant additional relative wage shifts. Smoothing the series by introducing and fading out the temporary shock gradually would improve the correspondence with observed labour market trends in the US further. As was mentioned above, the results are very sensitive to small changes in parameters. The reproduction of relative wage behaviour in numerical simulations is therefore more of a happy coincidence than a robust result in this specification. Note also that the introduction of ICT cannot have had very strong relative productivity effects in the R&D sector.

4.5   CONCLUSION

In this chapter the interaction between technical change and labour demand was analysed in the context of a general model of endogenous innovation. This model was simulated to verify the robustness of two hypotheses that explain why the relative demand for skilled labour increased in the US over the 80s.

Without completely dismissing the possibility of a strong market size effect as suggested in Acemoglu (2002a), it was shown that the parameter restrictions that such an effect requires are quite restrictive. The simulation of various specifications indicated that γ, the output elasticity for labour in R&D, plays a pivotal role in generating or preventing the strong market size effect. In addition the strong market size effect proved very sensitive to parameter variations in general and to small changes in innovation function parameters, γ and a_R, in particular.

With the introduction of the product life cycle, a new general-purpose technology provides an additional source of bias that is robust to model variations and causes a temporary relative demand shift in the model. With the introduction a new general-purpose technology, some effect on the relative productivity of product innovation should be expected. Although several specifications yielded the observed facts in Chapter 1, the moderate product life cycle specification of the model is the preferred specification that emerged. That model predicts that the recent ICT bubble extended itself to labour markets and the aging of the new economy may cause a reversal of fortune for low skilled workers in the near future.

Obviously the reproduction of stylised facts in a calibrated numerical simulation does not prove any hypothesis wrong or right. Instead it indicates that neither can be rejected at this stage. This may change when the international evidence is considered and the model is required to also reproduce European wage stability. As unemployment is a clear distinguishing element in the international context, however, the model will first have to be extended by generalising the labour market structure, such that it allows for unemployment, in Part II.

NOTES

[1] To construct a model that can hold both a closed economy interpretation of Grossman and Helpman (1991a) and a final output variety expansion version of Acemoglu (2002a) requires several minor changes to the assumptions. The general model will therefore not exactly reproduce their results as special cases but contains specifications in which their primary mechanisms are reproduced.

[2] These appendices are downloadable at www.marksanders.nl.

[3] Where

$$X_s \equiv \left(1 + \left(\frac{n_{-s}}{n_s} \right) \left(\frac{w_{-s}}{w_s} \right)^{\frac{-\alpha\beta}{1-\alpha\beta}} \left(\frac{b_{-s}}{b_s} \right)^{\frac{\alpha}{1-\alpha}} \right)^{-1} E^{\frac{1-\alpha}{1-\alpha\beta}}$$

[4] It is concave because demand is convexly downward sloping in the relative wage. Hence an ever-larger increase in n_H/n_L is required to push relative demand out and relative wages up

by the same percentage. This is easily verified by solving (4.1) for relative wages. The exponent on n_H/n_L is less than 1.

[5] Note that the short-run elasticity of substitution between high and low skilled labour can be derived and is strictly negative. Its absolute value is given by, $\sigma_{SR} \equiv 1/(1-\alpha\beta)$. This expression is identical to the elasticity of substitution in the Acemoglu (2002a) model for given A, see Equation (3E.10), but slightly different from the derived elasticity when A is interpreted as a variety of differentiated capital goods, see Equation (3E.46). The difference is the result of total demand for differentiated capital goods being proportional to labour when A is subject to optimisation. It also corresponds to the Grossman and Helpman (1991a) model (see Equations 3G.15 and 3G.16) that assume constant returns to labour ($\beta=1$).

[6] It can be verified in Cell 7 that the allocation of R&D resources will end up in a corner solution out of equilibrium otherwise. With constant returns in both applications, the entire available R&D resources would switch to one or the other type of innovation until the steady state is reached (or overshot). One can imagine that in the numerical simulations of transitional dynamics, in particular with endogenous allocation of high skilled labour over production and innovation, this is very inconvenient.

[7] This does not imply that the entire model is equivalent to theirs, only the innovation functions are. As was mentioned before, in the original Grossman and Helpman (1991a) model there is no perfect patent protection and international immobility of labour. The original Acemoglu (2002a) model has labour and a variety of intermediates combine into homogenous final output whereas here labour produces a variety of final output directly. This causes a slightly different relative profit and hence innovation value function but with similar characteristics.

[8] Strictly speaking φ now represents intrasectoral knowledge spillover in research whereas ψ represents joint knowledge or even cross-sectoral knowledge spillover in development. Also $(1-\psi)(1-\zeta)$, $(1-\varphi)\chi$, $(1-\psi)\zeta$ and $(1-\varphi)(1-\chi)$ have different interpretations. Still these parameters will be referred to below as intra-, cross- and joint-knowledge spillovers respectively to avoid confusion.

[9] See Appendix 4A.

[10] Ibid.

[11] See also Appendix 4B.

[12] The expansion of relative high skilled employment will rotate the *PMA* curve to the right and down.

[13] In Appendix 4A the two resulting steady state relationships between the high skilled wage level and the relative number of varieties per sector, n_H/n_L are derived. This extension is of little importance at this point, as it only implies that at lower high skilled wages there is not only a reallocation from low to high skilled labour using innovation within R&D but also a larger overall demand for and employment of high skilled labour in R&D. This ceteris paribus increases both innovation rates but has no implications for the market size effect or the relative position of low and high skilled labour. It is the relative allocation of R&D that matters for the evolution of the relative size of variety ranges that in turn determines the relative wage.

[14] See Appendix 4C.

[15] Empirical evidence suggests that the short-run elasticity of substitution lies between 1 and 2. See also subsection 4.3.1

[16] See also Equation (4.6).

[17] It is interesting to point out at this stage that Acemoglu (2002a) suggested that introducing diminishing returns to R&D effort would not affect his general conclusions and could overcome the Jones' (1995) critique that his model, like all innovation driven models, is also vulnerable to.

[18] Note also that the type II *RDA* in principle allows for multiple steady states. The stable ones are those where the *RDA* curve intersects the *PMA* from above. This theoretical possibility is less relevant here as multiple stable equilibria (at most 2) will not occur under realistic parameter values in the specifications analysed below.

[19] This number increased to about 0.8% by the early 90s.

[20] Note that in half of the specifications analysed in the next sub-section, the number of workers allocated to R&D is in fact an endogenous variable. There this observed R&D employment level is used to calibrate a parameter below.

[21] See also the references in Chapter 1, p. 16.

[22] This is known in the literature as the Daimond-McFadden-Rodriguez Non-Identification Theorem. The empirical estimates are typically obtained under the assumption that technology is the same over time or across firms and the observations represent different points on the same isoquant. In reality, however, the isoquants shift due to technical change and possibly these shifts are biased. See Binswanger (1974) for a discussion of the non-identification problem and the solutions he suggests.

[23] This is a property that Acemoglu (2002a) refers to as the LeChatelier principle.

[24] In that regression it turned out that using the number of product innovations and the number of process innovations yielded statistically indistinguishable coefficients. This implies that based on that observation the assumption of an identical γ in both innovation functions cannot be rejected and diminishing returns to R&D labour are comparable in both types of R&D. The data used and several other results are discussed in more detail in Van Zon and Sanders (2002).

[25] Jacobs, Nahuis and Tang estimate the elasticity of TFP with respect to R&D intensity, correcting for intersectoral and international spillovers. Acs and Audretsch (1988) use innovations as counted in trade journals and control for variables such as industry concentration, unionisation, advertising and capital intensity. The latter indicate that their sample is possibly biased towards product innovations.

[26] Numerical analysis with $\gamma=1$ will fail as $1-\gamma$ appears in some denominators and the allocation of R&D resources switches between corner solutions out of equilibrium.

[27] See for example Barro and Sala-I-Martin (1995).

[28] See Van Praag and Booij (2003) for a short summary of the evidence.

[29] It is larger than the above-mentioned 1.2% of the workforce by an order of magnitude.

[30] It does not matter for the model whether one exogenously doubles the required rate of return or exogenously halves the actual rate of return. In both cases the invested amount and thereby the employed labour is reduced by a similar amount. Using a higher ρ to capture this success rate saves one parameter in the model.

[31] The very high values are obtained when diminishing returns are assumed to be weak in R&D. This also strengthens the case against constant returns, made above.

[32] As was mentioned above γ is considered a specification parameter as well, since empirical evidence suggest a rather broad range and, as was argued in Section 4.2, the impact of γ on the strong market size effect is profound.

[33] Notably $\varphi=\psi=0$ and $\gamma=1$. See Table 4.3 below.

[34] As was shown above these versions will yield comparable results in terms of their market size effect and are considered in this chapter to merely illustrate the different transitional dynamics. The endogenous labour allocation versions have been calibrated to yield the same employment in R&D as was assumed in the exogenous allocation version. See below. Hence the long-term equilibrium results are identical and only transitional dynamics differ. The endogenous vs. exogenous allocation models will start to generate more interesting and different results when labour supply is endogenised and labour market institutions are considered in Part II.

[35] This model specification was discussed elaborately in Sanders (2002).

[36] The relative productivity shock in R&D in the next section is a natural experiment that provides a sensitivity test on this assumption.

[37] In fact this normalises the unit of output such that a unit of low skilled labour produces one unit of low skilled labour using output.

[38] The obtained ρ is not sensitive to the specification of the model and holds for all specifications with a given value of γ.

[39] These restrictions are in the lower part of Table 4.4 above. The equilibrium condition of the model provides the 4th restriction. In the exogenous labour allocation cases one actually solves only three equations in three variables. As was mentioned above p is inconsequential for the steady state in those cases. In addition, as in the exogenous allocation cases the supply of R&D labour is set at 1.2% of total labour, the steady state results are identical. The responses to shocks, however, differ slightly.

[40] Implying that given the normalisation of total labour supply to 1000 low skilled labour supply is reduced 1 for 1 from 775 to 600 over the same interval.

[41] But not between these steady states. See the figures towards the end of this chapter.

[42] Appendix 4D presents a table containing the elasticity of the steady state relative wage with respect to a 10% shock in α, p, a_R and b_H. The sensitivity to shocks in a_R is also illustrated in the simulations presented in the next section and Appendix 4E.

[43] Note that this is not a valid argument in no-PLC specifications as in these symmetric models there is no a priori reason why a GPT would be skill biased in general.

[44] In period 65 the market size effect starts to kick in for real in the models that exhibit the strong market size effect. In that period relative wages start to rise after falling in response to the exogenous rise in relative supply. In period 80 the exogenous rise in relative supply ends and the model starts to tend towards its new steady state.

[45] This implies a nice alternative way of introducing a GPT-shock would be to simulate a temporary shock to γ. The intuition for such a shock would be that a GPT temporarily lifts the diminishing returns in innovation as a large new field of possibilities is opened up and R&D efforts are not crowding each other out. As this implies varying elasticities in relative innovation functions by sector, however, the model is greatly complicated and the analysis of such an experiment is therefore left for future research.

[46] By trial and error until relative wages in period 80 were close to 1.6. In Chapter 5 a more sophisticated method is used to calibrate an R&D productivity shock such that the stylised relative wage developments are reproduced in the model.

[47] As was mentioned above, the relative wage in these specifications exceeds the required 1.6 in the steady state. Still the factor was calculated to get it at 1.6 in period 80. After that the relative wage continues to rise to its new steady state level of about 3.

[48] This specification is unstable and oscillates around some mean relative wage in the steady state. This is because the combination of high output elasticity, endogenous R&D employment and high skilled labour abundance leads to an explosive growth in n and always overshooting of the steady state.

[49] Relative supply increases between period 50 and 80 by some 100% and then remains stable, whereas the productivity shock is modelled as the blunt pre-multiplication of the productivity parameter on product R&D between periods 65 and 80.

PART II
TECHNICAL CHANGE
AND THE LABOUR MARKET

The last part focused on illustrating the interaction between innovation and labour demand. The model developed there explained a prominent US labour market trend, rising relative high skilled wages, as the result of an endogenous innovation driven shift in relative demand. But one rightfully wonders: Why only in America? Europe saw similar increases in relative labour supply and adopted similar technologies. Relative wages nevertheless remained stable or even fell in some countries. In addition, the model in Part I assumed the absence of unemployment, rather than considering the fact that it first rose and then fell in relative terms, be it at low levels in the US and high ones in Europe. To explain such quantity adjustments in the labour market and evaluate the possibilities to trade-off relative wage stability for unemployment, extensions to the basic model have to be considered. To that end Chapter 5 introduces endogenous participation and unemployment theories as potentially underlying a less than perfectly inelastic labour supply curve. Chapter 6 then proceeds with analysing the impact of such an extension in more detail and addresses the different US and European labour market trends. The main contribution in this part lies in the extension to more general labour market structures that allow one to address unemployment in general and the European situation in particular.

CHAPTER 5:

THE LABOUR MARKET

Obviously, the labour market model of Chapter 4 will not do to explain observed international labour market trends. People will generally not work at any wage level the market dictates and, as they have many alternatives to spending their time at work, they usually reduce the quality (effort) and quantity (hours) of their labour supply as wages fall. In addition workers who are perfectly willing and qualified to occupy a job at the going wage level, might fail to find one.

As unemployment levels are also linked to wage levels, the key implications of such quantity adjustments can be analysed by introducing an upward sloping aggregate relative supply curve as has been suggested in Section 1.2. In this chapter the aim is to introduce this general extension to the model and argue that it captures the essence of several models of participation and unemployment that have been developed in the literature.

The first section introduces upward sloping supply curves into the model by reformulating the labour market equilibrium conditions. A second section then shows how the resulting aggregate upward sloping relative supply curve can be linked to endogenous participation. In the final section of this chapter the main concern is with unemployment. Many potential sources for unemployment have been identified in the literature. Most theories of unemployment can be related to the so-called wage curve.[1] The implications of this negative relationship between unemployment and wage levels can be analysed in the model by an appropriate reinterpretation of the upward sloping relative labour supply curve proposed in Section 5.1.[2] Again all mathematical details are in the appendices and the extensions are presented in the familiar synopsis table format. Chapter 6 then proceeds by analysing the labour supply and unemployment extensions to the model.

Most of the analysis refers to relative rather than absolute levels and existing preconceptions may or may not apply in this context. Note also that relative levels always refer to the high over low skilled ratio except for the unemployment rate, where the conventional definition of low over high skilled unemployment rates was used.

5.1 QUANTITY ADJUSTMENTS

To introduce endogenous labour supply into the model at this point, only a few adjustments are required. When l_s represents the share of the available stock of workers of skill S that is willing and able to secure a job at a given wage level, the labour market equilibrium conditions in Cell 8 of the above synopsis tables have to be adjusted accordingly. Table 5.1 presents the adjusted equilibrium conditions.

Table 5.1:   FORMAL SYNOPSIS OF THE GENERAL MODEL
Extended

EQUILIBRIUM CONDITIONS S Indexes Sector/Skill			
		Equilibrium without Competition	Equilibrium with Competition
LABOUR MARKET(S)	8	$R_R + R_D = R^*$ $L_H^D = I_H(w_H)L_H^* - R^*$ $L_L^D = I_L(w_L)L_L^*$ $\dfrac{I_H(w_H)L_H^*}{I_L(w_L)L_L^*} = F(w_H/w_L)\dfrac{L_H^*}{L_L^*}$	$w_H = w_R$ $L_H^D + R_R + R_D = I_H(w_H)L_H^*$ $L_L^D = I_L(w_L)L_L^*$ $\dfrac{I_H(w_H)L_H^*}{I_L(w_L)L_L^*} = F(w_H/w_L)\dfrac{L_H^*}{L_L^*}$

The properties of $F(.)$ depend on the underlying theory of endogenous participation or unemployment. Still, $F(.)$ is increasing in the relative wage when the employment rate is positive in the wage level as is generally the case. Relative supply, interpreted as the relative number of workers that can be employed at any relative wage level, is now given in the last line:

$$\frac{L_H^S}{L_L^S} = F\left(\frac{w_H}{w_L}\right)\frac{L_H^*}{L_L^*} \tag{5.1}$$

Recall also that relative labour demand was given by Equation (4.1):[3]

$$\frac{L_H^D}{L_L^D} = \frac{n_H}{n_L}\left(\frac{w_H}{w_L}\right)^{\frac{-1}{1-\alpha\beta}}\left(\frac{b_H}{b_L}\right)^{\frac{\alpha}{1-\alpha\beta}} \tag{5.2}$$

Assuming that wages still clear labour markets, the expression in Equation (5.2) can be set equal to Equation (5.1). In the short run, for a given n_H/n_L, Equations (5.1) and (5.2) determine the relative wage and relative employment levels as in Figure 5.1 below.[4]

Figure 5.1: EQUILIBRIUM IN THE LABOUR MARKET

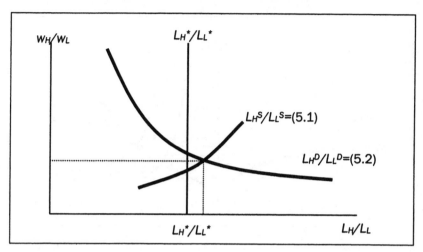

In the long run the equality of Equation (5.1) to Equation (5.2) dictates a relation between relative wages and n_H/n_L. Solving the labour market equilibrium condition for n_H/n_L yields a new (inverse) PMA curve:[5]

$$\frac{n_H}{n_L} = F(w_H/w_L)\frac{L_H^*}{L_L^*}\left(\frac{w_H}{w_L}\right)^{\frac{1}{1-\alpha\beta}}\left(\frac{b_H}{b_L}\right)^{\frac{-\alpha}{1-\alpha\beta}} \qquad (5.3)$$

By the fact that the right-hand side is now the product of an upwards-sloping convex factor in relative wages and the upward sloping function $F(.)$ in relative wages, Equation (5.3) is an upward sloping curve in the relative wage. The adjusted PMA curve can also be constructed graphically, as is illustrated in Figure 5.2. By plotting the relative wage that equilibrates the labour market on the right against different values of n_H/n_L, denoted by Z_0, Z_1 and Z_2, in the left panel, the new PMA curve (II) generally retains its original concave upward sloping shape.[6] The innovation part of the model, the RDA curve and all that underlies it, is not affected by the introduction of endogenous labour supply. Hence the structure and steady state properties of the model remain intact. A stable steady state solution exists as long as the RDA curve intersects the PMA curve from above and the model still generates the strong market size effect if the RDA curve is upward sloping.

Figure 5.2:   GRAPHICAL CONSTRUCTION OF THE *PMA* CURVE

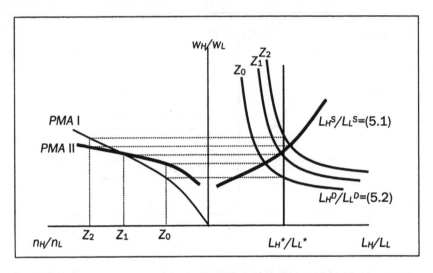

In Chapter 6 it will be shown that this extension indeed leaves the basic structure of the model unaffected and analyses its impact more elaborately. Before proceeding in that direction, however, some justifications for the upward sloping relative supply curve $F(w_H/w_L)$ are offered to guide its functional specification and provide an interpretation of its parameters. The models of labour supply and unemployment presented below are classics in economics and basically reproduced from textbooks by Layard, Nickell and Jackman (1991) (on bargaining and efficiency wages), Filer, Hamermesh and Rees (1996) (on labour force participation) and Davidson (1999) (on search models). Those familiar with that literature and satisfied with the claim that such models may underlie an upward sloping relative supply curve are advised to proceed to Chapter 6.

5.2   ENDOGENOUS LABOUR PARTICIPATION
BASED ON FILER, HAMERMESH AND REES (1996)

In the model of Chapter 4 workers supplied their labour at any given wage level. The *population* was assumed to be equal to the *labour force*.[7] In classical labour market theory, however, labour force participation is typically assumed to be the aggregate result of individuals' choices to spend their time on (looking for) paid employment rather than something else. The individuals in the population are assumed to value both the expected labour income and the leisure forgone, hence a trade-off has to be made. This trade-off can be formalised by introducing leisure as an argument in the utility function. The properties generally attributed to that utility function are substitutability between leisure and consumption, diminishing returns to both arguments and a marginal utility that tends to infinity when either leisure or consumption approaches 0.[8]

Substitutability implies that individuals are prepared to trade leisure for consumption.[9] In addition, diminishing returns cause a given amount of consumption to buy less and less additional leisure time.[10] This is captured in an individual labour supply curve like:

$$\frac{U_c(\overset{-}{C},\overset{+,0}{1-l})}{U_{1-l}(\overset{+,0}{C},\overset{-}{1-l})} = \left(\frac{w}{P}\right)^{-1} \tag{5.4}$$

where U_c and U_{1-l} are the marginal utility of consumption and leisure, which are constant or negative and positive in labour supply l, respectively, by the assumed diminishing marginal utility.[11] Equation (5.4) implies that l is positive in the real wage, w/P if the substitution effect dominates the income effect.[12] Aggregation over $L*$ identical atomistic price-taking individuals yields an aggregate labour supply curve $lL* = L^S$ (w/P) that increases in the real consumption wages earned.[13]

Assuming that both high and low skilled workers consume the same goods and make the trade-off described above one obtains:

$$\frac{w_H}{w_L} = \frac{U^L{}_c}{U^H{}_c}\frac{U^H{}_{1-l}(\overset{+}{l_H})}{U^L{}_{1-l}(\overset{+}{l_L})} \;\Rightarrow\; \frac{L_H{}^S}{L_L{}^S} = \frac{l_H L_H{}^*}{l_L L_L{}^*} = F(w_H\overset{+}{/}w_L)\frac{L_H{}^*}{L_L{}^*} \tag{5.5}$$

This implies that the parameters in the functional specification of $F(.)$ can be related to the parameters of the utility function. In Equation (5.5) the sensitivity of aggregate relative supply to relative wages depends on the sensitivity of low and high skilled individual labour supply with respect to their own consumption wages. In addition to the individual labour-leisure trade-off, skill-specific reservation wages, non-labour incomes, mixed households and endogenous human capital accumulation affect aggregate relative labour supply and the sensitivity of relative participation rates to relative wages.

For obvious reasons individual labour supply is strictly positive. Individual supply functions are therefore truncated. Although it is not immediately clear from the discussion above, there will be no supply of labour when the real wage falls below the *reservation wage*. This reservation wage represents the utility value of the first hour of leisure that has to be given up and includes the value of home production and the non-labour incomes lost when one accepts a job, such as unemployment benefits. As reservation wages typically depend on the prevailing wage levels in the market, through reservation wages, the impact of relative wage changes is increased.

Similarly all increases in non-labour income, also those that are not lost when employment is accepted, have a *wealth effect*. Higher non-labour income decreases labour supply, because the additional consumption reduces the marginal value of working and consuming relative to that of leisure. The aggregate relative supply may be more or less sensitive to relative wage changes when reservation wages and non-labour incomes differ by skill and depend on the market wage of the own or the other skill group.

Another factor of importance is the fact that labour supply is typically a *household* decision (see for example Gregg and Wadsford (1996) for an empirical investigation). Households consist of several individuals that pool their incomes and share consumption. They also decide how much labour every individual member will supply. In that case the incomes of the other members in the household will reduce an individual's labour supply, whereas there will also be some specialisation, possibly increasing the supply of some members beyond their individually preferred levels. Typically those with a comparative advantage in working, i.e. those with high wages, will then supply more labour. The existence of mixed households (containing skilled and unskilled labour) implies that relative wages matter for the relative supply of that household. In fact, due to the specialisation within households, relative labour supply will become more sensitive, and more elastic to the relative wage than when one considers atomistic agents.

A final issue that may affect the sensitivity of relative available labour to relative wages is the endogenous accumulation of skills. Not only do individuals decide on how much time to spend on labour and leisure, they also decide on how much time should be spent in education, necessary to acquire skills. In principle that decision is not much unlike the consumers' savings decision in the previous part, which brings one to the *human capital* approach. The idea in this approach is that individuals invest time in education and consider it an asset that yields a return. This idea goes back to Adam Smith (1776) but Schultz (1961) and Becker (1962) were among the first to seriously and precisely formulate and analyse this hypothesis.

The key result of the human capital approach is that the anticipated returns to education determine to a large extent the amount of time devoted to education. These returns are mainly higher wages and consequently the future stock of skilled labour will depend positively on anticipated relative wages. The human capital approach predicts that the elasticity of relative supply is larger in the long run. The argument is intuitively clear. Consider the long-run implications of a rise (fall) in the relative wage. The immediate effect is to increase (decrease) the returns to education and reduce (increase) the opportunity costs of education (since the low skilled wage is foregone while one is being educated). Hence the investment in education will rise (fall) and in the long run the relative supply of skilled labour rises (falls) even more than in the short run.

The inactivity discussed here is voluntary, both at the micro and macro level.[14] The resulting upward sloping relative supply curve must be interpreted as tracing out the relative numbers of participating workers of either skill type at a given relative wage. As it was argued in Section 1.2, however, the US and Europe shared similar trends in relative participation rates. US and European labour markets differ primarily in their involuntary unemployment levels, which will be addressed below.

5.3   UNEMPLOYMENT

The part of the population that voluntarily supplies its labour to the market at going wage levels makes up the labour force. A large part of the labour force will typically be *employed*. Not every individual in the labour force, however, has or instantly finds a job that matches his abilities and preferences and pays the going market wage. Those thus involuntarily out of work are defined as the *unemployed*.[15]

As opposed to voluntary entry and withdrawal from the labour force, involuntary unemployment poses a serious policy problem. It implies inefficiency as productive resources are left idle and in addition those affected suffer a serious income loss, potentially causing strong negative externalities.[16]

In most unemployment models the employers have the right to manage their firms, such that actual employment will always be on the labour demand curve and the going wage level reflects productivity. Unemployment can therefore be interpreted as the amount of labour that employers do not employ at the going wage level despite the fact that these workers would want to accept going or even slightly lower wages. If, for whatever reason, wages fail to adjust fully to this excess supply in the labour market, unemployment may persist in equilibrium.

Adjusting labour market equilibrium conditions accordingly one can write the inverted *PMA* curve in Equation (5.3) as:

$$\frac{n_H}{n_L} = \frac{(1-u_H)L_H{}^s}{(1-u_L)L_L{}^s}\left(\frac{w_H}{w_L}\right)^{\frac{1}{1-\alpha\beta}}\left(\frac{b_H}{b_L}\right)^{\frac{-\alpha}{1-\alpha\beta}} \tag{5.6}$$

where $L_H{}^s$ and $L_L{}^s$ are the amounts of high and low skilled labour supplied, $l_H L_H{}^*$ and $l_L L_L{}^*$, respectively. As Equation (5.6) illustrates, the levels of (un)employment equilibrate the labour market at going (relative) wages and unemployment arises for all the reasons that wages fail to adjust to excess supply.

Most models of unemployment would predict that wages are correlated negatively with unemployment levels and empirical research has indeed uncovered a robust negative relation between wage and unemployment levels.[17] This negative relationship has been labelled the *wage* curve. Introducing an inverted wage curve directly into the inverse *PMA* curve above would again imply adding terms in (relative) wages to the right-hand side as was the case with endogenous supply in Equation (5.3).[18]

Using a wage curve, the model in Chapter 4 can thus accommodate unemployment in much the same way as it accommodated endogenous supply. The required extensions can all be made to the labour market equilibrium conditions and without further specification voluntary and involuntary unemployment are indistinguishable in the model. Table 5.2 presents the extension below.[19]

There are many models of unemployment that identify possible causes for the failure of labour markets to clear. Consequently there are many possible specifications and interpretations of the wage curve. Traditionally economists distinguish seasonal, demand deficient, structural and frictional unemployment.[20]

The first two categories are not considered. As workers are usually assumed to dislike large income fluctuations, relative wages will respond very little to these types of unemployment. Workers absorb the seasonal and cyclical variation by working fewer or more hours and relative hourly wages remain quite stable over the cycles. Moreover Layard, Nickell and Jackman (1991) show that the bulk of the variation in unemployment rates cannot be attributed to conventional business cycles, so by implication demand deficient unemployment is of minor importance in explaining the development of unemployment itself over longer periods of time.

Table 5.2: FORMAL SYNOPSIS OF THE GENERAL MODEL
Unemployment

		EQUILIBRIUM CONDITIONS S Indexes Sector/Skill
LABOUR MARKET(S)	8	**Equilibrium without Competition** $R_R + R_D = R^*$ $L_H^D = (1 - u_H(w_H))L_H^* - R^*$ $L_L^D = (1 - u_L(w_L)L_L^*$ $\dfrac{(1 - u_H(w_H))L_H^*}{(1 - u_L(w_L)L_L^*} = F(w_H/w_L)\dfrac{L_H^*}{L_L^*}$ **Equilibrium with Competition** $w_H = w_R$ $L_H^D + R_R + R_D = (1 - u_H(w_H))L_H^*$ $L_L^D = (1 - u_L(w_L)L_L^*$ $\dfrac{(1 - u_H(w_H))L_H^*}{(1 - u_L(w_L)L_L^*} = F(w_H/w_L)\dfrac{L_H^*}{L_L^*}$

Finally, as the lifetime of a patent spans several years, the seasonal and cyclical variation in unemployment would normally be anticipated and has little impact on expected future profits.[21] For this reason these types of unemployment cannot be expected to affect the process of technical change much.

This leaves frictional and structural unemployment. Structural unemployment emerges when wages do not adjust in the equilibrium. The government may enforce this for example by setting a (binding) minimum wage. Supply will then exceed demand in the labour market, creating a pool of workers who cannot find a job at the going wage. Workers may also push wages above the market-clearing level in a wage bargain. Bargaining, by unions or workers individually, prevents labour markets from clearing because union members and insiders with other types of market power care less about the unemployment of outsiders than about their own wages.[22] Finally employers may set wages above market clearing levels to attract, motivate and retain a productive work force. In the minimum wage model unemployment simply assumes the role of the wage in equilibrating the labour market. In the latter two, unemployment and the wage level are simultaneously determined and unemployment serves to discipline workers.

Frictional unemployment emerges when the transition from the inactive to the employed population (and back) or from one job to the next takes time and effort. Labour turnover itself now becomes the source of unemployment. Wages play no direct role in the equilibrating process and are usually determined along similar lines as in bargaining models. Unemployment then serves to reduce the wage claim in these models, yielding a wage curve. But wages and unemployment are determined simultaneously with labour turnover and affected strongly by, for example, search costs and job destruction rates.

These models and the corresponding implications for the specification of the wage curve are discussed below in more detail. They will be referred to as the minimum wage, the insider-outsider, the efficiency wage and the search models of unemployment, respectively, in separate sub-sections.

5.3.1 Minimum Wages and Unemployment
Based on Muysken, Sanders and van Zon (2001)

Structural unemployment can emerge to absorb the excess supply of labour at the going statutory minimum wage in equilibrium. As a statutory minimum wage is only sensible if it is binding and since low skilled workers earn lower wages, the low skilled wage should be set at the minimum wage. Hence a binding minimum sets $w_L = w_{MIN}$. Now unemployment simply replaces the wage as the variable that adjusts to bring about the labour market equilibrium.[23] If the minimum wage is set exogenously and never adjusted, then the normalisation chosen matters for the long-run equilibrium.[24] In line with policy practice and avoiding the normalisation problem, the minimum wage can be set directly relative to average market wages. In a two worker-type model this implies that the minimum wage is fixed implicitly to the high skilled wage level.[25]

As long as the minimum wage is binding for the low skilled and specified in terms of the high skilled wage, for example by setting the minimum wage for low skilled at $\omega_{MIN}*w_H$, the relative wage is fixed. The relative supply curve is now kinked as in Figure 5.3 below. Below the fixed relative minimum wage low skilled workers earn more than the minimum and supply their labour inelastically. Above the relative minimum wage they cannot work and their unemployment rate is 1. Relative supply therefore becomes infinite and relative supply is a horizontal curve as has been illustrated in Figure 5.3 below.

Figure 5.3:   EQUILIBRIUM IN THE LABOUR MARKET
Minimum Wage

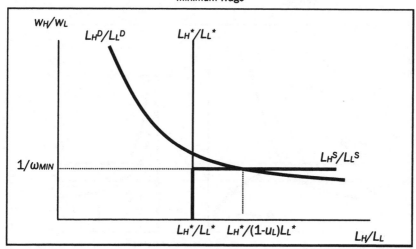

One obtains for the labour market equilibrium:

$$\frac{L_H^*}{(1-u_L)L_L^*} = \frac{n_H}{n_L}(\omega_{MIN})^{\frac{1}{1-\alpha\beta}}\left(\frac{b_H}{b_L}\right)^{\frac{\alpha}{1-\alpha\beta}} \tag{5.7}$$

where an exogenous labour force was assumed for convenience.[26] As the relative wage is fixed as long as the minimum wage is binding, the RDA curve determines the steady state ratio of n_H over n_L. Figure 5.4 illustrates the full response to an increase in the minimum wage. From the initial equilibrium at A, A' the demand for low skilled labour immediately falls along the demand curve to B. The lower relative wage also reduces the incentive to do low skilled complementary R&D at B' and n_H/n_L will rise, causing further adjustment in relative labour demand and unemployment. The new long-run equilibrium is at C, C' where low skilled unemployment is higher than at A and B.[27]

This implies that (low skilled) unemployment increases even further to increase marginal productivity in the low skilled sector. Hence one returns to a steady state at a higher unemployment level. With minimum wages this unemployment is involuntary at micro and macro level. Table 5.3 shows that the minimum wage extension can be introduced in the labour market equilibrium conditions in Cell 8 of the synopsis table in a very straightforward way.

Figure 5.4:   STEADY STATE IMPACT OF AN INCREASE IN THE MINIMUM
WAGE

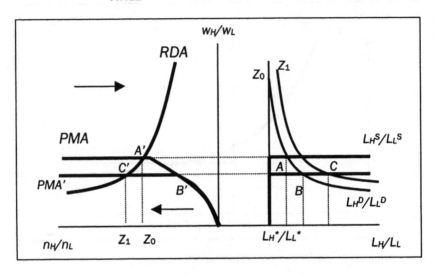

Table 5.3:   FORMAL SYNOPSIS OF THE GENERAL MODEL
Minimum Wage

		EQUILIBRIUM CONDITIONS S Indexes Sector/Skill
LABOUR MARKET(S)	8	**Equilibrium without Competition** $R_R + R_D = R^*$ $L_H^D = L_H^*$ $L_L^D = (1 - u_L)L_L^*$ $u_L = 1 - \dfrac{L_H^*/n_H}{L_L^*/n_L}(\omega_{MIN})^{\frac{-1}{1-\alpha\beta}}\left(\dfrac{b_H}{b_L}\right)^{\frac{-\alpha}{1-\alpha\beta}}$ **Equilibrium with Competition** $w_R = w_H$ $R_R + R_D + L_H^D = L_H^* - R^*$ $L_L^D = (1 - u_L)L_L^*$ $u_L = 1 - \dfrac{L_H^*/n_H}{L_L^*/n_L}(\omega_{MIN})^{\frac{-1}{1-\alpha\beta}}\left(\dfrac{b_H}{b_L}\right)^{\frac{-\alpha}{1-\alpha\beta}}$

A minimum wage model, with its horizontal relative supply curve, presents the extreme case of the trade-off hypothesis discussed in Section 1.2. All technology driven demand shocks are absorbed by quantity adjustment alone and relative unemployment absorbs all relative wage pressure. [28] The minimum wage differential is, however, unlikely to explain much of the EU-US unemployment differences. Theoretically the fact that the minimum wage is lower in the US than in Europe implies that (low skilled) Europeans will experience a higher unemployment rate.[29] It is immediately clear that higher minimum wages also predict higher relative unemployment rates, u_L/u_H.[30] As was shown in Section 1.2, this not supported in the data. Unemployment in Europe is generally higher for both skill groups, but relative unemployment rates are comparable or even more favourable for the low skilled than in the US.

In addition Brown, Gilroy and Kohen (1982) find little evidence to suggest that the minimum wage contributes significantly to overall unemployment levels. Other institutional features of the US and European labour markets prove to be much more important in explaining even these level differences. These results should not come as a surprise if one realises that even of the least skilled workers only a small fraction actually earns the minimum wage. Most jobs pay higher wages than the legally required minimum. The minimum wage is therefore not binding for many low skilled workers, and a much larger fraction of workers, in the US and in particular in Europe is affected by collective bargaining, which is introduced in the next sub-section.

5.3.2 WAGE BARGAINING AND INSIDER-OUTSIDER MODELS OF UNEMPLOYMENT
BASED ON LAYARD, NICKELL AND JACKMAN (1991)

Minimum wages are not the only difference between European and US labour markets. As is well documented in the literature, union bargaining extends to a much larger percentage of the work force in Europe and their bargaining position is strengthened further by high replacement rates, strict firing regulations etc.[31] This stronger bargaining position is another potential explanation for high unemployment levels.

Unemployment performs the function of reducing wage claims by unions or individual wage bargainers. If unemployment is very high the wage claim is reduced because the prospect of being fired when claiming a high wage is not very appealing. If, on the other hand, unemployment is very low, then wage claims can be high, since one easily finds another job when one is fired.[32] This mechanism yields a wage curve that can be represented by an upward sloping supply curve as was suggested above.

Bargaining theory starts from the assumption that employers and employees are not price takers in the labour market but instead bargain over the wage. Both parties to a bargain will aim to maximise their own objective function and use all their bargaining power to do so. Standard bargaining theory has developed the Nash product as a way to formalise bargaining.[33] The outcome of a simple wage bargain would be the solution to a maximisation problem of the form: [34]

$$\max_{w} : \left(V(w) - V_0\right)^{\omega} \left(\Pi(w) - \Pi_0\right)^{1-\omega} \tag{5.8}$$

where ω is a parameter that represents the bargaining power of the worker, $V(w)$ is his value function which obviously depends positively on the wage and $\Pi(w)$ is the profit of the employer that usually depends negatively on the wages paid.[35] V_0 and Π_0 are the fallback positions, the incomes the parties receive when they fail to agree, of the employees and employers, respectively. For the employee one should think of unemployment benefits, strike income and the like. For the employer the fallback position is the value of firing the worker and posting a vacancy.

The worker is usually assumed to care about his expected income only. This expected income consists of two components. The wage he bargains for, times the probability he will continue to earn that wage, plus his *outside option*, the value of being unemployed, times the probability that he loses his job.

The probability of survival in the job depends (negatively) on the wage and can be written as $s(w_S(i))$, the *survival function* of worker i of skill S. Appendix 5B shows that, if one assumes that all workers and firms are identical within skill groups, sets $\Pi_0 = 0$ and assumes for simplicity that the fallback position V_0 is equal to the workers' outside option, A_S, one obtains that the wage will solve:

$$\max_{w_S} : \left(\left(w_S - A_S\right)s(w_S)\right)^{\omega} \left(\Pi(w_S)\right)^{1-\omega} \tag{5.9}$$

It is also shown in Appendix 5B that, using identical monopolistic firms implies that the wage mark-up over the workers' outside option equals:

$$\frac{w_S - A_S}{w_S} = \frac{1}{-\sigma_{sw}(w_S) + ((1-\omega)/\omega)(\alpha\beta/(1-\alpha\beta))} \tag{5.10}$$

This wage mark-up depends positively on the bargaining power of the worker, ω, and the profit share in output, $(1-\alpha\beta)$.[36] It also depends positively on the (negative) elasticity of the survival probability with respect to the wage, σ_{sw}. Intuitively, when the probability of being fired is very sensitive to the wage claimed, a worker will settle for lower wages.

The survival elasticity is the product of the (positive) elasticity of survival with respect to employment and the (negative) elasticity of employment with respect to wages. It is shown in Appendix 5B that the elasticity in Equation (5.10) depends (negatively) on the demand elasticity of labour, the voluntary quit rate and the steady state growth rate.[37]

As all workers were assumed to be homogenous within skill groups, the equilibrium probability of being unemployed is equal to the aggregate unemployment rate. If the wage bargain fails, expected income equals that probability times benefits B_S plus $(1-u_S)$ times w_S, which represents the probability of finding another job earning the market wage. Substitution into Equation (5.10) and solving for wages over benefits one obtains the wage curve:[38]

$$M_s(u_s) \equiv \frac{w_s}{B_s} = \frac{u_s}{u_s - x_s} \tag{5.11}$$

Appendix 5B defines x_s as a skill specific positive constant (function of constant parameters only). It is easily verified that the wage level is negative in the unemployment rate as empirical evidence on the wage curve suggests. The same increase in unemployment will increase the numerator by a smaller percentage than the denominator, causing the fraction to go down. Note also that the wage tends to infinity when the denominator falls to 0. This defines a positive level, $u_{s0} \equiv x_s$, of unemployment that the workers do not care to reduce any further. Finally the mark-up of wages over benefits falls to its minimum at $m_{s0} \equiv 1/(1-x_s)$ when unemployment reaches its maximum at 1.[39]

If unemployment benefits are constant or defined in terms of the group specific wage alone, then the equilibrium unemployment rate is independent of the wage level and determined by Equation (5.11). As this would eliminate the short run responsiveness of wages to unemployment, however, the wage curve would not have been introduced properly. The problem can be avoided when benefit levels are set in terms of both wages. Consider for example:

$$B_S = \rho_S w_S{}^{\delta_S} w_{-S}{}^{1-\delta_S} \qquad S \in \{H,L\}, -S \neq S \tag{5.12}$$

Solving Equation (5.11) for unemployment one then obtains:

$$u_S = \frac{x_S}{\left(1 - \rho_S w_S^{\delta_s-1} w_{-S}^{1-\delta_s}\right)} \tag{5.13}$$

It can be verified that the unemployment rates are now negatively related to one's relative wage. Using these unemployment rates in a model with an exogenously fixed relative labour force would then generate an upward sloping relative supply curve, where supply must be interpreted as the amount of employable labour at the relative wage levels offered.[40]

Table 5.4:   FORMAL SYNOPSIS OF THE GENERAL MODEL
Wage Bargaining

		EQUILIBRIUM CONDITIONS S Indexes Sector/Skill
LABOUR MARKET(S)	8	**Wage Bargaining** $w_S = \dfrac{u_S}{u_S - x_S}\rho_S w_S^{\delta_s} w_{-S}^{1-\delta_s} \qquad \Rightarrow$ $u_S = \dfrac{x_S}{1 - \rho_S\left(w_S/w_{-S}\right)^{\delta_s-1}}$ **Equilibrium without Competition** $R_R + R_D = R^*$ $L_H^D = (1-u_H)L_H^* - R^*$ $L_L^D = (1-u_L)L_L^*$ $\dfrac{(1-u_H)L_H^*}{(1-u_L)L_L^*} = F(w_H/w_L)\dfrac{L_H^*}{L_L^*}$ **Equilibrium with Competition** $w_H = w_R$ $L_H^D + R_R + R_D = (1-u_H)L_H^*$ $L_L^D = (1-u_L)L_L^*$ $\dfrac{(1-u_H)L_H^*}{(1-u_L)L_L^*} = F(w_H/w_L)\dfrac{L_H^*}{L_L^*}$

Wage bargaining therefore gives rise to an upward sloping aggregate relative supply curve. Some additional issues in bargaining structures may make that relative supply curve more elastic to the relative wage. Unions may have skilled and unskilled workers, leading to bargaining over the relative wage. In addition the wages of one group affect the employment and thereby survival probabilities of the other group. As long as the two are substitutes, as has been assumed from the outset, this will increase the elasticity of relative supply when bargaining is reasonably centralised.[41] In Table 5.4 the adjustment to the equilibrium conditions in Cell 8 can be made to introduce wage bargaining.

The adjustment implies that the formal structure of the model is not affected over and beyond what has already been discussed. The functional form of $F(.)$, however, is now fully specified and its parameters and variables can be related to the bargaining process. These parameters have been routinely estimated in the huge empirical literature on US and European labour markets, which facilitates the numerical simulations that are presented in the next chapter. Unemployment is involuntary at the micro level only when a bargaining model is employed.[42] As there are large international differences in the bargaining position of workers, this is a promising extension that will be analysed in detail in Chapter 6 below.

5.3.3 Unemployment and Efficiency Wages
Based on Layard, Nickell and Jackman (1991)

A final reason why wages may structurally fail to clear labour markets is that employers pay their workers more than is required to attract them to a job. Employers may have good reasons to pay above market clearing wages. When asked they argue that higher wages allow them to recruit, retain and motivate a more productive workforce, when searching, selecting, training and monitoring workers is costly.[43] Consider the motivation argument. The underlying assumption of this model is that employers cannot fully monitor their workers. The worker therefore has some discretion in choosing the effort level he will provide. As effort affects productivity it also affects profits and it might pay for the employer to offer higher wages to induce additional effort. Assume for example that a worker's effort depends positively on the mark-up of the firm wage over the outside option.[44] As the outside option depends negatively on unemployment and positively on the expected wage level outside the firm, the effort level in the firm increases in unemployment and the firm wage relative to the wage expected outside the firm. Suppose employer j knows that his employees of skill type S choose effort according to:[45]

$$e_S = e\left(\frac{w_{Sj}}{w_S}, u_S\right) \tag{5.14}$$

Taking the firms in the model of Chapter 4 and assuming e_s^β replaces the exogenous productivity parameter b_s implies that profits are given by:[46]

$$\pi_{sj} = (1 - \alpha\beta)E\left(\frac{E}{P}\right)^{\frac{-\alpha}{1-\alpha\beta}}\left(\frac{w_{sj}}{e_{sj}}\right)^{\frac{-\alpha\beta}{1-\alpha\beta}} \tag{5.15}$$

Maximising this expression with respect to the firm level wage, given Equation (5.14), implies that the firm will set:

$$w_{sj} = \frac{e(w_{sj} / w_s, u_s)w_s}{e_1(w_{sj} / w_s, u_s)} \tag{5.16}$$

where $e_1(.)$ is the partial derivative of the effort function with respect to its first argument, the firm's relative wage. Assuming all firms are equal implies that they will all make the same trade-off and drive up wages in the aggregate equilibrium until $w_{sj}/w_s=1$. Unemployment is now the only variable that can generate the desired motivation for workers in the aggregate and is given by substituting $w_{sj}/w_s=1$ into Equation (5.16) and solving:

$$e_1(1,u_s) = e(1,u_s) \tag{5.17}$$

As the effort function was assumed to be positive in both arguments, unemployment reduces the need for high wages to motivate workers. If firms pay efficiency wages for motivation the wage curve will therefore emerge.[47] Paying efficiency wages to reduce voluntary quitting generates a similar result. A quitting function of employees intuitively depends negatively on both the firm's relative wage and the aggregate unemployment rate. Assuming labour turnover is costly to the employer, he sets higher wages to avoid quitting and as workers quit more at low unemployment rates he (and all other employers) will set a higher wage. Finally, when high relative wages and unemployment both increase the number of job applicants per vacancy, then recruiting competition among identical firms also implies that unemployment generates the desired job queues in equilibrium.[48] Like bargaining models, efficiency wages may therefore justify introducing a wage curve and the corresponding upward sloping relative supply curve.

Table 5.5 illustrates how efficiency wages, in this case motivated by the effort model above, generates a wage curve that can be introduced in the model.

Table 5.5: **FORMAL SYNOPSIS OF THE GENERAL MODEL**
Efficiency Wages

		EQUILIBRIUM CONDITIONS S Indexes Sector/Skill
LABOUR MARKET(S)	8	**Efficiency Wages** $$E(w_{sj}/w_s, u_s) = \frac{dE(w_{sj}/w_s, u_s)}{dw_{sj}} \frac{w_{sj}}{w_s} \quad \Rightarrow$$ u_s solves $E(1, u_s) = \dfrac{dE(1, u_s)}{dw_{sj}}$ **Equilibrium without Competition** $R_R + R_D = R^*$ $L_H^D = (1-u_H)L_H^* - R^*$ $L_L^D = (1-u_L)L_L^*$ $\dfrac{(1-u_H)L_H^*}{(1-u_L)L_L^*} = F(w_H/w_L)\dfrac{L_H^*}{L_L^*}$ **Equilibrium with Competition** $w_H = w_R$ $L_H^D + R_R + R_D = (1-u_H)L_H^*$ $L_L^D = (1-u_L)L_L^*$ $\dfrac{(1-u_H)L_H^*}{(1-u_L)L_L^*} = F(w_H/w_L)\dfrac{L_H^*}{L_L^*}$

There is a lot of empirical evidence supporting efficiency wages theory. Capital-intensive firms with high profits pay higher wages, as do large and unionised ones. Productivity differences, compensating differentials and wage bargaining all fail to explain these inter and intra industrial wage structures.[49] Efficiency wages models may also have some explanatory power when it comes to the international patterns of unemployment and wage inequality that this part aims to explain. The large international differences could be explained when effort, quitting and recruiting functions differ sufficiently between the US and Europe. European workers could, for example, be much less sensitive to unemployment in a motivation model as job protection and high unemployment benefits reduce the possibility and severity of losing your job. Similarly, European employers could have to offer much higher wages to attract a queue of applicants as the generous social benefits system reduces people's incentives to apply for any job. There is little empirical evidence to support this hypothesis, but the possibility presents an interesting research agenda for the future.

As evidence is scarce at the moment, however, and because international differences are probably too large to rely heavily on efficiency wages for an explanation, the implications of efficiency wages are not pursued further below. Chapter 6 will focus on the bargaining model instead.

5.3.4   FRICTIONAL UNEMPLOYMENT AND SEARCH
BASED ON DAVIDSON (1990)

Friction unemployment emerges when the transition from unemployment or an old job to a new one requires costly search on behalf of both parties in the labour market. The focus in search models is therefore mainly on the flows in the labour market.

Figure 5.5:   **FLOWS IN THE LABOUR MARKET**

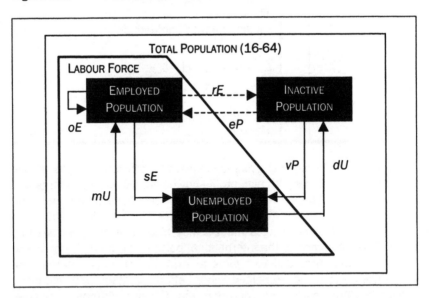

Figure 5.5 illustrates the flows in the labour market. The labour market is in *full stock equilibrium* when all stocks remain stable relative to the total population, hence when the sums of outflows equal the sums of inflows in

each stock. Defining N, U, and P as the stocks of employed, unemployed and inactive persons, the flows can be expressed as a fraction of these stocks. The flows out of employment are voluntary quits or involuntary dismissals.

Of those leaving their current job, qN, some may find a new one immediately, oN, for example when there is on-the-job search. Some may withdraw from the labour force altogether, rN, and some will experience a spell of unemployment, sN. Those unemployed may flow back into employment, mU, or withdraw from the labour force, dU, whereas the inactive population may enter the labour force through unemployment, vP or directly acquire a suitable job, eP.[50] The full stock labour market equilibrium is then characterised by:

$$oN + sN + rN = qN = mU + eP + oN$$

$$mU + dU = vP + sN \qquad\qquad (5.18)$$

$$rN + dU = eP + vP$$

The labour force, $LF \equiv N + U$ and the unemployment rate, $u \equiv U/LF$ are defined as usual. It can now be shown that the equilibrium unemployment rate is given by:[51]

$$u^* = \frac{s + (vr/(e+v))}{m+s+r} \qquad\qquad (5.19)$$

Empirical research has shown that the matching rate, m, and the (involuntary) separation rate, s, have the most profound impact.[52] Search models have therefore focussed on explaining these flows. Some early work on job search models was done by Stigler (1961) and McCall (1970) and with the papers by Diamond (1981, 1982, 1984), Mortensen (1982) and Pissarides (1984a, 1984b) this approach took root in mainstream labour economics.[53] In these papers jobs are viewed as the result of active searching on behalf of supplying and demanding parties in the labour market. An underlying 'matching technology' is introduced to describe how search results in employment. As Davidson puts it:

> *This technology may be viewed as a production function with jobless workers, their search effort, vacancies and the search effort of firms as the inputs and jobs as the output.*
> -Davidson (1990), p. 32 -

Formally one could write:

$$m = M(U/V, se_U, se_V) \qquad\qquad (5.20)$$

where U/V is the number unemployed per vacancy and se_x is the search effort of unemployed, $x=U$, and firms, $x=V$, respectively. Intuitively the matching rate is positive in all arguments. Obviously wages are an important variable in stimulating workers and firms to search. But note that in these models wages do not equilibrate the labour market. Jobless workers search for vacancies. Once one is found, they bargain over the wage and, assuming that they agree, production starts, generating a surplus that is shared between the worker and the firm. Hence wages are determined in pretty much the same fashion as in the insider-outsider models presented above. Unemployment, by reducing the workers outside option, again puts a downward pressure on wages and the wage curve will emerge. The aggregate or average wage levels usually play a role in endogenously determining the search effort on both sides of the market.

High wages will induce workers to search harder. This generates a wage curve on the supply side as higher search effort would reduce unemployment by increasing the matching rate for given separation rates.[54] But as employers will reduce their search efforts and aggregate unemployment falls relative to the vacancies, the effect on matching is compensated for and as higher wages imply that fewer jobs will generate a surplus, unemployment must rise in equilibrium.[55] For given separation rates, this implies that the search model of unemployment can be represented by an upward sloping supply curve. In addition to the usual bargaining parameters, however, now the elasticity of the workers' search intensity to the wage level will have an impact.

Equilibrium unemployment is also determined by separation rates. Search models of unemployment usually assume that separation is random and a job is destroyed at a positive probability in each period. The separation rate, s, itself is usually exogenous and invariant in the wage level but sometimes made to depend on other variables in the model. In the latter case these other variables and the sensitivity of the separation rate with respect to these variables will enter the specification of the upward sloping supply curve. As is shown in Aghion and Howitt (1994) the separation rate can for example be set equal to the rate of innovation in a quality ladder model of product innovation. They show that in a steady state equilibrium the number of jobs that is destroyed each period is equal to the number of new jobs created, which in their model is equal to the rate of product innovation.[56]

Similarly, in the model of Chapter 4, the rates of high and low skilled job destruction could be set equal to the rates of innovation in these sectors. As can be verified in the firm's labour demand equation in Cell 4 of Table 4.1, the demand for labour at firm *j* falls in proportion to the number of firms in its sector. Hence firms will continuously shed labour at a rate that is equal to the rate of (sectoral) innovation. This implies that one can write:

$$s_S = \dot{n}_S / n_S \tag{5.21}$$

In terms of modelling implications search unemployment is therefore of a different breed altogether. It results in unemployment being the unintended side effect of job turnover, which can be directly related to technical change and the resulting reallocation of labour.

Table 5.6:   **FORMAL SYNOPSIS OF THE GENERAL MODEL**
Search Unemployment

		EQUILIBRIUM CONDITIONS S Indexes Sector/Skill
LABOUR MARKET(S)	8	$s_S = \dot{n}_S / n_S$ $m_S = M(U_S / V_S, se_{U_S}(\overset{+}{w}s), se_{V_S}(\overset{-}{w}s))$ $\Rightarrow u_S^* = \dfrac{s_S}{m_S + s_S}$ **Equilibrium without Competition** $R_R + R_D = R^*$ $L_H^D = (1 - u_H)L_H^* - R^*$ $L_L^D = (1 - u_L)L_L^*$ $\dfrac{(1 - u_H)L_H^*}{(1 - u_L)L_L^*} = F\left(\dfrac{w_H}{w_L}, \dfrac{\dot{n}_H}{n_H}, \dfrac{\dot{n}_L}{n_L}\right)\dfrac{L_H^*}{L_L^*}$ **Equilibrium with Competition** $w_H = w_R$ $L_H^D + R_R + R_D = (1 - u_H)L_H^*$ $L_L^D = (1 - u_L)L_L^*$ $\dfrac{(1 - u_H)L_H^*}{(1 - u_L)L_L^*} = F\left(\dfrac{w_H}{w_L}, \dfrac{\dot{n}_H}{n_H}, \dfrac{\dot{n}_L}{n_L}\right)\dfrac{L_H^*}{L_L^*}$

The search model of unemployment suggests an adjustment to the labour market equilibrium conditions as presented in Table 5.6. Note that unemployment is now, as before, a decreasing function of the wage level and consequently relative supply is upward sloping in the relative wage. Through the separation rate, however, relative supply in now also decreasing in the relative innovation rates in the model.[57] The friction unemployment models thereby suggest some additional parameters that may help explain international differences in unemployment. Notable ones are the sensitivity of search intensity to wages and the efficiency of the matching technology captured by parameters in $M(.)$.The aim of this chapter, however, is to find the extensions that help explain relative unemployment dynamics at high and low levels in Europe and the US respectively, while reconciling these observations with rising relative wages in the US only.

As separation rates are equal for both skill levels in the steady state and higher for high skilled in the transition after a new general-purpose technology is introduced, friction unemployment would counterfactually predict equal or lower relative unemployment rates in the US at higher levels ceteris paribus. Eliminating that channel from the friction unemployment model basically reduces it to a matching model in which wage bargaining establishes the relationship between wage and unemployment levels. Therefore friction unemployment need not be considered further below.

5.4   CONCLUSION

This chapter introduced an extension to the model that allows one to analyse the impact of quantity adjustments in the labour market. This extension is required for two reasons. First, such quantity adjustments, caused by participation and unemployment responses to relative wage shifts, may cause feedback effects on technical change and interfere with the mechanisms explaining wage divergence in the US identified in Part I. Second, with this extension the model predicts participation and unemployment dynamics, which can be confronted with the stylised facts on the US and EU presented in Chapter 1.

The extension was made in general terms in Section 5.1. Two subsequent sections then presented several rather standard and definitely mainstream models of labour supply and unemployment, respectively. It was shown that all these models can explain the existence of an upward sloping aggregate relative supply curve. Moreover, the specification of that upward sloping relative supply curve, or rather, the endogenisation of participation and unemployment rates, leaves the rest of the model intact and provides a simple and tractable way of analysing the most important impact of introducing the labour-leisure trade-off, minimum wages, wage bargaining, efficiency wages and finally labour market frictions. It was also argued that the wage bargaining interpretation holds most promise for addressing the divergent labour market trends in the OECD. Focussing on that interpretation the next chapter will analyse and simulate the extended model numerically to check for the predictions and implications of endogenous unemployment.

NOTES

[1] Blanchflower and Oswald (1994a) used this term to refer to the robust negative relationship between wage levels and regional unemployment rates they found in many countries.

[2] For those able or willing to accept the claims made in Section 5.1 without a review of labour supply and unemployment theory, the latter sections are less relevant.

[3] See also Cell 4 of Table 4.1.

[4] It should be noted that, unlike the more familiar supply curve in levels that typically has a vertical asymptote, the relative supply can lie both left and right of the exogenously given relative availability of labour.

[5] Note that the no-competition specification was used to keep things tractable. The model can also be solved when R&D and production compete over high skilled labour but then relative labour demand is much more complex, as was shown in Chapter 4.

[6] The exact shape obviously depends on the parameters in the model. The point of intersection with the original *PMA* curve (I) is defined by the relative wage at which relative supply equals relative availability, i.e. where participation or unemployment rates are equal. In the extreme case of perfectly elastic relative supply, the *PMA* curve, like the relative supply curve, is horizontal. Other properties, such as horizontal asymptotes and positive intercepts, also carry over from relative supply to the *PMA*. Chapter 6 will be more elaborate on the issue.

[7] In this chapter 'population' is used to refer to the population of working age, typically between 16 and 65 years of age.

[8] See for example Filer, Hamermesh and Rees (1996).

[9] There are also models of labour supply that assume that leisure and consumption are complements. Both time and goods are used as inputs to 'produce' utility. See for example Abbott and Ashenfelter (1976), Kooreman and Kapteyn (1987) and Biddle and Hamermesh (1990). These models aim to explain certain aspects of individual labour supply that are of lesser concern when relative aggregate supply is analysed. See Filer, Hamermesh and Rees (1996) for a more elaborate overview.

[10] A logical implication of that assumption is that a very large (infinite) amount of additional consumption is required to make the individual give up his last hours of leisure, and at the other extreme, he is willing to give up all his leisure for the first unit of consumption. In Appendix 5A it is shown that, when utility is maximised, the individual will supply hours of labour until he is indifferent between spending his last hour as leisure or at work, consuming the wages earned.

[11] U_x is the partial derivative of utility with respect to x. In general these partial derivatives are themselves functions of the arguments in the utility function. The signs are above the arguments.

[12] Individual supply curves can be backward bending. Then further wage increases beyond some point reduce the supply of labour, as people prefer to consume more leisure when

their income rises. At the aggregate level, however, this effect is not likely to be strong. See Box 5.1 below.

[13] Consequently, if one interprets (1-l) as voluntary unemployment, then Equation (5.4) defines a wage curve that relates the wage level negatively to the voluntary unemployment rate.

[14] And therefore it is also Pareto-efficient and no cause for (policy) concern. Still low participation is generally perceived to be problematic as the non-participation can be induced by generous social security benefits. In that case non-participation generates a negative externality and is cause for concern.

[15] Involuntary part-time employment also fits this definition. When unemployment exists, the rational forward looking individuals that decide to participate in the labour force will take the probability and expected duration of unemployment into consideration and discount the observed market wage accordingly. This implies that participation will vary with unemployment rates and duration, even though going wages may remain constant. To introduce unemployment into the labour-leisure trade-off in the previous section, the wage, w, must be interpreted as *expected income* when deciding to participate. The results are not qualitatively affected by such a reinterpretation.

[16] See for example Freeman (1997), who links unemployment rates to crime rates.

[17] See for example Blanchflower and Oswald (1990, 1994a and b and 1995).

[18] Blanchflower and Oswald contrast their wage curve to the classical Phillips (1958) curve that suggests a negative relationship between the level of unemployment and the change in wages. The Phillips curve, however, is based on inflation expectations and assumes a degree of money illusion. As the model has no monetary sector and assumes perfect foresight, the introduction of a Phillips curve is less straightforward in this setting. The causality in the wage curve, however, is less clear and it is not an unchallenged hypothesis in the literature. The possibility that the wage curve is in fact a mis-specified Phillips curve, as for example Card (1995) seems to argue, is an important qualification to the conclusions drawn below.

[19] Where $u_S(w_S)$ is the inverted wage curve for workers with skill $S=\{H,L\}$.

[20] See for example Lipsey (1968) or any modern textbook on the labour market such as Ehrenberg and Smith (1996) or Filer, Hamermesh and Rees (1996).

[21] It does have an impact on the variance of profits but arguably to the same extent for high and low skilled labour using firms.

[22] The union reduces competition among workers, creating monopoly power. Due to asymmetric information, however, hiring and firing is costly to firms and as they try to reduce labour turnover they also create market power for the insiders. Another class of insider-outsider models, referred to as hold-up models (i.e. Teulings and Hartog (1991)), argue that workers have the power to bargain for higher wages because the employer has fixed costs. Whatever the source of market power, insiders will bargain for wages that exceed market-clearing levels, as they accept unemployment in exchange for higher wages as long as their own employment is not threatened.

[23] Basically this specifies the wage curve as a discontinuous curve defined by $u_S=0$ if $w_S>w_{MIN}$ and $u_S=1$ otherwise.

[24] Normalising income implies a falling price in the model that ensures that the minimum wage is fixed in terms of total income and grows in terms of utility (at the same rate as total income and other wage levels). Since the price index is sort of an average of wages this normalisation implicitly defines the minimum wage in terms of low and high skilled wages. If the price level is normalised, however, as for example in Acemoglu (2002a), fixing the minimum wage nominally implies that it falls relative to marginal productivity and eventually becomes non-binding.

[25] At least in the steady state when the weights of high and low skilled labour in employment do not change.

[26] A constant relative wage implies a constant relative participation rate, even if it is endogenous.

27 Note that the market size effect cannot be present as an upward sloping *RDA* curve can never intersect the now horizontal *PMA* curve from above. Acemoglu, shortly mentioned in Section 1.2, argued that a binding minimum wage for low skilled makes the employers the full residual claimant of any productivity increases, implying that they would invest more, not less, in low skilled complementary innovations when minimum wages rise. According to Acemoglu (2002b) the higher minimum wage in Europe has put a brake on the market size effect and reduced the supply induced outward shift in relative demand. The result comes from his implicit assumption that employers do not adjust their employment levels when minimum wages exceed marginal productivity. Employment is not on the relative demand curve. If it were, as was assumed in the model above, the value of low skilled complementary innovations falls with higher minimum wages, implying that demand should have shifted more in Europe.

28 Note that high skilled unemployment was assumed to be 0. It might as well have been set to some small positive level due to for example friction.

29 The differences in minimum wages, however, are not large enough to explain the large differences in unemployment. The US hourly minimum wage was 5.15 dollars in 1997. In Europe it ranged between 1.78 in Portugal to 7.23 in Luxembourg with France, Belgium and the Netherlands around 6.5. See OECD (1998) Table 2.2.

30 One should assume a given low but positive level of unemployment for high skilled workers, for example due to friction.

31 Union coverage is 70-90% in Continental Europe. In the US only 18% of workers are covered by a union bargain. The UK, Canada and New Zealand hold the middle ground between 38 and 67%. Ireland is an outlier in the Anglo-Saxon group at 85%. A similar picture emerges from the employment protection ranking in the OECD *Jobs Study* and replacement rates. See for example OECD (1994b, 1997) and Mühlau and Horgan (2001) Table 1. These factors all strengthen the bargaining position of European workers.

32 Of course a more appropriate measure would be the unemployment over vacancy ratio, but in wage bargaining models vacancies are usually fulfilled without friction. See for example Layard, Nickell and Jackman (1991).

33 See Nash (1950).

34 There are complex game-theoretical foundations for the Nash product in many different bargaining settings. See for example the annex to Chapter 2 in Layard, Nickell and Jackman (1991).

35 The profits can depend positively on wages because, as was shown in Chapter 4, profits are proportional to the wage bill. Hence if labour supply to the firm is more than inversely proportional to wages, an increase in wages will also increase profits. Because prices reflect the wage change, however, the utility value of profits will fall when wages increase. Higher wages therefore cause redistribution of utility from profit earners to wage earners in the model of Chapter 4 as well.

36 The bargain redistributes the monopoly rents in product markets towards the worker, who has some market power in the labour market.

37 The steady state growth rate basically defines an involuntary separation rate as workers have to move from existing to new varieties.

38 See Appendix 5B.

39 It is shown in Appendix 5B that this mark-up will exceed 1 under reasonable assumptions.

40 The employable labour is equal to the available less the unemployed required to reduce the wage claim of those employed to the given wage.

41 Which implies that the union realises and cares about these second order effects.

42 It can be argued that is voluntary at the aggregate level as the bargaining parties, usually unions, trade-off unemployment for wages and choose to bargain for non-market clearing wages.

43 See for example Kaufman (1984) who presents evidence from several employer surveys.

44 These models are known as gift-exchange models. See Akerlof (1982) and Kaufman (1984).

[45] Underlying this function one might again imagine some utility maximisation of the employee in which effort affects utility negatively while expected income has a positive impact.

[46] Hence productivity is a function of effort and effort enters the model as purely labour augmenting. This implies that doubling effort is equivalent to supplying twice the amount of labour. Due to diminishing returns in production, however, this does not generate twice the amount of output.

[47] This wage curve, however, is not originating on the supply side as for bargaining. The equilibrium unemployment level equates the supply of and demand for effort adjusted labour.

[48] See Layard, Nickell and Jackman (1991), Chapter 3 for the formal proof.

[49] Ibid, Table 1.

[50] Natural and demographic in- and outflows such as immigration, emigration, births and deaths may affect the size of all stocks, including the total working age population. Such flows, although potentially important empirically, are not relevant here. The equilibrium conditions are easily adjusted to such exogenous in- and outflows.

[51] It was assumed that the retirement rate r is equal to the withdrawal rate d. See Appendix 5C.

[52] See Davidson (1990).

[53] See Davidson (1990) and Pissarides (1990, 2000) for excellent and more complete overviews of this literature.

[54] These are usually assumed to be insensitive to wages. See below.

[55] This is the normal shift along the demand curve.

[56] They assume one firm employs one worker and as is usual in quality ladder models, each quality improvement implies one firm replaces another, creating job destruction and creation.

[57] In the steady state these innovation rates are equal and while generating unemployment, they do not explain different unemployment rates.

CHAPTER 6:
THE MODEL EXTENDED

In Chapter 5 it was shown that the model can be extended to include voluntary and involuntary unemployment by introducing a wage curve. The aim in this chapter is to evaluate the impact of this extension in terms of its contribution to explaining observed differences in relative wage trends and unemployment levels. As the general model has no closed form analytical solution this requires a numerical simulation approach and further specification of the labour market is required. [1]

The first section of this chapter therefore presents a parameterisation of the wage curve, based on Gregg and Manning (1997). Of course in general the specification of this curve and the interpretation of its parameters depends on the underlying theory of unemployment or non-participation, but their functional specification is empirically inspired and the parameters can be interpreted in terms of various underlying theories of unemployment.

In section 2 the extended model is analysed numerically. As in Chapter 4 this requires careful estimation and calibration of the new parameters. The focus will be on the wage bargaining interpretation of the wage curve, as Chapter 5 has concluded that this holds most promise for explaining the differences between Europe and the US.

The analysis shows that, under the specifications chosen below and in light of the evidence on the parameters, endogenous unemployment adjustments have a very limited moderating effect on relative wage developments. The observed differences in relative wage trends in the US and EU can therefore not be attributed to differences in labour market institutions. Unemployment and participation rates, on the other hand, are very sensitive to the parameters of the wage curve. These results suggest that wage inequality is technologically determined whereas high unemployment levels are largely due to inflexible labour market institutions.

Relative wages do remain sensitive to changes in the skill composition of the working age population and the labour force. Hence relative wage dynamics are driven primarily by what Tinbergen (1975, p.79) referred to as the *race between education and technology*. The model of Chapter 4 already established an endogenous link from education to technology through the labour market. The endogenous education extension to the model was mentioned only briefly in Chapter 5 and remains an interesting issue for further research. In this chapter the focus is on relative quantity adjustment through unemployment changes.

6.1   A SPECIFICATION OF THE WAGE CURVE

This section presents a specification of the wage curve due to Gregg and Manning (1997). This specification can be interpreted as introducing endogenous participation and involuntary unemployment into the model. The Gregg and Manning paper analyses the implications of skill biased technical change on the labour market. After deriving a simple relative demand curve that is assumed to shift in favour of the high skilled, they introduce a wage curve. They argue that, in addition to unemployment, the wage of the other skill group also determines the wage that workers bargain for. Thus relative wages are linked directly to the unemployment level of both skill groups and by implication relative supply is a function of the relative wage. Their specification of the wage curve is empirically inspired and they present various arguments to justify its functional form. As some of their arguments are linked to endogenous participation and some to wage bargaining theory, their specification can be thought of as an attempt to capture the essence of both.

In line with the arguments offered in subsection 5.2.2 they suggest that the wage is set as a mark-up, $M(.)$, over the value of unemployment, u_S:[2]

$$w_S = M(u_S) * u_S \tag{6.1}$$

They then propose to set the latter equal to a replacement rate $0 < \rho_S < 1$ times the average wage:

$$U_H = \rho_H w_H{}^{\delta_H} w_L{}^{1-\delta_H} \text{ and } U_L = \rho_L w_L{}^{\delta_L} w_H{}^{1-\delta_L} \tag{6.2}$$

where $0 < \delta_S < 1$ sets the exponential weights of the two wages.[3] As was shown for the bargaining model in subsection 5.2.2, they assume that:

$$\frac{dM(u_S)}{du_S} < 0 \quad \lim_{u_S \uparrow 1} M(u_S) = m_{S0} \quad \lim_{u_S \downarrow u_{S0}} M(u_S) = \infty \tag{6.3}$$

where m_{S0} is a parameter in the mark-up function that defines the minimum mark-up required for workers to accept a job. By the definition of the reservation wage one therefore obtains:

$$w_S{}^{RES} = m_{S0} u_S \tag{6.4}$$

A statutory minimum wage, the value of leisure and the option value of unemployment could underlie parameter m_{SO} in a model of unemployment.[4] Appendix 6A shows that utility maximisation on behalf of individual workers can also underlie a specification of the wage curve as in Equations (6.1)-(6.4). In that case non-labour income or social security benefits determine the minimum mark-up in Equation (6.4).

Gregg and Manning do not suggest any further interpretation of this parameter nor present a specification of the mark-up function as they focus on the implications of introducing the other group's wage in the wage curve.[5] To evaluate the impact of voluntary and involuntary unemployment in the model, however, a full specification of the mark-up function is required. A specification that satisfies the properties of Equation (6.3) above:[6]

$$M(u_S) = \left(\frac{u_S - u_{SO}}{1 - u_{SO}}\right)^{-\varepsilon_S} m_{SO} \qquad (6.5)$$

In this specification u_{SO} can be interpreted as the level at which unemployment becomes ineffective in reducing the wage claim in the bargaining model.[7] If Equation (6.5) is to represent the labour supply decision as in Section 5.2, then u_{SO} is a level of inactivity that workers are unwilling to give up regardless of the wages offered.[8]

In a bargaining context, ε_S (>0) is the elasticity of wages with respect to effective unemployment, u_S-u_{SO}. In the context of endogenous labour supply, this elasticity is inversely related to minus the elasticity of labour supply and can be linked to the elasticity of substitution between leisure and consumption.[9] Both interpretations bring this parameter close to routinely estimated elasticities, which facilitates the numerical specification of this important parameter below.

The wage curves are now given by:

$$w_H = \left(\frac{u_H - u_{HO}}{1 - u_{HO}}\right)^{-\varepsilon_H} m_{HO} p_H w_H^{\delta_H} w_L^{1-\delta_H}$$

$$ \qquad (6.6)$$

$$w_L = \left(\frac{u_L - u_{LO}}{1 - u_{LO}}\right)^{-\varepsilon_L} m_{LO} p_L w_L^{\delta_L} w_H^{1-\delta_L}$$

These wage curves are easily rewritten as standard labour supply curves where the supply of skill level S now depends positively upon the relative wage. Figure 6.1 below illustrates those supply level curves. Note that wage inflexibility enters the model by setting very low values for ε_S. In that case shifts in unemployment have a limited effect on the wage levels until unemployment approaches the lower bound u_{SO}. In the limit the standard labour supply curves will be kinked and horizontal until employment reaches $(1-u_{SO})$ L_S^* where supply curves have a vertical asymptote.

Figure 6.1:   LABOUR SUPPLY LEVEL CURVES

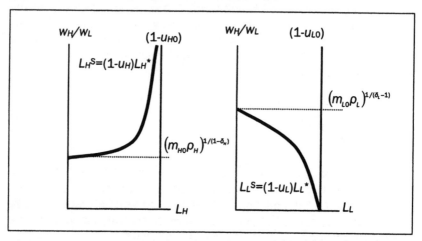

Now consider the implications for the aggregate *relative* labour supply curve. Given the curves in Figure 6.1, the relative supply curve has an S-shape around the vertical exogenous maximum labour availability curve, given by $(1-u_{HO})L_H^*/(1-u_{LO})L_L^*$ as in Figure 6.2 below. This shape can be verified analytically. Solving Equation (6.6) for unemployment and substituting this solution into the standard definition of employment, $L^S=$ $(1-u)L^*$ for both skill types allows one to write relative aggregate labour supply as:

$$\frac{(1-u_H)L_H^*}{(1-u_L)L_L^*} = \frac{1-\left((w_H/w_L)^{\delta_H-1}m_{HO}\rho_H\right)^{\frac{1}{\varepsilon_H}}}{1-\left((w_H/w_L)^{1-\delta_L}m_{LO}\rho_L\right)^{\frac{1}{\varepsilon_L}}} \frac{(1-u_{HO})L_H^*}{(1-u_{LO})L_L^*} = F(\overset{+}{w_H}/w_L)\frac{L_H^*}{L_L^*} \quad (6.7)$$

Note that Equation (6.7) has a positive intercept, is upward sloping over its entire domain and has a horizontal asymptote at the relative wage level that reduces the denominator to 0. This implies the relative supply curve must be S-shaped. It can also be verified in Equation (6.7) that for every relative wage level between an upper and lower bound there is a unique relative supply.

Figure 6.2:   EQUILIBRIUM IN THE LABOUR MARKETS

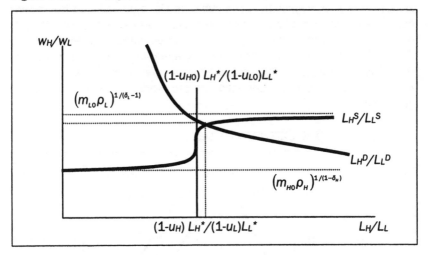

The upper and lower bounds are reached when the unemployment of one group approaches 1.[10] At those relative wage levels the relative supply falls to 0 or becomes infinite.

Consider again the case of extreme wage inflexibility where one has nearly horizontal supply level curves that become near vertical at $(1-u_{S0})L_S^*$. In that case the relative supply curve will be horizontal up to and beyond the relative exogenous availability. This, however, also implies that the relative supply curve becomes nearly vertical at the original relative exogenous availability. In that section of the relative supply curve, large changes in relative wages are required to generate small changes in relative (un)employment. The reason for this rather peculiar result, a near vertical section in an otherwise horizontal relative supply curve, is that both individual supply curves were assumed to have a vertical asymptote. This vertical section of the relative supply curve may explain why the trade-off hypothesis fails to explain the data. As any equilibrium that has significant employment of both skill types will be found close to the original relative exogenous availability, the trade-off between wage inequality and unemployment is unlikely, ironically the more so in countries with high wage inflexibility. Hence if workers, implicitly or explicitly, bargain over relative rather than absolute wage levels, the trade-off between relative wage stability and high unemployment levels does not exist.[11]

Now consider how the interaction with technological change is affected. Chapter 5 already indicated that, as long as $F(.)$ is upward sloping in relative wages, the *PMA* curve needs to be adjusted but retains its concave, upward sloping shape. For the model specifications that do not have competition over high skilled labour between production and R&D, this implies that the model still has a stable equilibrium, where the *RDA* curve intersects the thus adjusted *PMA* curve from above.[12] In Figure 6.3 below these curves, adjusted for the wage curve, are presented graphically.

Figure 6.3:   **THE EXTENDED MODEL**

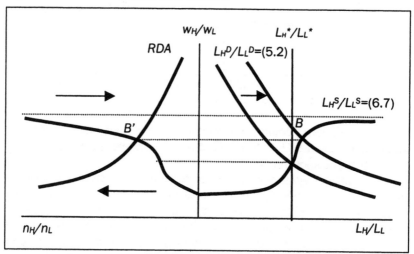

Given technology, n_H/n_L, the right panel determines the relative wage and relative unemployment rates simultaneously, in a point such as *A*. But the model is not in steady state equilibrium at *A*. The left panel shows the familiar *RDA-PMA* diagram. The *PMA* curve essentially captures the labour market equilibrium in the right hand panel for various levels of n_H/n_L so in the short run the economy is always on the *PMA* curve, in point *A'*.[13] As was shown in Chapter 4, when that point lies below the *RDA* curve, n_H/n_L will rise, indicated by the black arrow. It should be noted that relative demand is conditional on technology, in this case on n_H/n_L. A higher n_H/n_L intuitively increases the demand for high skilled workers at every relative wage and therefore would shift the curve to the right. Induced innovation thus shifts the demand curve in the right panel until in the long run relative wages, relative employment rates and n_H/n_L all stabilise in points B and B'.

Competition over high skilled workers between manufacturing and R&D considerably complicates the mathematics but not the principles involved. As in Chapter 4 it requires the equality of the marginal value product of labour in manufacturing and R&D. Appendix 4A showed that the solution could be computed when labour supply was exogenous by numerically solving a single equation for n_H/n_L. The same procedure will yield a solution here, as the *RDA* curve can be used in Equation (6.7) to write the previously exogenous relative supply as a function of n_H/n_L.[14]

As in Chapter 4, competition over high skilled labour does not affect steady state results and by the calibration of the discount rate its impact is also quantitatively limited in the transitional dynamics.[15] Both steady state and transitional dynamics analysis in the moderate product life cycle model require full numerical specification and simulation, as analytical solutions do not exist in the moderate product life cycle model.

6.2   THE IMPACT OF THE WAGE CURVE

In the previous section it was shown that the Gregg and Manning (1997) specification of the wage curve yields an S-shaped aggregate relative labour supply curve. The upper and lower bounds imply that relative wages must move within a limited but still potentially wide band. The slope of the curve determines how exogenous shocks translate into relative wage and relative employment adjustments.

The trade-off hypothesis, discussed in Chapter 1 and often offered as an explanation for relative wage stability in Europe, claims that the band is narrower and the slope is flatter in Europe than it is in the US. Although Chapter 1 has already dismissed the trade-off hypothesis based on the absence of predicted relative unemployment responses, the present model extension allows one to carefully trace that failure to the wage curve parameters by investigating the evidence available on their values in Europe and the US.

The first sub-section below concludes from the available evidence on these parameters that the *relative* supply curve in the mid 70s was not that different, causing the trade-off hypothesis to fail. In the process the baseline numerical values for the parameters in the model are obtained. The baseline simulations illustrate that the introduction of the wage curve hardly changes the relative wage response to a given increase in the relative availability of skilled labour. As unemployment is linked to relative wages through the wage curve, however, that also implies that the baseline fails to reproduce stylised facts on unemployment.

This requires one to seriously consider the possibility that the wage curve was misspecified. A calibration exercise in the second sub-section, however, illustrates that stylised facts on relative wage and unemployment dynamics can easily be reconciled within the model when empirically justifiable shifts in the wage curve parameters are considered. From this analysis it can be concluded that while differences in unemployment dynamics can easily be attributed to diverging labour market institutions, labour market rigidity has not prevented relative wage changes in Europe. Relative wage stability in Europe indicates that relative demand, and thereby the technology driving it, moved more in line with demand than in the US.

In the final subsection it is shown that the endogenous technology response to a more moderate relative availability shock and the lagged adoption of a new general-purpose technology both reduce the relative demand shifts that emerge in the model. In a numerical simulation it is shown that a slower and more gradual increase in relative availability allows for technology to respond and relative demand to keep up. The initial relative wage drop and consequently the subsequent rise in relative wages are smaller when the growth rate of relative availability is reduced. Still, in this experiment, the pattern of long-term wage adjustments is fully determined by the degree of diminishing returns in innovation, captured by the value of γ, as was the case in Part I.

The existence of the product life cycle may cause the development of a general-purpose technology to be quite different in terms of its impact on relative demand, than the adoption of that general-purpose technology after a few years of development. In the latter case the initial shock to product innovation is smaller, the subsequent shock to process innovation larger, due to knowledge spillovers. In calibrated simulations it is shown that the observed European and US relative wage trends can be reproduced when the general-purpose technology introduction/adoption is modelled as a composite shock on the innovation productivity parameters.

6.2.1 A NUMERICAL EVALUATION OF THE TRADE-OFF HYPOTHESIS

The interpretation of the parameters in the wage curve is presented for the wage bargaining and the labour/leisure model in Table 6.1. As Chapter 5 has already concluded that the wage bargaining extension holds most promise in explaining US-EU differences, the focus will be on the former and the evidence regarding the latter is presented in the endnotes. Observation, estimation and calibration can be used to obtain the numerical values for these parameters and variables. Before turning to the latter, consider the stylised facts that the model is required to explain. First recall that the skill availability shocks were quite comparable throughout the OECD.

Table 6.1:   INTERPRETATION OF PARAMETERS AND VARIABLES

PARAMETER/ VARIABLE	DESCRIPTION/INTERPRETATION where S={H, L}	
	WAGE BARGAIN	LABOUR/LEISURE
w_S	Hourly wage for skill group S.	Hourly wage for skill group S.
u_S	Unemployment rate for skill group S.	Inactivity rate or one minus participation rate, measured as hours of labour supplied divided by hours available.
u_{S0}	Ineffective unemployment level. For example equal to long-term unemployment.	Minimum hours of leisure never supplied.
ε_S	Elasticity of wage level to effective unemployment rate, which equals the elasticity of the wage to unemployment after correcting for long-term unemployment.	Elasticity of wage level to inactivity rate which equals minus one over the elasticity of supply to the wage level times the average inactivity rate.
m_{S0}	Mark-up of reservation wage over unemployment benefits.	Mark-up of reservation wage over social security benefits.
ρ_S	Replacement rate of unemployment benefits over reference wages.	Replacement rate of social security benefits over reference wages.
δ_S	Exponential weight of own and other groups wage in reference wages.	Exponential weight of own and other groups wage in reference wages.

In the model these shocks are exogenous and originate in educational policies and demographic developments. The data for the US were presented in Chapter 1 and show a strong upward trend in the relative availability of high skilled workers. This increase was particularly strong in the mid 70s. Acemoglu (2002b) attributes this to large cohorts of Vietnam draft avoiding college graduates entered the labour market. In Europe the availability of high skilled workers also increased, arguably by the same magnitude over the entire period. In Europe this was due to relatively large post-war baby boom cohorts that entered the labour market and increased the average educational level more gradually than in the US.

Now consider the endogenous variables. Recall from Chapter 1 that the relative wage dropped from 1.4 in the mid 70s to 1.3 in the early 80s and then rose to about 1.6 in the early 90s in the US. Over the same period it remained stable in most continental European countries with the UK and Ireland holding an intermediate position.[16]

Most of the OECD shared similar trends in the relative participation of high and low skilled workers. Overall labour force participation measured in persons remains quite stable in most OECD countries and hovers between 85 and 90% in the US and UK, around 80% in Germany and 75% in France.[17] This does not imply that relative participation remained stable. The large shifts between the skill groups, however, are remarkably comparable across the OECD. In the OECD *Jobs Study* (1994a) it is shown that participation ratios rose by 20% from about 1 in 1970 to about 1.2 in 1990 in the US.[18] Over the same period it rose by 25% from 1.2 to 1.5 in France. For both countries most of the rise occurred over the 70s and stabilised over the 80s. The relative stability of this ratio at around 1.03 over the 80s in Germany and the UK suggests that relative participation rates rose over the 70s and stabilised in the 80s throughout the OECD.[19]

Trends are quite different for involuntary unemployment. In the early 70s unemployment was higher in the US than in the EU. Over the following decade unemployment increased on both sides of the Atlantic but Europe overtook the US towards the end of the 70s. By 1979 unemployment rates had risen to between 2-3% and 5-8% for low and high skilled respectively on both continents. Over time high skilled unemployment rates went up to 3-4% in the US and Europe respectively in 1984. Over that same period the rates rose to 12-16% for the low skilled.[20] European unemployment then continued to rise to levels about one and a half times the US levels that had fallen back to their 1979 levels by the end of the 80s.

As Chapter 1 has shown, however, relative unemployment consequently developed similarly on both sides of the Atlantic, despite the marked differences in level. It rose over the early 80s and then declined again.[21] The underlying trends only start to diverge in the mid 80s. In the US the recovery in the late 80s and early 90s brought both unemployment rates down but low skilled rates fell faster than high skilled ones, causing relative unemployment to fall. A similar pattern was observed in the UK but at a later stage, as overall unemployment rates dropped below 5% only towards the end of the 90s.[22]

Because unemployment in the US and Europe started out at comparable levels in the mid 1970s, it is justified and convenient to calibrate both to a common starting position. As stylised facts Table 6.2

below suggests, at a relative wage of 1.4 high skilled unemployment stood at about 1.5% whereas the low skilled experienced some 5% of unemployment.

Table 6.2:   SUMMARY OF STYLISED FACTS

VARIABLE	COUNTRY/ PERIOD					
	US			EU		
	Mid 70s	Early 80s	Early 90s	Mid 70s	Early 80s	Early 90s
w_H/w_L	1.4	1.3	1.6	1.4	1.4	1.4
u_H	0.015	0.03	0.03	0.015	0.04	0.05
u_L	0.05	0.12	0.10	0.05	0.16	0.15

In Europe on the other hand, relative unemployment rates initially rose due to a strong increase in low skilled unemployment, which stabilised at the high level. Relative unemployment came down as high skilled rates went up further to about 5%.[23] Table 6.2 presents a summary of the stylised facts on unemployment and relative wage dynamics. Below the model will be calibrated in such a way that these stylised facts are reproduced.

Now consider the parameters of the wage curve. Under the specification of the wage curve in Equation (6.6) above it is the effective unemployment rate, $u_S - u_{S0}$, that reduces wage pressure.[24] Nickell (1987) finds that rising long-term unemployment compensated for a lot of the downward pressure exerted by higher unemployment in the period 1957-1985 in Britain. According to Bean (1994) this is the case in the rest of Europe as well. Long-term unemployment can therefore be regarded as ineffective and this provides an interpretation of u_{S0}. On average between 5 and 10% of the unemployed remained unemployed for more than a year in the US over the entire period under consideration. In contrast, Germany, France and the UK have experienced much higher long-term unemployment at shares between 30 and 50%.[25]

Long-term unemployment is and has been concentrated among the low skilled both in the US and EU over the entire period under consideration.[26] Taking the mid 70s as the baseline situation implies using long-term unemployment rates at about 5% and 10% for the high and low skilled respectively for the US. As overall long-term unemployment hovered around 20% in France at that time, the only country in the EU for which the OECD (1994a) presents data, 15 and 30% were used for high and low skilled labour in Europe.

The subsequent rise in long-term unemployment over the 80s must be interpreted as an exogenous shock to the model as the duration of unemployment has not been endogenised. It can be verified in Equations (6.6) that this shock will, all else equal, drive up wage levels and unemployment rates. It might therefore also affect relative unemployment and relative wages in the short and long run and explain part of the unemployment divergence between the US and EU.[27]

Evidence on the elasticity of wages with respect to effective unemployment rates, ε_S, can be found in the empirical literature on the wage curve. This wage curve has been estimated for many countries including the ones of prime interest here, the US, Germany, France and the UK. Usually the studies in this field run a regression of the form:

$$\log w_{ict} = \alpha_0 + \alpha_1 \log(u_{ct}) + \beta X_{ict} + v_{ict} \qquad (6.8)$$

where i indexes individuals or groups, c indexes a country or region and t indexes time. α_1 is now the elasticity of the wage level to changes in the unemployment rate. Typically empirical studies find a negative coefficient of between minus 0.01 and minus 0.2. See for example Blanchflower and Oswald (1990, 1994a). Their results suggest that Europe is closer to the upper end of the range although t-statistics are quite low, implying that they are not significantly different from the estimates for the US.

The empirical evidence presented in for example Card (1995), Gregg and Manning (1997), Johansen (1999), Black and Fitzroy (2000), Kingdon and Knight (2001) suggests that the elasticity should indeed be negative and significantly below 1. Guichard and Laffargue (2000), using a panel of OECD-countries, make a case against international differences in this elasticity. Black and Fitzroy (1990), Card (1995), Johansen (1999) and Bartik (2000) find evidence that low skilled wages are about twice as responsive to changes in unemployment than high skilled wages. Nickell and Bell (1995) and Gregg and Manning (1997) on the other hand find that this elasticity is quite similar between skills.[28] All studies suggest a very low and similar value for both skill groups throughout the OECD.

Note, however, that in the specification of the wage curve in Equation (6.6) above ε_S is the elasticity with respect to the *effective* unemployment rate. Hence the estimated elasticities must be corrected for the differences in long-term unemployment rates if they are to provide an adequate value for ε_S in the numerical simulations below. The unemployment elasticity of wages is now given by:

$$\frac{dw_S}{du_S} \frac{u_S}{w_S} = -\varepsilon_S \frac{u_S}{u_S - u_{SO}} \qquad (6.9)$$

Hence the elasticity with respect to effective unemployment must be set equal to:

$$\varepsilon_S = \left(u_{S0} / u_S - 1\right)\alpha_1 \qquad (6.10)$$

where α_1 is about minus 0.1, the coefficient estimated in Equation (6.8) above. Long-term unemployment was a low (5-10%) and similar share of total unemployment for both skills in the US throughout the period under consideration, so the required correction is minimal and ε_S is set equal to (minus) the estimated elasticities at minus 0.1 for the US.[29] The high long-term unemployment rates in Europe, however, call for a downward adjustment of this parameter for the EU. Averaging long-term unemployment over the period under consideration, the elasticity with respect to effective unemployment might be set to 0.75 and 0.5 times the estimated elasticity of wages to unemployment, for high and low skilled workers respectively.[30] This reduces the elasticity of wages with respect to effective unemployment for both skill levels relative to the US and reduces that of low skilled workers by more.

Wage levels, both in the US and EU, therefore hardly respond to changes in unemployment.[31] By implication both relative supply curves are very flat. Indeed, as was argued above, when the elasticity approaches 0 the supply curve will become perfectly elastic at the upper and lower bound with a vertical section at $(1-u_{H0})L_H{}^*/(1-u_{L0})L_L{}^*$.[32] As observed unemployment rates are much closer to u_{S0} than to 1, however, the calibrated equilibrium will lie on the almost vertical section of the relative supply curve.

The lower elasticity for Europe, although consistent with the commonly accepted observation that European workers have to accept more unemployment to offset wage reductions, also causes the relative supply curve to be steeper around the equilibrium than in the US. For the relative supply curve to enforce wage stability in the face of demand shifts it is therefore required that the upper and lower bound are much closer together in Europe. The upper and lower bounds to the relative wage are given by:

$$UB = \left(m_{L0}\rho_L\right)^{1/(\delta_L - 1)}$$
$$LB = \left(m_{H0}\rho_H\right)^{1/(1-\delta_H)} \qquad (6.11)$$

Therefore consider the evidence on the parameters in Equation (6.11). As was shown in Chapter 5 a wage bargaining context implies that the mark-up is defined relative to the unemployment benefit level, $\rho_s w_s^{\delta_s} w_{-s}^{1-\delta_s}$. As benefit levels are usually linked to average and own wage levels, the exponential weights, δ_s, may differ in the reference wage, $w_s^{\delta_s} w_{-s}^{1-\delta_s}$, for high and low skilled workers. But hard evidence on these parameters is difficult to obtain as little empirical research has been done.

Gregg and Manning (1997) provide an estimate of the wage curve for the UK. Their results suggest that both wage levels are important to both skill types. They find δ_H=0.46 and δ_L=0.71. As is intuitively plausible they thus find that the weight of low skilled wages is larger for high skilled than the wage of high skilled wages is for the low skilled. Still it is remarkable that their estimate of δ_H is actually below 0.5. They argue that this can be attributed to the large share of low skilled in their sample. If benefits are set relative to average rather than own group wages, than through average wages the low skilled labour share pushes the estimated weight on high skilled wages down.

As high skilled workers constitute a larger share of the workforce in Germany, the US and France all three are likely to have a larger δ_H and smaller δ_L, although decentralised bargaining structures in the US may reduce this effect.[33] But since comparable estimates are not available for Germany, France and the US, the Gregg and Manning estimates are used below. Relatively wide bounds for the sensitivity analysis are set to avoid numerical specificity. The domain is {0,1} for both parameters and the numerical results will be tested for robustness on that interval.

The replacement rate varies a lot with income. High-income groups typically have lower replacement rates. In 1999 at 100% of the average production worker wage, replacement rates are around 50% for the US and as high as 80% in France. The OECD summary measure is an average replacement rate over four income levels, which implies that higher income levels have far lower replacement rates. Consequently one should set $\rho_L > \rho_H$.

In addition the evidence suggests that the European replacement rate is about 1.6 times that of the US for low skilled and possibly more for high skilled.[34] Ceteris paribus this higher replacement rate lowers the upper bound and increases the lower bound of the relative supply curve as would be required for obtaining stable relative wages. Whether these differences show up in the upper and lower bound relative wages, however, also depends on the minimum mark-up, m_{s0}, over unemployment benefits that workers require for leaving unemployment. This parameter is unobservable and can be used to calibrate the model to historical unemployment levels in the US and EU. Table 6.3 summarises the evidence presented above and lists the chosen parameter values as well as the sensitivity range over which they were tested.

Table 6.3: NUMERICAL SPECIFICATION OF PARAMETERS

PARAMETERS		VALUE US	VALUE EU	SOURCE	SENSITIVITY TEST RANGE
OBSERVED PARAMETERS	u_{H0}	$0.05*u_H$	$0.15*u_H$	OECD (2003b)	0.01-0.1
	u_{L0}	$0.1*u_L$	$0.3*u_L$	OECD (2003b)	0.01-0.2
	ρ_H	0.65	0.65	See Text	0
	ρ_L	0.65	0.65	See Text	0
ESTIMATED PARAMETERS	ε_H	0.1	0.075	0.01-0.2	0.01-0.2
	ε_L	0.1	0.05	0.01-0.2	0.01-0.2
	δ_H	0.5	0.5	Gregg and Manning (1997)	0-1
	δ_L	0.7	0.7	Gregg and Manning (1997)	0-1
(RE-) CALIBRATED PARAMETERS	m_{H0}	Calibrated to get u_H=0.015		NA	+/-50%
	m_{L0}	Calibrated to get u_L=0.05		NA	+/-50%
	ρ	Calibrated to get R_R+R_D=0.012* $((1-u_H)L_H^*+((1-u_L)L_L^*)$		0.02-0.92	+/-50%
	a_R	Calibrated to get $G_{nL}=G_{nH}=G_n$=0.03		NA	See the GPT-experiment below
	a_D	a_R		NA	See the GPT-experiment below
	b_H	Calibrated to get w_H/w_L=1.4		NA	+/-50%
	b_L	1		Normalised	Normalised

Figures 6.4-6.5 present the baseline simulations for the moderate PLC model with low and high γ respectively. As the replacement rate only appears multiplicatively with the calibrated parameter m_{S0}, its numerical value is inconsequential and has been set to 0.65 to ensure that m_{S0} always lies above 1.[35]

Now consider the model predictions regarding relative wages and unemployment rates. As in the simulations of Chapter 4, the relative availability of skilled labour was increased by 100% over a relatively short interval from period 50 to 80. The bold lines represent the results from Chapter 4 (without a wage curve) for reference.

Figure 6.4:   SIMULATION OF RELATIVE SUPPLY SHOCKS
Strong Diminishing Returns in R&D (γ=0.4)

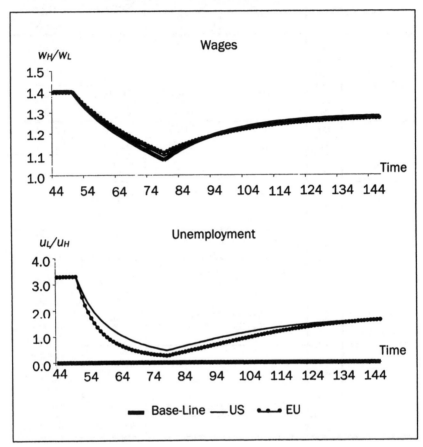

The thin lines were generated with a wage curve as specified above, where the full line represents the US and the dotted one the EU.[36] In the top panels it can be verified that relative wages closely follow the original results. This indicates that, as has been predicted, the demand curve intersects relative supply in a relatively vertical section.[37] The supply shock shifts the relative supply curve to the right causing wages to drop. As the endogenous technology response materialises, demand shifts out and relative wages recover. The strong market size effect in Figure 6.5 pushes relative wages beyond their baseline value.

Figure 6.5:   **SIMULATION OF RELATIVE SUPPLY SHOCKS**
Weak Diminishing Returns in R&D (γ=0.9)

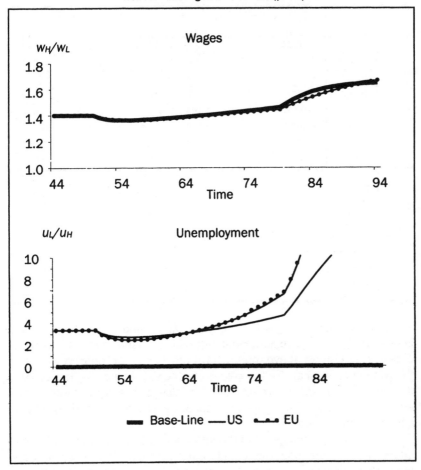

The strong increase in European long-term unemployment rates stabilises relative wages somewhat but has a very limited impact. Table 6.4 shows that the full model in general and relative wages in particular are not very sensitive to the parameters of the wage curves, both in the short run (given technology) and in the steady state.[38] The elasticities in Table 6.4 were computed numerically by shocking all wage curve parameters individually by 10% while keeping all other parameters at the values given in Table 6.3. The computed elasticities never exceed 0.4 and for most parameters they lie below 0.1.

Table 6.4:   ELASTICITIES WITH RESPECT TO WAGE CURVE PARAMETERS [39]

γ	X	SHORT TERM			STEADY STATE		
		$\sigma_{wh/wl,x}$	$\sigma_{ul/uh,x}$	$\sigma_{uh,x}$	$\sigma_{wh/wl,x}$	$\sigma_{ul/uh,x}$	$\sigma_{uh,x}$
0.4	δ_H	0.0134	-1.461	1.759	0.0027	-1.528	1.815
	δ_L	0.0544	-1.770	-0.267	0.0108	-2.020	-0.054
	$m_{HO}\rho_H$	0.1120	-5.780	14.500	0.0239	-6.060	15.600
	$m_{LO}\rho_L$	-0.3621	9.187	2.023	-0.0830	14.080	0.425
	ε_H	0.0342	-3.024	4.484	0.0071	-3.165	4.660
	ε_L	-0.0807	2.428	0.413	-0.0169	3.050	0.085
	ltu_H	0.0004	-0.047	0.050	0.0001	-0.050	0.051
	ltu_L	-0.0027	0.085	0.013	-0.0006	0.103	0.003
0.9	δ_H				-0.0036	-1.569	1.850
	δ_L				-0.0141	-2.170	0.071
	$m_{HO}\rho_H$				-0.0322	-6.237	16.330
	$m_{LO}\rho_L$		As for γ=0.4		0.1261	18.430	-0.607
	ε_H				-0.0094	-3.250	4.775
	ε_L				0.0229	3.466	-0.113
	ltu_H				-0.0001	-0.516	0.053
	ltu_L				0.0007	0.113	-0.004

The fact that for example the signs on $m_{HO}\rho_H$ and $m_{LO}\rho_L$ are reversed implies that shifts in replacement rates in the same direction, such as observed in Europe above, hardly have any impact on relative wages as the two effects cancel. For low values of γ the sign of the long-run effect is the same as in the short run but the elasticity is significantly lower, indicating that an endogenous technology response partially offsets labour supply shocks.

That sign changes with the introduction of the strong market size effect (γ=0.9), creating the counterintuitive result that positive wage pressure shocks cause the wage of the group involved to decline relative to their colleagues. As wage pressure shocks make a given type of labour artificially scarce, that result, however, is what one would expect from the strong market size effect. Still the effects, as for the more intuitively plausible weak induced innovations model, are quantitatively limited.

The only shock on the supply side that really matters for relative wages seems to be the exogenous increase in the availability of skilled workers. This conclusion, although to some perhaps suspect and disappointing, is very much in line with results obtained by for example Gregg and Manning (1997), who claim that educational policy is much more important in driving relative wages than labour market institutions.

Given the limited impact of wage bargaining, it will not come as a surprise that the mechanisms identified in Chapter 4 still work more or less unaffected in the extended model as well. The US relative wage behaviour can still be reproduced as the permanent impact of the strong market size effect, the temporary impact of introducing a new general-purpose technology or a combination of the two.

This does not mean that labour market institutions do not make a difference. The elasticities on relative unemployment and the unemployment levels are very large by comparison, even in the long run. Note also that the sign of the effect on relative unemployment is the same for the short- and long-term even with strong market size effect.[40] This implies that an increase in the wage pressure of one skill group, regardless of the impact on its relative wage, will always increase the unemployment rate of that group relative to that of the other. The high elasticities also indicate that wage pressure shocks primarily affect unemployment and hence are the prime suspect for explaining the observed differences in unemployment dynamics.

As relative wages are negatively related to unemployment rates by the wage curve, the relative unemployment rate, defined as the ratio of low over high skilled unemployment, will follow the pattern of relative wages closely when wage curve parameters are stable. In the lower panels of Figures 6.4-6.5 the predicted impact of the relative availability shock on relative unemployment is illustrated. The trade-off introduced by the relatively flat wage curves (low ε_s) generates large predicted shifts in relative unemployment rates. This effect is most pronounced in the European (almost) constant returns to scale ($\gamma=0.9$) specification.[41] But even without the strong market size effect and European style increases in long-term unemployment rates, the wage curve extension predicts an initial drop, followed by a rise in relative unemployment rates. Such shifts, as was shown in Section 1.2, are clearly counterfactual and the interaction between technology and the labour market fails to explain unemployment dynamics on either continent. To reconcile stylised relative wages and unemployment levels of Table 6.2 in the model, some significant shifts in the wage curve parameters must be introduced.

6.2.2 RECONCILING UNEMPLOYMENT DYNAMICS AND RELATIVE WAGE TRENDS

The simulations presented above were generated under the hypothesis that the parameters of the wage curve remained stable at their baseline levels. That generated counterfactual predictions for unemployment in both the US and Europe. From that observation two conclusions are possible. The bargaining structures and wage determination have not remained stable over time and between the two regions or the wage curve have been misspecified.

Assuming the wage curve was not misspecified, the sensitivity analysis suggests that unemployment in general and relative unemployment in particular has been driven by shifts in wage curve parameters. It was already argued above that diverging long-term unemployment experiences are part of the story but in addition the Reagan and Thatcher Administrations in the US and UK clamped down on union power while in Continental Europe they remained powerful key players in the labour market. In addition over the 80s replacement rates in Europe increased whereas in the US and UK they fell significantly, in particular at the lower ends of the pay scale.[42] Such developments seriously affected the bargaining position of workers and cause diverging trends in wage pressure. To verify that the wage curve in its current specification can reproduce the stylised facts, the m_{SO} parameters were recalibrated to reconcile the predicted unemployment and relative wages with those presented in Table 6.2. The results are presented in Table 6.5. The computed parameter changes can be interpreted as the combined effect of exogenous shifts in replacement rates on the one hand and union bargaining power on the other.[43] The table shows that wage pressure should have increased for both skill levels in the late 70s by some 5-7% in the EU whereas in the US the high skilled experienced a modest 3% wage pressure increase while low skilled wage pressure rose by some 14%.

Table 6.5:   THE REQUIRED WAGE PRESSURE SHOCKS

VARIABLE	COUNTRY/ PERIOD					
	US			EU		
	Mid 70s	Early 80s	Early 90s	Mid 70s	Early 80s	Early 90s
w_H/w_L	1.4	1.3	1.6	1.4	1.4	1.4
ltu_H	0.05	0.05	0.05	0.15	0.2	0.3
m_{HO}	1.19005	1.22916 (+3.3%)	1.36363 (+10.9%)	1.31261	1.40701 (+7.2%)	1.4173 (+0.7%)
u_H	0.015	0.03	0.03	0.015	0.04	0.05
ltu_L	0.1	0.1	0.1	0.3	0.5	0.6
m_{LO}	1.02044	1.16572 (+14.2%)	1.05126 (-9.8%)	1.17701	1.24107 (+5.4%)	1.21829 (-1.8%)
u_L	0.05	0.12	0.10	0.05	0.16	0.15

Union militancy may have been a factor in explaining this pattern while the acceleration in the availability of college graduates might have dampened the upward trend in wage pressure in the US for high skilled. Over the 80s the general recession, de-unionisation, Reaganomics and Thatcherism caused wage pressure to drop for the low skilled in Anglo-Saxon countries. High skilled wage pressure, however, might have increased, as the new general-purpose technology increased their bargaining power.

In Europe there were some further but very modest changes in wage pressure over the 80s as union power and replacement rates remained high.[44] Such shifts in wage pressure would make observed relative wage behaviour consistent with observed unemployment levels and explain the latter given the former. To the extent that introducing such shifts is justified empirically, the wage curve is not seriously misspecified. However, relative wages remain to be explained endogenously and wage stability in Europe still requires an explanation. The sub-section below will argue why it is likely that relative labour demand evolved more gradually and more in line with supply in Europe.

6.2.3 ADJUSTMENT SPEED AND ADOPTION LAGS

In Section 1.2 two hypotheses were put forward to explain relative wage stability in Europe. First an endogenous innovation version of Tinbergen's (1975, p.97) *race between education and technology* was presented. It was argued that endogenous technology responses are better able to offset gradual rather than sudden increases in the relative availability of skilled labour. A second hypothesis relied on the product life cycle and attributed more gradual demand shifts to (endogenous or exogenous) lags in adoption. The feasibility of both can be illustrated in numerical simulation experiments.

First consider the impact of a more gradual increase in relative supply. Figure 6.6 presents the results in a graph. Doubling the interval over which relative availability increases exogenously by 100% yields a relative wage response that is much more moderate. The upper panel presents the explosive (fast) and more gradual (slow) relative availability shock. The lower panel shows the relative wage response. The fast lines were reproduced from Figures 6.4 and 6.5 for reference.[45] The added lines now present the corresponding relative wage response to a more gradual relative availability shift in the same model. As should be expected, the steady states are identical but in the transition the endogenous technology response reduces the required relative wage shifts for the model with and without the strong market size effect. The absence of the Vietnam Draft and the more gradual entry of post-war baby boom cohorts in the labour market, may exogenously explain the more gradual increase in the relative availability of in Europe.

Figure 6.6:   THE RACE BETWEEN TECHNOLOGY AND EDUCATION

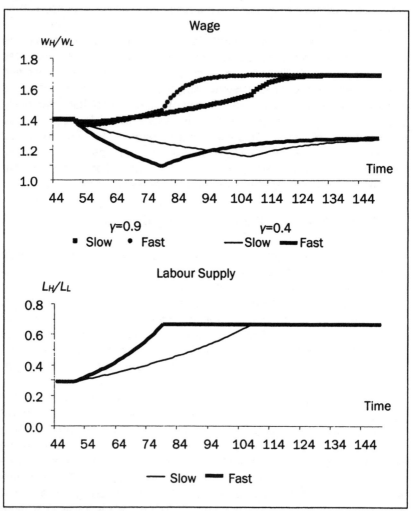

To the extent that educational policy was responsible, it contributed to the stability of relative wages. Gregg and Manning (1997) indeed concluded from their analysis that it did much more so than the usual suspect, institutional wage rigidity. The simulations show that their result is even more pronounced when technology is allowed to respond endogenously to relative availability shifts.

Figure 6.7:   GENERAL PURPOSE TECHNOLOGIES AND KNOWLEDGE SPILLOVERS

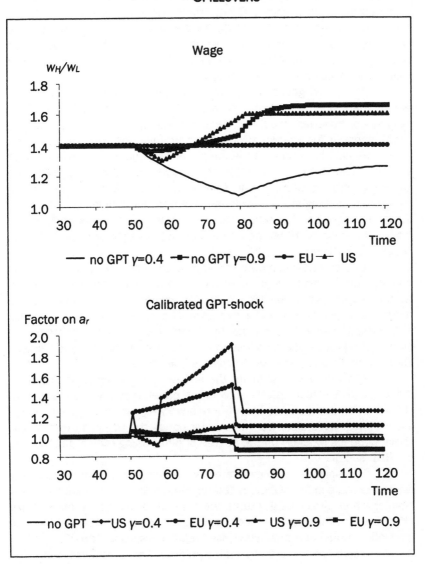

But although the model predicts a more stable relative wage, this hypothesis takes a rather closed economy approach, as the technology response in Europe is supposedly driven entirely by domestic availability shocks and is not affected by events in the US.

In addition, the predicted pattern of wage adjustments still mimics that in the US, whereas some European countries saw stable or even falling relative wages. Clearly more moderate availability shocks cannot be the entire story and the lagged adoption hypothesis is more promising on both accounts. To illustrate the lagged adoption hypothesis one would ideally combine the US and EU economy in one model and specify their trade and technology ties explicitly.[46]

The 'new' goods in the US, and the knowledge they embody, would then also be (partially) available for European R&D. Such extensions, however, require quite some issues to be considered.[47] A useful shortcut for analysing the impact of such spillovers on European labour markets is to analyse the impact of exogenous changes in a_R and a_D. As these parameters enter the model multiplicatively with the knowledge stocks, see Cell 7 in Table 4.1, any changes in them can be interpreted as exogenous knowledge spillovers that originate outside the model. Because only the ratio of the two parameters seriously affects the model, the value of a_D can be normalised to the calibrated values for the baseline simulation.

One can now compute the knowledge spillovers that predict the relative wage levels for a given shock to the relative availability of skilled labour. Recall that a similar yet cruder experiment was suggested to represent the introduction of a new general-purpose technology in the US in Chapter 4. Figure 6.7 presents the results. The thick lines represent the predicted relative wage response in the absence of knowledge spillovers. These were already presented in Figures 6.4-6.6 above.

The thin lines represent the stylised relative wage behaviour in the US and EU, respectively. The lower panel shows the sequence of shocks on a_R computed to keep the relative wage at that stylised level in every period. As is clear from the upper panel, the response to a supply shock depends crucially on the degree of diminishing returns to labour in the R&D sector.

The spillover was calibrated with strong and weak diminishing returns to scale in innovation. It can be verified that the required shock is smaller when diminishing returns are weak and the strong market size effect exists. The largest shock is required to get the weak induced innovation model to reproduce stylised relative wages for the US.

Reproducing perfectly stable relative wages requires a smaller shock, which can be interpreted as the loss of information as the general-purpose technology spills over to Europe or, and more intuitively plausible, as a simultaneous increase in the spillover to low skilled complementary process innovation due to lagged adoption.[48] The product life cycle explanation argues that a new general-purpose technology makes product innovation more productive immediately. Due to the lag in adoption, however, the productivity of development will also increase in the EU. Hence a_R/a_D will rise in Europe, but not as much as it did in the US. In that case the model without the strong market size effect can be calibrated to yield stable relative wages under a rising relative supply.

Stable wages in the model with the strong market size effect would imply that a_R first rises but eventually falls relative to a_D, which is quite an extreme assumption. It should be interpreted as Europe not being able to grasp the fundamental principles of the underlying general-purpose technology and only adopting it through developing low skilled labour intensive production processes for products already on the market in the US. This might be a more adequate description of technology spillover to third world countries.[49]

The shifts in the labour market parameters calibrated above, can now be added to generate the observed patterns of relative unemployment. In the early 70s wage pressure increased in the US for low skilled and in the EU for both. With the recession of the 80s low skilled wage pressure dropped in the US but in the EU much less so as social security entitlements, high replacement rates and long-term unemployment kept the pressure up. High skilled increased their bargaining position in the US as they could start cashing in on the new general-purpose technology.

In Europe pressure remained high and rising long-term unemployment reduced the effective downward wage pressure from unemployment in the EU. This caused high levels of unemployment in the EU, whereas especially the low skilled unemployment rate dropped in the US. As unemployment dynamics, even in Europe, hardly affect relative wages, this extension does not affect the interaction between relative skill availability, relative labour demand and innovation. Consequently it can be concluded that relative unemployment and relative wages are unrelated in the model although the wage curve, a robust empirical relation between wage and unemployment levels within skill groups might have suggested otherwise. The policy implications of that conclusion will be discussed further in Chapter 7 but at this stage one obvious point can be made. Wage inequality reduction and low unemployment are not mutually exclusive policy goals and there is no trade-off between them.

6.3   CONCLUSION

In this chapter the aim has been to evaluate an existing and some newly formulated hypotheses on the US-EU differences in relative wage and unemployment dynamics. It was shown that the trade-off hypothesis couldn't explain relative wage behaviour under realistic parameter settings. This might strike one as odd, as the correlation between wage stability and unemployment rates is very obvious and the trade-off hypothesis provides a simple and intuitive explanation for that correlation.

Of course that makes one weary and the possibility of misspecification, either of the wage curve in this part or the interaction between technology and labour demand in the previous one, must be considered. It should also be noted that the calibration of the model on relative wage and unemployment levels rather than, for example, their growth rates, might have to some extent driven the results. Further research is required to address these issues.

Keeping in mind these qualifications, however, the chapter did explain why things might not be as obvious as they seem. In the context of the extended model, institutional differences allow both high and low skilled European workers to bargain for higher wages. This implies that they both suffer higher unemployment levels than their American colleagues. Relative wages cannot be stabilised by that mechanism, however, as that would require unemployment to seriously affect *relative* supply. As both groups' unemployment rates are much closer to 0 than to 1, even in the EU, their relative employment rate is always close to 1 and relative supply will be close to the relative availability of skills.

Relative wages will still be sensitive to relative availability shocks and the endogenous technology responses affecting relative demand. Analytical and numerical analysis has shown that this conclusion can be squared with the evidence and unavoidably follows from the assumptions made in modelling the interaction between technology and labour demand in Part I and introducing the wage curve in this part.

To reconcile international differences in relative wage developments the model suggests that one must look at differences in innovation and relative labour availability. Two alternative hypotheses, a more gradual relative availability shock and lagged international technology spillovers, proved effective in explaining different relative wage dynamics. Given relative wages, the unemployment dynamics seem to be driven by the differences in labour market institutions.

That gives rise to the conclusion that there is no trade-off. It is the interaction between the relative availability of skills and technology that drives the relative wage. Unemployment differences are largely due to institutional factors. Low unemployment and rising wage inequality are a coincidence in the US as are high unemployment levels and wage stability in Europe. The policy implications of that conclusion are significant.

American policy makers can tackle their huge poverty problems without having to fear European unemployment levels, whereas in Europe unemployment can be addressed without accepting US inequality.[50] What policy makers on both sides of the Atlantic should be made aware of, however, is the fact that labour market policies, income policies, science and technology policies and educational policies will all interact. Making choices in one area defines the room for manoeuvre in other areas but policies may also be mutually reinforcing. That interaction and its policy implications will be dealt with in the final part below.

NOTES

[1] In this chapter the model refers to the moderate PLC version of the model for low and high values of γ. As was argued in Chapter 4 these two versions allow one to illustrate the market size effect and product life cycle dynamics that were identified as the prime sources of technology driven demand shocks.

[2] This may be the replacement rate of unemployment benefits or of the reservation wage over average wages. See Table 6.1 below.

[3] Gregg and Manning (1997) refer to this average wage as the reference wage.

[4] The minimum wage puts a floor in the labour market, typically at above unemployment benefit levels. Everything the worker requires for giving up his unemployment status will cause m_{S0} to exceed 1.

[5] They do suggest that the mark-up function has a constant elasticity with respect to unemployment by estimating an equation:

$$\log(w_{si}) = \alpha_0 + \alpha_1 \log(u_{si}) + \alpha_2 \log(w_{si-1}) + \alpha_3 \log(w_{-si}) + \beta X_i + v_i \,,$$

where v is the error term, βX is a vector of control variables and i indexes an individual, S skill and t time.

[6] Obviously there are many others. This specification was chosen for convenience and the availability of empirical evidence on the parameters, both for the endogenous supply and wage bargaining interpretation. This evidence is presented in the sections below.

[7] There are several reasons why this parameter may be positive. Empirical research, for example by Nickell (1987), has shown that, for example, long-term unemployment is less effective in putting a downward pressure on wage claims. In the bargaining model of Chapter 5 the acceptable unemployment level was shown to be positively related to the profitability of firms, bargaining power and labour turnover. Intuitively this is the case because they increase both the gains from accepting unemployment and the market power of workers and reduce the threat of unemployment respectively. The acceptable unemployment level was also negatively affected by the elasticity of survival with respect to employment and the discount rate. See the definition of $u_{S0} = x_S$ in Appendix 5B.

[8] As their total available time is usually normalised and might as well be considered net of this inelastic amount of leisure consumed, this parameter can then be set to 0 without loss of information.

[9] See Appendix 6A. Due to the income effect these parameters may then actually be negative. In that case the higher relative wage reduces relative supply. As was argued in Chapter 5 this property is very unlikely to arise when labour supply is aggregated over many individuals.

[10] As was mentioned in the figures, the upper and lower bounds are given by:
$w_{_H} / w_{_L} = (m_{_{L0}}\rho_{_L})^{1/(A-1)}$ and $w_{_H} / w_{_L} = (m_{_{H0}}\rho_{_H})^{1/(1-A)}$ respectively.
It is argued below that both terms in brackets are likely to be smaller than 1, which implies that the lower bound is smaller and the upper bound larger than 1.

[11] It should be noted here that a trade-off does exist between wage and unemployment *levels.*

[12] In general multiple equilibria cannot be ruled out. It is possible for the *RDA* (of type II) to intersect the adjusted *PMA* more than once and the model may even have two stable equilibria. The moderate PLC model, however, will not generate multiple stable equilibria. As numerical simulations below will generally not converge to an unstable equilibrium, the issue is less relevant and will be dealt with in the endnotes when it is required.

[13] Note that the S-shape caries over to the *PMA* curve. In the figure a type I *RDA* curve was drawn as it guarantees that the model has a stable steady-state equilibrium. For the type II *RDA* curves, a unique equilibrium is not guaranteed. See Section 6.2 below.

[14] To obtain the equation one should solve Equation (6.6) yielding unemployment as a function of relative wages. Using the *RDA* curve to write that expression as a function of n_H/n_L substituting one minus that expression times available labour for both Ls^* in Equation (4A.34) yields the steady state condition.

[15] By calibrating the model such that a mere 1.2% of the labour force is in R&D the relative employment levels in manufacturing are hardly affected.

[16] Due to problems with international consistency in educational classifications observed relative wages can be quite different from 1.4. Wage stability is stylised by assuming the relative wage remains about 1.4 for Europe over the 80s. One can interpret this as normalising educational classification systems such that a high skilled worker is defined as one earning 1.4 times the wage of an unskilled worker in 1975. As a parameter was calibrated to obtain this result, it is a rather arbitrary value. Assuming an equal starting position for the US and EU facilitates the comparison of simulation results.

[17] See OECD (2002) *Labour Force Statistics.* Pencavel (1986) presents participation rates for several countries stretching back as far as 1890 and concludes that in the long run overall participation rates are remarkably stable.

[18] The participation ratio is defined as the ratio of high over low skilled participation rates.

[19] The similarity in participation trends indicates that they have little to add in explaining different relative wage developments.

[20] See OECD (1994a).

[21] Recall that, following custom in the literature, relative unemployment is defined as u_L/u_H.

[22] See OECD (2002a).

[23] A notable exception is Germany where reunification first caused both unemployment rates to fall as in the US. By the mid 90s, however, Germany too joined the European high unemployment level club.

[24] The minimum inactivity level, u_{S0} can be normalised to 0 for both skill levels when a labour-leisure model underlies the wage curve.

[25] See OECD (2003b) and Gazeley and Newell (1999).

[26] Reliable data on relative long-term unemployment rates by skill were unavailable for the countries and period under consideration. Bollens (2002) presents a figure for 1997 for the EU. That shows the incidence of long-term unemployment for the low skilled labour force is about 3 to 4 times as high as that for high skilled. As normal unemployment rates are about 2 to 3 times higher for low skilled, this seems to suggest that the incidence of long-term unemployment among low skilled unemployed is between 1 and 2 times higher than that of the high skilled. This sets a range for sensitivity testing.

[27] Its impact on relative wages is negligible as long as the long-term unemployment shock is introduced symmetrically.

[28] Nickell and Bell (1995) find -0.05 and -0.06 for low and high skilled respectively. Gregg and Manning (1997) introduced relative wages in their specification of the wage curve and

find -0.04 and -0.02 respectively but these estimates are not significantly different from each other.

[29] Correcting for the differences in long-term unemployment partially reverses the higher elasticities found for low skilled.

[30] The correction is based on an average long-term unemployment rate of 25 and 50% of total unemployment for high and low skilled, respectively. See the data above. Such a correction would not be warranted if parameters are given a labour/leisure interpretation.

[31] It is likely that this was the case for different reasons. The US is close to its natural rates of unemployment, whereas in Europe institutional rigidity and long unemployment duration play a role.

[32] At the upper (lower) bound the low (high) skilled will switch from supplying $1-u_{S0}$ to 0.

[33] A similar argument applies in the labour/leisure interpretation of the model. To the extent than non-labour incomes, incomes foregone, household income and the value of home production vary with the own and average wage level, the exponential weights may vary. As the entire domain is checked in the sensitivity analysis, these parameters are adequately considered.

[34] Benefit entitlements do not fall as quickly as in the US.

[35] Setting it higher reduces m_{S0} proportionally such that the product is constant. The product is generally smaller than 1 as all calibrated values for m_{S0} lie below 1.5. The same applies to the labour/leisure interpretation, as there this parameter is the replacement rate of social benefits over some reference wage and also enters multiplicatively with a calibrated parameter.

[36] The only differences at this point being that for the EU case long-term unemployment was allowed to rise and the elasticity in the wage curve was adjusted downwards to account for higher average long-term unemployment rates. The two cases can therefore also be used to illustrate the sensitivity of the model predictions with respect to u_{S0}.

[37] Which is the result of calibrating the model to generate observed unemployment rates, which forces the relative employment rate, $(1-u_H)/(1-u_L)$ to lie close to 1, and hence close to the vertical section in the relative supply curve.

[38] Only the results for the moderate PLC model with competition are presented here.

[39] Appendix 6B presents the sensitivity analysis as announced in Table 6.2. In this table all parameters were shocked by 10%. In the appendix the impact of setting parameters to the minimum and maximum of the sensitivity testing range is evaluated.

[40] For the level of unemployment these signs may differ.

[41] Note that in Figure 6.4 the line representing Europe has not reached a new steady state in period 95. In fact, the strong rise in long-term unemployment that distinguishes it from the US case causes the long-term stability of the model to collapse entirely. The *PMA* curve simply rotates out of range for the concave upward sloping *RDA* curve in this specification. Consequently relative wages grow to infinity as the low skilled wage falls to 0 and similarly, and more exaggerated, relative unemployment explodes as relative wages rise.

[42] See for example OECD (1994b) Table 8.B.1.

[43] See also Appendix 5B, where union power was identified as one of the parameters that defines m_{S0}. Union bargaining power is obviously not directly observable. Union density dropped significantly throughout the OECD but bargaining extension laws still ensure coverage is high in Europe (over 90% in France and Germany versus less than 20% for the US with the UK at 50% in the middle, see Nickell et al. (2003) Tables 4 and 5).

[44] Note, however, that wage pressure is already significantly higher in Europe than in the US in the mid 70s as well. This is primarily due to the fact that replacement rates were set to 0.65 for both skill types and continents. The higher levels of m_{S0} thus primarily reflect differences in replacement rates.

[45] Figure 6.5 presents the model without adjustment for higher long-term unemployment rates to the elasticity of the wage to unemployment and long-term unemployment rates remain constant over time. This was done to avoid the instability in the $\gamma=0.9$ case. It has

been verified, however, that up to the point where the simulation breaks down numerically, the pattern is similar to those presented above.

[46] Davis (1992) is an example of a two-country model with such trade and technology ties.

[47] Assuming for example also trade in goods implies that prices are equal and through the factor price equalisation theorem wages will also converge. Non-tradables could be introduced to deal with this counterfactual prediction but these issues are better left for further research after the analysis below has established that international knowledge spillovers are important.

[48] Recall that a_R should be interpreted as a_R/a_D as a_D was normalised.

[49] In developing countries low R&D intensities might also make the assumption of (almost) constant returns to scale in R&D less problematic. Empirical evidence, however, is lacking to substantiate such claims.

[50] That implies that relative poverty need not be a concern. Of course the absolute wage levels of the low skilled should also be a concern. These may drop below acceptable levels when social security is completely abandoned.

PART III
THE ROLE OF GOVERNMENT

In the previous two parts the aim was to explain the 'natural' interaction between technological change and the labour market without explicitly considering the role of government. In Part I the effects of labour market shocks on technological change (the market size effect) and of technology shocks on the labour market (life cycle effect of a general-purpose technology) were analysed. It was concluded that wages, through profits, are the key transmitter of such shocks. In Part II wage rigidity was shown to affect the transmission mechanism only marginally, mostly because if both wages are equally rigid, relative wages are still flexible, even at high unemployment levels.

This final part turns to the implications of and for policy in general and taxation, labour market and science and technology policy in particular. It will evaluate the effectiveness of policy instruments in light of the interactions between technology and the labour market uncovered above and investigate whether feedbacks through the government budget reinforce or dampen the shocks. The analysis is presented in one single chapter that will discuss the aims, introduce the instruments and analyse the impact of policy in the model. The chapter concludes with some suggestions to improve the position of the unemployed in Europe and the low skilled in the US. Its contribution to the debate on policy making is the idea that these policy areas are linked and the goals can be conflicting. If this part provides insufficient arguments to cause politicians to revise, then at least it should cause them to reconsider their technology, labour market and income policies.

CHAPTER 7:

THE GOVERNMENT IN THE MODEL

The analysis of policy serves a dual purpose. On the one hand, policy may help explain observed facts. On the other, as the model hopefully helps one to understand a relevant part of reality, policy advice summarises the implications of that understanding. A common and straightforward way of doing both is to analyse the impact of changes to exogenous variables in the model that to some extent are under the control of policy makers in the real world.[1]

Based on the analysis so far one could for example conclude that unemployment benefits drive up the outside option of employees and thereby drive up wages and cause unemployment. As was argued above, this helps explain the unemployment differentials between the US and Europe. The obvious policy advice for Europe would be to lower unemployment benefits as many have indeed advocated.[2] As unemployment benefits have been treated as exogenous variables in the model, analysing such policies is equivalent to the sensitivity analyses that were conducted above.

Likewise the experiments on parameter a_R indicate that, to combat wage inequality, it would be possible to subsidise low skilled complementary process R&D. However, such policy analyses overlook the fact that the government is part of the economy and should be analysed as part of the model. In this chapter the aim is therefore to take the analysis of policy some steps further. The first step is to assume that the government finances all expenditures out of taxes. Through the tax system such financing constraints may strengthen or weaken the effectiveness of any given instrument in achieving a policy goal. The next step is to analyse if and how instruments may help or hinder other instruments aimed to achieve other goals. Trade-offs and double-edged swords may exist and are important to identify before, switching to normative analysis, the policy implications can be formulated.[3]

The first section addresses the goals, instruments and constraints for the government. Then in Section 7.2 the model is extended with a government that is financially constrained and has several instruments to raise taxes and implement policy. In Section 7.3 the focus is on trade-offs and double-edged swords in current policies. Section 7.4 formulates the policy implications and concludes.

7.1   AIMS, INSTRUMENTS AND CONSTRAINTS

One cannot fruitfully formulate policy advice without some agreement on the aims of policy. In reality a political process underlies the policy aims and frequent adjustments are made.[4] To avoid being caught in the complexities of politics this chapter will focus only on the big issues and assume that there is agreement. Goals like steady and sustainable economic growth, full employment and an equitable distribution of wealth and income rank among the top priorities of governments throughout the OECD.

It is a well-known fact that the United States and other Anglo-Saxon countries tend to put more emphasis on the former two than on the latter and consequently put more faith in the market, whereas continental European countries stress the latter goal and seem willing to accept lower rates of growth and unemployment. The political and historical processes behind these priorities will not be modelled here, even if it were possible to do so adequately.[5] The analysis below treats them as given. As the model only distinguishes two groups of workers, the goal of equity must be interpreted as keeping relative wages at a level that yields a fair return, r^*, on investments in education but no more. The goal of full employment can also be interpreted as keeping unemployment as close as possible to a low target level, U^*.[6]

Stable sustainable economic growth is a bit trickier but can be interpreted to mean stimulating a stable rate of steady state product innovation as that ultimately determines the rate of economic growth in the long run. Here too the government will aim for a target growth rate, T^*.[7]

In pursuing their aims governments have a wide array of instruments. A first categorisation of these instruments, often used in environmental policy analysis, is market-based versus command and control instruments.[8] The former are instruments that change relative prices but leave the optimisation problem of other agents in the model intact. One could think of taxes, wage-subsidies, excise taxes, import tariffs, R&D subsidies etc. These instruments may affect the outcomes but not the way people choose their behaviour. The latter are much harder to model and would imply changing the optimalisation problems by adding constraints to other agents in the economy in ways that help the government to achieve their goals. They include for example import quota, quality and sanitation regulation, active labour market policies, government R&D and so on. Needless to say it is quite an involved operation to model the implications of such instruments.

In addition the changes to the model would be specific to every single policy one would like to consider. Hence the analysis below will consider only market-based instruments. As the number of market-based instruments is limited to the number of markets the model allows for taxes and subsidies on final products, factors of production and innovations. One additional policy instrument that was already introduced as an exogenous variable in Chapter 6, is unemployment benefits. To insure workers against sudden income losses due to, for example, unemployment, the government provides social security.[9]

The generosity of the social security system, to some extent a policy instrument, was already identified as one of the key explanatory variables in the trans-Atlantic unemployment differences. Note at this point that all policy is conducted exclusively through transfer payments. This brings one to the constraints the government has to consider when setting market-based instruments to achieve its goals. Social security and subsidies require financing. This financing is obtained through taxation.

The key constraints on government policy are thus an economic and a financial one.[10] The financial constraint is required to ensure that the government can maintain the level of transfer payments. A balanced budget constraint is therefore imposed in the model.[11] The economic constraint is merely the way the 'world', in which the government operates, works. The behaviour of consumers, producers and innovators in the economy is fully specified and perfectly predictable in the model and the government is constrained, i.e. must consider their responses to policy changes.

7.2   INTRODUCING THE GOVERNMENT IN THE MODEL

In the previous section taxes, subsidies and unemployment benefits were identified as the instruments of policy. It is relatively straightforward to introduce the market-based instruments, taxes and subsidies, market by market, by adjusting the corresponding cells of the model's formal synopsis Table 4.1. Table 7.1 illustrates how that table is affected by introducing various taxes and subsidies.

In the top two cells are the consumers. They can be taxed by levying a consumption tax. Section 1.3 has shown that most industrialised countries have a consumption tax in one form or another. Value added taxes, excise taxes, environmental charges etc. drive a wedge between consumer and producer prices. Although in the real world these taxes are often set to promote or discourage the consumption of one good rather than another, it is unheard of that consumption taxes discriminate between otherwise equal goods on the basis of the skill level of the labour used in production. Hence it is reasonable to assume that the consumption tax rate is a flat tax, levied on all products in the model.

Table 7.1:   FORMAL SYNOPSIS OF THE GENERAL MODEL[12]

The Government

AGENT(S)		PROBLEM(S) SUBJECT TO CONSTRAINT(S) S indexes Sector/Skill	⇒ RESULTS
CONSUMERS	1	$\max_{B(t)} : \int_t^\infty e^{-\rho(\tau-t)} \log U(E(\tau))d\tau$ s.t. $Y(t)+rA(t)=B(t)+dA(t)/dt$ $\Rightarrow \dfrac{\dot{E}(t)}{E(t)} = r - \rho$	
	2	$\max_{c(i)} : U(.) = \left(\int_0^n c(i)^\alpha di\right)^{\frac{1}{\alpha}}$ s.t. $\int_0^n \tau p(i)c(i)di \le E$ $\Rightarrow c^0(i) = \left(\dfrac{\tau p(i)}{P}\right)^{\frac{1}{\alpha-1}} \dfrac{E}{P}$ $\Rightarrow P \equiv \tau\left(\int_0^n p(i)^{\frac{\alpha}{\alpha-1}} di\right)^{\frac{\alpha-1}{\alpha}}$	
GOVERNMENT	A	Consumption Tax Revenue	$\Rightarrow \dfrac{\tau-1}{\tau}E$

It is mathematically convenient to introduce this tax as a mark up over consumption prices. Hence in the model consumers pay $\tau p(i)$ with $\tau>1$ whereas producers receive only $p(i)$ per unit of good i. This leaves price setting by producers unaffected. The government in additional Cell A now receives:

$$T = (\tau - 1)(n_N p_H c_H + n_L p_L c_L) = \frac{(\tau-1)}{\tau} E \qquad (7.1)$$

In the next two cells are the producers. They make profits and pay wages to their employees. At this level one could thus introduce corporate and labour taxes. Consider the latter first. As Section 1.3 has shown, labour taxes including social security contributions are a very common and important means of generating revenue in industrialised countries. In addition it was argued that labour taxes are used to redistribute income from high to low income earners. As income is (perfectly) correlated to skill in the model, it would be natural to introduce a separate tax rate for high and low skilled.

Table 7.1:		FORMAL SYNOPSIS OF THE GENERAL MODEL	
(Cont'd)		The Government	
AGENT(S)		PROBLEM(S) SUBJECT TO CONSTRAINT(S) ⇒ RESULTS	
		S indexes Sector/Skill	
PRODUCERS	3	$\max\limits_{p_s(i)} : \pi_{s_c}(i) = c_s(i)p_s(i) - tc_s(i)$ s.t. $c_s(i) = c_s^{D}(i)$ $$\Rightarrow p_s(i) = \frac{1}{\alpha}mc_s(i)$$	
	4	$\min\limits_{l_s(i)} : t_s w_s l_s(i)$ s.t. $c_s^{D}(i) = b_s l_s(i)^{\beta}$ $$\Rightarrow l_s^{D}(i) = \frac{\alpha\beta}{n_s t_s w_s}X_s \;^{13}, \; L_s^{D} = \frac{\alpha\beta}{t_s w_s}X_s$$	
	5	$\pi_{s_c}(i) = (1-\alpha\beta)X_s / n_s$ $\forall i \in n_s$ iff $\dfrac{\dot{X}_s}{X_s} = 0 \Rightarrow \dfrac{\dot{\pi}_s(i)}{\pi_s(i)} = -\dfrac{\dot{n}_s}{n_s}$	
GOVERNMENT	B	Labour Tax Revenue⇒ $(t_L - 1)w_L L_L^{D} + (t_H - 1)w_H L_H^{D}$	

Assuming that workers care about after tax incomes in bargaining or deciding to participate, the easiest way to introduce the income tax is to add the tax to marginal labour costs. This implies that, as is shown in Cell 4, firms pay $t_H w_H$ or $t_L w_L$ per high and low skilled unit of labour employed, where t_H, $t_L > 1$ should be interpreted as 1 plus the average tax rate. Consequently labour tax income from manufacturing is equal to:

$$T = (t_L - 1)w_L L_L^{D} + (t_H - 1)w_H L_H^{D} \tag{7.2}$$

Progression in taxes implies that the average rate is an increasing function of the gross wage level. To capture that progression, the tax rate should be set in function of the wage level. Consider the tax function:

$$t_s = 1 + t_0 w_s^{t_1} \tag{7.3}$$

where $t_0 w_s^{t_1}$ is the average tax rate. Parameter t_0 shifts the level of the labour tax whereas $t_1 > 0$ determines the degree of progression in the tax system.[14] These parameters can be considered the relevant policy instruments.

Corporate taxes, like consumption taxes, typically do not discriminate between producers on the basis of the skill level of their employees. Hence a uniform rate would be in order, since all corporate income or profits are used to repay the initial R&D investments in the model. Uncertainty on future corporate tax rates adds to the uncertainty of after tax returns to R&D investments and there is a strong argument for keeping these rates constant.[15] But if these rates are assumed constant and uniform, they merely reduce the value of a firm from discounted flow of pre- to after tax profits and corporate taxes could be introduced in the model as a tax on patents/innovations.[16]

Table 7.1:   FORMAL SYNOPSIS OF THE GENERAL MODEL[17]
(Cont'd)   The Government

AGENT(S)		PROBLEM(S) SUBJECT TO CONSTRAINT(S) S indexes Sector/Skill	⇒ RESULTS
	6	Price taking in R&D $\Rightarrow v_H = \left(\dfrac{\pi_H(i) + \dot{v}_H(i)}{r} \right) = \left(\dfrac{\pi_H + \dot{v}_H}{r} \right)$ $\Rightarrow v_L = \left(\dfrac{\pi_L + \dot{v}_L}{r} - \dfrac{\pi_H + \dot{v}_H}{r} \right)$	
R&D	7	$\max\limits_{R_R} : \pi_R^{R\&D} = \sigma_H \dot{n}(R_R)v_H - t_R w_R R_R \quad \text{and} \quad \dot{n}_H = \dot{n} - \dot{n}_L$ $\text{s.t. } \dot{n}(R_R) = a_R n \, n_H^{(1-\varphi)X} n_L^{(1-\varphi)(1-X)} R_R^{\gamma}$ $\Rightarrow w_R = \dfrac{a_R n \, n_H^{(1-\varphi)X} n_L^{(1-\varphi)(1-X)} R_R^{\gamma-1} \sigma_H v_H}{t_R}$ $\max\limits_{R_D} : \pi_D^{R\&D} = \sigma_L \dot{n}_L(R_D)v_L - t_R w_R R_D$ $\text{s.t. } \dot{n}_L(R_D) = a_D n^{\psi} n_H^{(1-\psi)X} n_L^{(1-\psi)(1-\zeta)} R_D^{\gamma}$ $\Rightarrow w_R = \dfrac{a_D n^{\psi} n_H^{(1-\psi)X} n_L^{(1-\psi)(1-\zeta)} R_D^{\gamma-1} \sigma_L v_L}{t_R}$	
GOVERNMENT	C	Labour Tax Revenue $\Rightarrow (t_R - 1)R^*$ Innovation Subsidies $\Rightarrow (1-\sigma_H)\dot{n}v_H + (1-\sigma_L)\dot{n}_L v_L$	

This brings one to the the R&D sectors. As governments typically would consider subsidising R&D, the net effect of corporate tax and R&D subsidy would be some fraction on the value of innovations in the model.

As R&D subsidies may be targeted at one rather than the other type of innovation, two rates should be introduced here as well. Table 7.1 introduces the subsidies on R&D as additional income to the R&D sector. Hence the value of an innovation to the producer in Cell 6 need only be v_H or v_L while the R&D firms still receive the value $\sigma_H v_H$ or $\sigma_L v_L$ in Cell 7.

Table 7.1:   FORMAL SYNOPSIS OF THE GENERAL MODEL
(Cont'd)   The Government

		EQUILIBRIUM CONDITIONS S indexes Sector/Skill
LABOUR MARKETS	8	**Wage Bargaining** $w_s = \left(\dfrac{u_s - u_{so}}{1 - u_{so}}\right)^{-\varepsilon_s} m_{so}\rho_s w_s^{\delta_s} w_{-s}^{1-\delta_s} \Rightarrow$ $u_s = u_{so} + (1-u_{so})\left((w_s/w_{-s})^{\gamma_s-1}\rho_s m_{so}\right)^{\frac{1}{\varepsilon_s}}$ **Equilibrium without Competition** $R_R + R_D = R^*$ $L_H^{\ D} = (1-u_H)L_H^{\ *} - R^*$ $L_L^{\ D} = (1-u_L)L_L^{\ *}$ **Equilibrium with Competition** $w_H = w_R$ $R_R + R_D + L_H^{\ D} = (1-u_H)L_H^{\ *}$ $L_L^{\ D} = (1-u_L)L_L^{\ *}$
GOVERNMENT	D	**Unemployment Benefits** $\Rightarrow B = u_H L_H^{\ *}\rho_H w_H^{\delta_H} w_L^{1-\delta_H} + u_L L_L^{\ *}\rho_L w_H^{1-\delta_L} w_L^{\delta_L}$
ASSET MARKETS	9	$\dfrac{\dot{n}}{n} = \dfrac{\dot{n}_H}{n_H} = \dfrac{\dot{n}_L}{n_L}$ $\Rightarrow \dfrac{\dot{v}_H}{v_H} = \rho - \dfrac{(1-\alpha\beta)(\tau-1)E_H/\tau}{\sigma_H v_H n_H}$ $\Rightarrow \dfrac{\dot{v}_L}{v_L} = \left(1+\dfrac{\sigma_H v_H}{\sigma_L v_L}\right)\rho - \dfrac{(1-\alpha\beta)(\tau-1)E_L/\tau}{\sigma_L v_L n_L}$ **Equilibrium** $d\dfrac{n_H v_H + n_L v_L}{Y} = 0 \quad \Rightarrow \quad \dfrac{\dot{n}}{n} = -\dfrac{\dot{v}_H}{v_H} = -\dfrac{\dot{v}_L}{v_L}$
GOVERNMENT	E	Balanced Budget $\Rightarrow T + T_H + T_L + T_R - B - \Sigma = 0$
STEADY STATE	11	$\Rightarrow$ no closed form solution for g

It can be seen that subsidisation and taxation are in fact two sides of the same coin as one now merely can assume σ_H and σ_L <1 to have a tax on innovation. The costs of this scheme are given by: [18]

$$\Sigma = (\sigma_H - 1)\dot{n}v_H + (\sigma_L - 1)\dot{n}_L v_L \tag{7.4}$$

In addition the government will usually levy an income tax on those working in the R&D sector. As the key input in R&D is labour, their incomes are treated as other labour incomes, using the labour tax rule in Equation (7.3). R is therefore considered labour and taxed progressively. The tax rate depends on the level of R&D-sector wages.

Table 7.1 is completed with the equilibrium conditions. In Cell 8, unemployment is introduced into the labour market equilibrium conditions, like before in Chapter 6. The government is introduced here as the provider of social security. It now explicitly provides the main source of non-labour income through unemployment benefits and social security transfers and thereby affects the outside option and reservation wages for workers.

The level of unemployment benefits per worker of skill S, B_S, or alternatively their replacement rates, parameters ρ_S, in Equation (5.12), are considered the final two policy variables in the model. Wage bargaining then yields the equilibrium wage and unemployment levels as before. The costs of the social security scheme are given in Cell D by:

$$B = u_H L_H{}^* B_H + u_L L_L{}^* B_L \tag{7.5}$$

Unemployment, u_S, can be interpreted as voluntary or involuntary and B_S should correspondingly be interpreted as the level of welfare benefits or unemployment benefits, respectively. The benefit level was already introduced in the model in Chapter 6 so this completes the introduction of the government into the model. In Equation (7.5) one might also add an exogenous transfer component, that can be calibrated to set total government expenditures to the levels observed in Section 1.3. The relevant budget constraint in Cell E is a balanced budget. Adding outlays and subtracting incomes the deficit of the government is given by:

$$D \equiv$$
$$\left(B_H u_H L_H{}^* + B_L u_L L_L{}^* + (1 - \sigma_H)\dot{n}v_H + (1 - \sigma_L)\dot{n}_L v_L \right) - \tag{7.6}$$
$$\left(\frac{(\tau - 1)}{\tau}E + t_0 w_H{}^{t_1+1} L_H{}^D + t_0 w_L{}^{t_1+1} L_L{}^D + t_0 w_R{}^{t_1+1}(R_R + R_D) \right)$$

With τ, t_0, t_1, ρ_H, ρ_L, σ_H and σ_L as policy instruments, the number of different policy experiments, even under the balanced budget constraint, quickly multiplies.[19] To limit the analysis two key issues are raised. First a check is done on the direct and indirect effects of the policy instruments introduced above. Tax progression, for example, usually aims at reducing the after-tax income inequality. In the model above, the effectiveness of progression in doing so can be evaluated. Under wage bargaining, however, a progressive tax system also affects the unemployment of high and low skilled workers. And, through its impact on relative wage costs, progression also affects relative profits and ultimately the direction of technical change. Hence progression may have an impact on growth and unemployment.

Similarly policies aimed at reducing unemployment and boosting economic growth may have implications for the distribution of income. In addition all policies have implications for the government's financial position and therefore require adjustments in other policy areas. A complete analysis of the direct and indirect effects of policy changes constitutes the positive analysis of the government in the model. It helps explain the problems in US and European labour markets and correctly identifying the linkages is a necessary first step in acting upon them.

7.3   A POSITIVE ANALYSIS OF POLICY INTERACTIONS

In this section the aim is to analyse the interactions in the model. The model in Table 7.1 can be analysed graphically and numerically to identify the direct and indirect channels through which policy instruments affect the outcomes of the model. The key variables of interest, also constituting the main differences between the US and EU discussed in Chapter 1, are relative wages, unemployment levels and the steady state growth rate. Relative wages rose in the US and remained stable in Europe. Europe has the higher unemployment levels while the US has led the early exploration and commercial exploitation of the ICT-revolution. Key policy instruments that were shown to differ between the US and EU in Section 1.3, are the degree of progression in the tax system, the level of unemployment benefits and the policy stance on Research and Development. This section will investigate to what extent these different policy stances may help explain the observed labour market trends.

First consider the impact of increased progression. As it is intended to reduce wage inequality, one would expect the model to predict this. In addition, however, progression will also cause wage stability, as increases (decreases) in wage costs are partially compensated by increases (decreases) in the average tax rate and do not fully transmit to take-home wages.

Figure 7.1:   THE IMPACT OF PROGRESSIVE TAXATION ON THE LABOUR MARKET

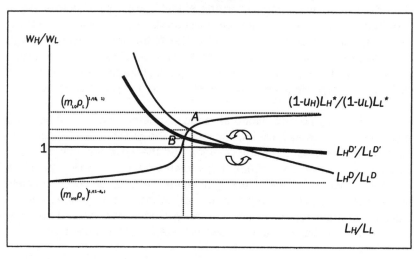

The impact of a progressive tax system can be illustrated in the graph for the labour market, presented in Figure 7.1. With relative take-home wages on the vertical axis, the relative demand curve will shift due to progression, as employers pay take-home wages plus taxes. Where both take-home wages are equal, the relative gross wage costs must equal 1 as the tax rule implies that both pay the same tax rate. Consequently, at that relative wage, relative demand is equal to relative demand without progressive taxes. As the relative take-home wage rises, so must relative wage costs and more than proportionately so, hence relative demand falls. As one moves away from 1, this difference increases and the demand curve rotates counter-clockwise.

Figure 7.1 indicates that, in addition to causing the predicted relative wage compression, progression also reduces relative employment.[20] At the given relative availability of labour this implies that low skilled unemployment falls relative to high skilled unemployment.

As has been argued extensively in the chapters above, a shift in gross relative labour costs will also cause technology to respond. Presenting the full figure and putting gross relative labour costs on the vertical axis yields Figure 7.2. In that figure the relative supply instead of the relative demand curve is rotated and consequently the *PMA* curve also rotates around 1.

Figure 7.2: **THE STEADY STATE IMPACT OF TAX PROGRESSION**

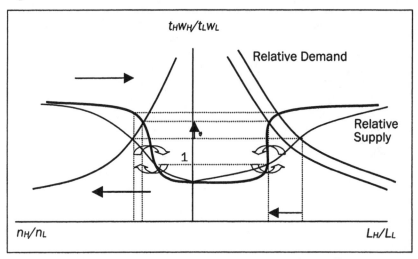

Starting in equilibrium in points *A*, *A'* this puts the model off the steady state at points *B*, *B'*. As progression makes low skilled labour artificially cheaper and more abundant at given relative labour costs, the innovation sector will respond by reducing n_H/n_L. This reduces relative demand and eventually the economy settles in points such as *C*, *C'*.

The figure shows an increase in relative labour costs while relative employment and unemployment rates drop.[21] In Figure 7.1 the inward shift in relative demand can be shown to reduce relative take-home wages by more than the initial effect of progressive taxation. Due to the endogenous technology response, the income redistributing effect of progression in the tax system is enhanced, although progression itself limits the impact of relative demand shifts on relative take-home wages.[22]

The model thus predicts that a more progressive tax system causes relative wages to be lower and more stable. Perhaps more surprisingly, the implications for unemployment are also in favour of the low skilled. As Section 1.3 has shown that Europe has the more progressive tax system, relative wage stability and relative unemployment performance are consistent with this observation. Also the trend towards reducing progression in the tax reforms of the 80s fits well within the general picture. Such reforms would be expected to increase wage inequality, directly and indirectly through technology responses.

Figure 7.3:   THE IMPACT OF INCREASING PROGRESSION

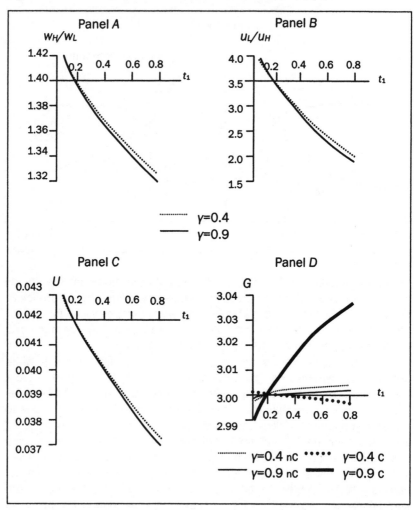

Consider shortly what the model would predict if the strong market size effect were in place.[23] In that case the technology response would be so strong that progression actually causes a reduction in relative labour costs, causing an even stronger relative take-home wage reduction. Progression in the tax system is therefore a powerful policy instrument in improving the overall labour market position, relative wage and unemployment of the low skilled. What about that other policy goal? How does progression affect long-term growth? This cannot be derived from analysing the graphs above. As the model has been fully calibrated in the chapters above, however, a numerical analysis is easily conducted. The results of this analysis are presented in Figure 7.3.

To verify the predictions made above panels A and B show the steady state relative wage and relative unemployment rates in function of the progression parameter t_1. Recall that the parameter t_0 is recalibrated to maintain budget balance in the steady state. The baseline values for policy instruments were set at $t_1=0.2$, $\tau=1$, $\sigma_H=\sigma_L=1$, $\rho_H=\rho_L=0.65$. Hence in the baseline there are no consumption taxes, no innovation subsidies and replacement rates are set at the values chosen in Chapter 6. The progression parameter implies that the average tax rate rises by 20% when income doubles.[24] All other parameters and exogenous variables were set or recalibrated as described in Chapters 4 and 6.

Although Panels A and B do show that the market size effect increases the effectiveness of progression, the size and difference in effects is marginal. This is the case because relative employment levels, and therefore relative marginal productivity and gross relative labour costs, change only marginally due to increased progression in the calibrated model. With the parameters set at the values of Chapter 6, the supply curve is very steep to begin with and rotating it counter-clockwise will shift the equilibrium only marginally.[25]

It can be verified in Panel B of Figure 7.3 that progression significantly reduces relative unemployment rates. Panel C shows that the impact on overall unemployment levels is also beneficial as the larger share of the population is still low skilled. The impact on the growth rate, depicted in Panel D, is small, in the order of hundredths of percentage points. It is worth noting, however, that the non-competition versions of the model show a positive impact, whereas the competition versions predict a reduction in growth for the weak induced innovations model but a relatively large increase under the strong market size effect. This is due to the endogenous reallocation of high skilled labour. The combination of strong diminishing returns and higher marginal tax rates drives skilled workers out of innovation in the first case, whereas constant returns cause innovation to attract workers from manufacturing in the second.[26]

It can be verified in the graphs that the impact of progression is positive in all target variables for all model specifications except one in growth, where the negative effect is very limited. Growth rates fall to 0.2995 when progression is increased to 0.8.[27] Progression is therefore a two-sided sword as it simultaneously improves the relative unemployment and relative take home wage position of low skilled. It makes high skilled labour artificially scarcer by pushing up its price but in doing so, it compensates for the artificial scarcity of low skilled workers, caused by wage bargaining.[28] Its effectiveness is therefore enhanced through endogenous innovation responses, but without seriously reducing growth. The latter result emerges because higher progression does not disturb the allocation of high skilled over R&D and manufacturing.[29] Also the progression in taxes has been increased without affecting the total labour tax revenue, such that other policies are not affected and the buck stops here. There seems to be no trade-off between equity and growth, even when endogenous technology responses and financial constraints are considered.[30]

The second instrument to be evaluated is the level of unemployment benefits and social security transfers. As was shown in Chapter 6, the manipulation of the replacement rates directly affects the shape of the relative supply curve in Figures 7.1 and 7.2. The sensitivity analysis on parameter $msops$ can be regarded as a first analysis of labour market policy. By changing the upper and lower bound and the slope of the curve, the unemployment benefit system had a direct impact on relative wages and unemployment. As was shown in Chapter 6 also, however, the impact on relative labour costs is limited. Consequently there is little additional innovation response and the level of benefits mainly affects the level of unemployment rates. As Europe was shown to have the more generous unemployment benefits and social security systems, this was already offered as the key explanation for the marked difference in unemployment levels between the US and Europe.

Social security and unemployment benefits schemes, however, also involve transfer payments from the government budget, which is an additional channel through which the generosity of the benefits system may affect the economy. In addition, the sensitivity analysis in Chapter 6 evaluated the impact of changes in benefit generosity for both skill types separately. For a given factor of proportionality of 0.2, the implications of changing both replacement ratios simultaneously is illustrated in Figure 7.4. As in Figure 7.3, Panel A shows the impact on relative wages, Panel B that on relative unemployment. Panels C and D show the effect on unemployment and growth. On the horizontal axis is the replacement rate, which remains equal for both skill groups. The largest impact is seen in Panel C where total unemployment rises quickly in all model specifications as replacement rates are increased.

Figure 7.4:   THE IMPACT OF INCREASING REPLACEMENT RATES

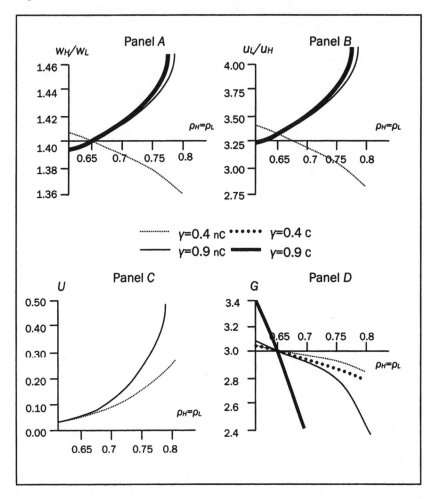

This drop in employment causes growth rates to drop, as less labour is now available in R&D.[31] As can be seen in Panels *A* and *B* the impact on the relative labour market position of the low skilled depends on the value of γ. With strong diminishing returns to labour in R&D, the model predicts that the position of the low skilled improves, whereas the market size effect will cause it to deteriorate. This is due to the rising tax burden.[32] At a given level of progression the wedge between relative take-home wages and relative wage costs decreases, causing high skilled labour to become artificially more abundant. Under the market size effect this causes

relative wages to increase, whereas under weak induced innovations the
relative after tax wages will fall. As relative unemployment responds
strongly to relative wages, the same pattern is observed here.[33] The
reductions in benefit levels, proposed in Chapter 6, therefore also
constitute a double-edged sword in the model. They increase both growth
and employment. However, there is a possible trade-off as costs may
come in terms of increased inequality. These costs depend on γ and are
not very likely to be large, though.

Figure 7.5:   THE IMPACT OF INCREASING INNOVATION SUBSIDIES

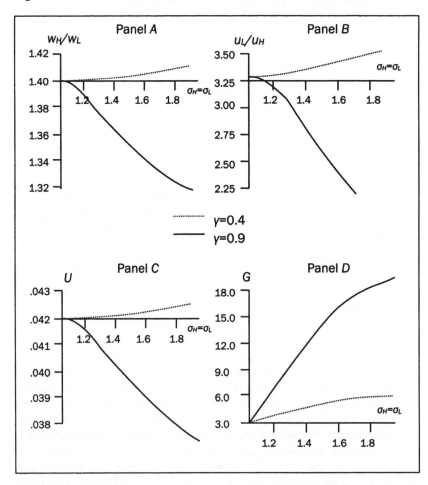

The final policy to be considered here are R&D subsidies. In the model such subsidies reduce the price of an innovation to producers, increasing the demand for them. In the exogenous allocation model, however, the number of R&D workers is fixed and innovative output cannot increase as long as unemployment levels are unaffected. A general subsidy would only increase wages in the R&D sector. Through the tax system there is therefore a redistribution of income from production to R&D workers but because the R&D sector was calibrated to be very small, the impact on the total tax burden is very small and the no-competition models hardly show any change. General subsidies only work in the endogenous allocation model. Figure 7.5 presents the simulation results when the general level of subsidies is raised from 1 to 2.[34]

In Panel *D* it can be verified that the subsidy is effective in stimulating overall growth. It is most effective under the market size effect, as diminishing returns in R&D are almost absent. The growth rate increases to a staggering 20% in that model. If diminishing returns are present, the subsidy increases growth to some 5% at most. The impact on all other variables depends on the value of γ.

For strong diminishing returns the unemployment level will rise, as do relative wages and relative unemployment rates. The subsidy drives up returns in R&D causing higher high skilled manufacturing wages. This reduces the demand in manufacturing as innovation does not cause n_H to rise fast enough. Unemployment rises, particularly for the low skilled, as they bargain for higher wages when high skilled wages increase. When constant returns characterise R&D, the situation is different. Relative wages actually fall as the subsidy makes high skilled labour scarcer to manufacturing.

This sets the market size effect in motion and although employment and wages now rise for both skill groups, they do for the low skilled in particular. Consequently relative unemployment also falls. Hence the effectiveness of this instrument totally depends on the degree of diminishing returns to scale in R&D. If it is high, then growth performance is only marginally improved at great costs to inequality and unemployment and there is a trade-off to be made. If diminishing returns are weak, however, growth performance, unemployment and relative wages may all move in the right direction following an increase in innovation subsidies. Once more γ turns out to be crucial for the result.[35]

In Section 1.3 it was shown that direct government spending on R&D is higher in the US than in Europe. Also a larger share of their expenditure is channelled through tax exemptions and general R&D subsidies, whereas in Europe the bulk of government R&D is in fact just that, government R&D.

The high level of general R&D subsidies would put the US to the right of Europe in Figure 7.5. In Panel *D* this implies higher growth rates and although US growth rates have been somewhat higher over the 90s, this panel suggest that both should have strong diminishing returns in R&D.

Figure 7.6:   THE IMPACT OF SHIFTING INNOVATION SUBSIDIES

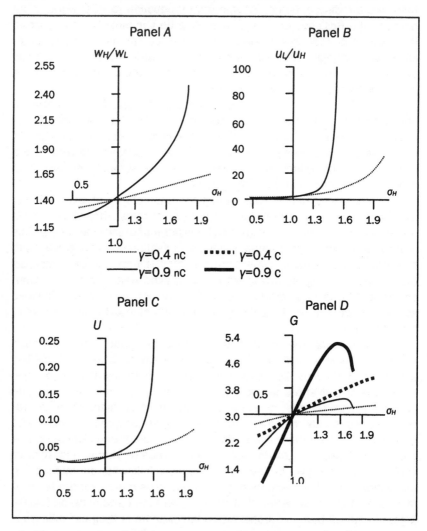

In the other panels that would imply higher relative wages, higher relative unemployment rates and slightly higher unemployment levels. The results are easily brought in line with the stylised facts when one considers that here both economies were assumed to have the same unemployment benefit schemes in this simulation.

As Figure 7.4 has indicated, a more generous system will seriously affect the overall unemployment level without affecting the other target variables very much. The government, however, also has the option to favour one type of innovation over the other. In Figure 7.6 the impact of varying σ_H/σ_L between 0.5 and 2 is illustrated.[36] Panel *D* shows that, by shifting R&D resources towards product innovation, the subsidies generate a slightly higher knowledge spillover and create higher steady state growth. This higher growth rate, however, comes at very large costs in all models.

Relative wages, relative unemployment and the overall unemployment level rise to very high levels, even though high skilled unemployment is all but eliminated. The tax burden will not change much due to the subsidy itself but indirect spillovers through the budget are quite large. Taxing product innovation, on the other hand, is a very powerful tool to reduce inequality, but severely reduces growth performance. The US targets its government R&D primarily at the defence industry, whereas European governments support the development and dissemination of basic knowledge. As was argued in Section 1.3, this could be interpreted as relatively more support for product innovation in the US. Hence, once more, the US should be placed to the right of Europe in Figure 7.6.

Now the direction of the predictions of the model does not depend on the value of γ. Once more the observed higher relative wages, higher relative unemployment rates and (marginally) higher growth rates are in line with the stylised facts and the more generous unemployment benefit system in Europe overturns the counterfactual prediction of higher unemployment levels in the US. The size of the differences makes it unlikely that diminishing returns in R&D are absent.

In addition to offering further explanations for the observed trends in OECD labour markets, the above analysis also indicates how current policy should be changed to avoid further deterioration or even improve the low skilled labour market perspective. A first and very important lesson to be learnt from the above is that the policy tools and aims are usually not linked one-on-one. Feedbacks through the budget and the economy cause seemingly unrelated policy instruments to affect the entire economic system in various directions, reinforcing and weakening each other.

This is the case in the very limited model presented above and is probably the case in a more complex real world too. As the executive branch of most Western democracies is very much segmented, policy makers are unaware or care little about such policy spillovers. Tax authorities in the OECD have aimed to broaden tax bases while cutting marginal rates. Their aim is to increase tax revenue while reducing price distortions. Meanwhile they reduce progression and in addition to causing after-tax income inequality this causes relative demand to shift away from the low skilled in the long run.

At some other department many industrialised countries have a task force that is trying to target innovative sectors in the economy for subsidies to increase economic growth, unknowingly causing rising relative wages and unemployment rates as new products enter the economy faster. At the department of labour, finally, as part of its overall strategy to reduce unemployment, benefit levels and entitlements become less generous to make work pay. While reducing unemployment and enhancing growth, however, their policies may alleviate or aggravate the plight of the low skilled as unanticipated technology responses shift relative labour demand. This chapter has shown the obvious, that tunnel vision can cause policy accidents.

7.4   POLICY IMPLICATIONS AND CONCLUSION

Having considered the policy instruments in isolation, the question is now, what instruments are most effective in achieving the aims of government when the full interactions in the model are considered? Although it is in principle possible to derive the optimal policy mix by specifying the government objective function and maximising its value given the constraints in the model of Table 7.1, it is not possible to analyse this graphically or analytically.[37]

For the numerically specified models analysed in simulations above, one might derive the optimal policy mix by evaluating a numerically specified objective function and conducting a grid search of the four dimensional policy space.[38] The specification of the objective function makes the actual outcome completely arbitrary, even if the calibrations in previous chapters do reflect the facts adequately. What this exercise does show, however, is what policy instruments are important in the fully interacting model.[39] Without presenting the results in full, a few relevant policy conclusions can be drawn.

Table 7.2 presents the results of the partial analyses to serve as a starting point. First, and not surprisingly perhaps, the models analysed above are particularly sensitive to innovation subsidies. By the assumed or calibrated small size of the R&D sector, subsidies have little impact on the budget. As Figure 7.6 already indicated, the relative subsidy level has a powerful impact on the relative rates of innovation and by the assumed link to relative labour demand these policies are very effective in changing relative wages, even under the assumption that total R&D resources are exogenously given.

Table 7.2:   IMPACT OF INSTRUMENTS ON OBJECTIVES

OBJECTIVES	INSTRUMENTS			
	t_1	ρ_H, ρ_L	σ_H, σ_L	σ_H/σ_L
w_H/w_L	-	0	-/+	++
u_L/u_H	-	0	-/+	+
U	0/-	++	0	+
g	0	0/-	++	+

The general level of R&D subsidies, on the other hand, fails to attract additional resources in that case and growth rates hardly respond to it. Under the competition version of the model, however, the level of subsidies enhances growth and relative growth rates are also much more sensitive to relative subsidies.[40]

Relative wage reduction through technology policy is therefore costly in terms of growth.[41] This trade-off implies that relative subsidies in particular must be set much higher to be optimal and column one shows that the progression of taxes then becomes important as a tool to reduce the relative after tax wage, both directly and indirectly through endogenous technology responses.

As was also clear in the partial analysis, the benefit levels should be reduced when the unemployment level is high. This will cause little relative wage pressure and if the strong market size effect exists, the relative wage may actually fall. These relative wage effects are easily compensated in the progression of the tax system or, even more effectively it would seem, in technology policy. [42] Table 7.2 shows that the channel from benefits to overall unemployment is relatively isolated from the rest of the model. This would suggest, as has been done in Chapter 6, that European policy makers need not fear the equity implications of the fight against unemployment, as long as they fight it on all fronts with equal zeal.[43]

The interaction between technology and labour demand suggests to policy makers on both sides of the Atlantic that R&D subsidies should not be aimed at the strengthening of current trends but rather should try to stabilise the natural cycles in technological development. As the general-purpose technologies of tomorrow emerge from the laboratories, science and technology policy should be redirected towards developing the previous one. As the frenzy of new products and services starts to dry up, the government could switch back to more basic research, stimulating the development of a next wave of innovations.

As trivially as such policies can be implemented in the model, so hard will it be in practice.[44] Given the uncertainties involved and the unavoidable policy lags, a fine tuned stabilisation policy is probably beyond the capabilities of any political system. What policy makers should attempt instead is to avoid obvious inconsistencies in their policies. Stimulating knowledge intensive production while at the same time maintaining an egalitarian stance on income distribution is having your pie and eating it too. As technology will evolve in response to the availability of skilled workers, there is no case for additional government support. Instead, that tax money is better spent on programmes to stimulate the lower end of the labour market and targeted R&D subsidies towards development.

In the chapter above, a host of policy experiments had to be left unattended. Shifting the tax burden from labour to another tax base, which is often advocated in the literature to stimulate employment, is ineffective in the model above, as both consumption and labour taxes will ultimately be borne by labour as it is the sole factor of production. Adding capital or energy to the model could make such experiments interesting and increases the relevance of financial constraints. In the experiments above, the government financed its transfers essentially by increasing or decreasing its tax burden neutrally. In that sense the analysis above is as crude as those assuming lump sum taxes. Policy experiments that shifted the burden from low to high skilled labour have shown that such policy changes have serious implications in the steady state as technology responds. These responses are to be expected in richer models.

Similarly the already mentioned open economy extension would allow for many more feedbacks and leaks, that could affect the outcomes and consequently the implications for policy. The analysis above, however, does suggest that these issues are a theoretical possibility. Further research is required to formulate the hypotheses on policy interactions more precisely. Then it's up to the empiricists to analyse their practical relevance.

NOTES

[1] See for example Barro and Sala-I-Martin (1995).
[2] See for example OECD (1994b). The OECD suggests many more ways in which the benefit system can be improved in terms of its impact on unemployment. A tight benefit administration and limits to the duration are examples of suggested labour market reforms.

In the model above the benefit level captures the value of being unemployed, which includes such aspects as duration and administrative hassle.

[3] Still the analysis is several steps short of the most sophisticated policy analyses. In a further step the government can be treated as a rational agent in the model who, given its competing aims, the limited number of instruments to achieve them and fully aware of the structure of the model, maximises his performance. This is the way in which for example the models of inflation in Walsh (1998) introduce government. Taking the analysis of government one step further still there is the literature on political economy. See for example Persson and Tabellini (2000). In that literature politicians are usually assumed set policy to maximise the probability of their re-election. Hence the government's priorities become endogenous. These extensions will not be considered further.

[4] Persson and Tabellini (2000) model this process.

[5] Some efforts are even made in this area. Alesina and Angeletos (2003) for example make an attempt at explaining the different attitudes towards income redistribution in a model where attitudes towards fate interact with the democratic system to generate self-reinforcing equilibria.

[6] This target level may be positive due to friction.

[7] A representation of these goals and the exogenous prioritisation is given in the objective function:

$$G(.) = \left(\left((1+r^{*}) - \frac{w_{H}}{w_{L}} \right)^{2} \right)^{\eta_{1}} \left(\left(U^{*} - \frac{u_{H}L_{H}^{*} + u_{L}L_{L}^{*}}{L_{H}^{*} + L_{L}^{*}} \right)^{2} \right)^{\eta_{2}} \left(\left(T^{*} - \frac{\dot{Y}}{Y} + \frac{\dot{P}}{P} \right)^{2} \right)^{1-\eta_{1}-\eta_{2}}$$

where it can be verified that the government would want to minimise this function and equity, full employment and economic growth have weights η_1, η_2 and $1-\eta_1-\eta_2$, respectively. The use of objective functions for governments is widespread in the monetary literature; see for example Walsh (1998). Without uncertainty the objective function is merely a convenient tool to represent the policy goals.

[8] See Siebert (1998).

[9] This additional aim must be introduced in the objective function in Note 7, otherwise the government would choose to abandon the system as it causes unemployment and has negative consequences for growth. The objective function could for example be augmented by adding a factor that is positive in the share of the population below some pre-defined poverty line times the distance to that poverty line.

[10] Obviously there can also be technical, political, social, legal or ethical constraints, but those are not explicitly modelled here and cannot be addressed.

[11] Lenders would require a return that translates in higher taxes in the future. As the required return equals the return on innovative investments, consumers are indifferent about postponing the tax bill. Meanwhile the deficit may crowd out innovative investments by increasing interest rates.

[12] In Cell 1 t and τ obviously represent time. In Cells 2-7 the symbols t and τ represent labour and consumption taxes, respectively.

[13] X_S was defined in Note 3 in Chapter 4 in Table 4.1.

[14] The marginal tax rate is given by:

$$t_1 t_0 w_s^{t_1 - 1}$$

The elasticity of average taxes with respect to after tax income is now given by t_1. Both average and marginal tax rate are given here with respect to after tax income. In the literature it is more common to express these rates in terms of the pre-tax wages but that complicates the mathematics without qualitatively changing the results. In principle t_1 could exceed 1 but that implies that doubling the income level more than doubles the average tax rate. Tax systems are unlikely to be that progressive.

[15] As the model has no uncertainty, this aspect is not captured by it. Unpredictable corporate tax rates would thus introduce uncertainty where it was assumed away for simplicity.

[16] Note that this is the case only because the patent is the only type of capital. Corporate taxes will have a different impact when physical capital is considered.

[17] Note that only the product life cycle specification is presented in Cells 6 and 7.

[18] Models without a life cycle would have:

$$\Sigma = (1 - \sigma_n)\dot{n}_n v_n + (1 - \sigma_L)\dot{n}_L v_L .$$

[19] The balanced budget constraint implies one of the instruments is lost and must be set to balance the budget. In the analyses below t_0 was used for this purpose. This tax level parameter is neutral, as labour is the only factor of production and must ultimately pay all taxes. By applying the same income tax rule in manufacturing and R&D the tax level is fully and neutrally shifted onto labour. In reality labour taxes are distortionary as there are more factors of production. A consumption tax is probably a less biased revenue generator in reality and the role could also have been played by τ. The other parameters are less suitable candidates as they change relative prices in the model and provoke innovation bias.

[20] The same result can be obtained by putting gross relative wage costs on the vertical axis. Then the relative supply curve must be rotated counter-clockwise around 1. This predicts an increase in gross relative wage costs and a reduction in relative unemployment rates. When supply is less than perfectly inelastic, the progression thus causes a relative wage and unemployment response. If it is inelastic, the supply curve will not shift and the burden of the tax falls on labour alone. Relative gross wage costs are unaffected while relative after-tax wages are reduced.

[21] Note that the relative employment rate is defined as high over low whereas the relative unemployment rate was defied as low over high skilled rates.

[22] As the demand curve is now flatter due to the counter-clockwise rotation.

[23] Imagine a similar shift in the relative supply and *PMA* curve but combined with a concave upward sloping *RDA* curve.

[24] In the US in 1992 the average tax rate at 66% of APW was 25%. For 133% of APW at around 30%, increasing the tax rate by 20% when the wage was doubled. Higher in the income distribution this progression is less in the USA. For Europe comparable rates are found at low-income levels and slightly higher ones at the higher levels. A notable exception is Germany, where average tax rates are considerably higher for all income groups. Hence Europe is more progressive. See OECD (1995) and Section 1.3.

[25] This issue was discussed at length in the previous chapter and the same caveats made there apply where these results are concerned.

[26] Recall that in manufacturing there are diminishing returns as well. The output elasticity was set at 0.8, between the 0.4 and 0.9 used in R&D to distinguish the weak and strong diminishing returns version of the model.

[27] Which implies that the average tax rate increases by 80% for a doubling of the take-home wage. To achieve that in actual tax systems that would imply an even larger increase in the marginal rate. 0.8 is chosen as the upper bound as it is the most progressive tax system for which the model can be solved numerically. For the same reason the extreme case of a proportional tax system, with $t_1=0$, has not been included.

[28] Note that low skilled unemployment is usually higher than high skilled unemployment. As the bargaining parameters were calibrated to reflect this in the baseline, the unemployment benefit system makes low skilled artificially more scarce than the high skilled.

[29] In the competition versions of the model R&D will attract high skilled labour from manufacturing to work on relatively profitable process development. In the non-competition versions the reduction in overall unemployment also implies that R&D employment goes up.

[30] In the literature there is an ongoing debate on the relation between growth and equity. Aghion and Howitt (1998) give an excellent overview in their Chapter 9. Indivisibilities in investment and incentives are key arguments in support of the trade-off. Aghion and Howitt show that capital market imperfections may reverse those arguments. To that debate this section adds the argument that redistribution may cause favourable biases in labour demand.

---

[31] Even in the exogenous allocation version the supply of R&D resources is set to 1.2% of total employment. Unemployment thus indirectly reduces the supply of R&D resources. The effect is obviously stronger when competition for high skilled labour is assumed.

[32] Recall from Chapter 6 that without the tax channel changes in replacement rates had a very limited impact on relative wages.

[33] Once more it is shown that under the assumptions made here these quantity responses do not prevent large relative wage movements.

[34] Implying that producers now only pay half of the costs of innovation and the R&D sector receives twice the value of an innovation.

[35] More generally the knowledge spillover structure in the innovation functions, analysed in Chapter 4 is equally crucial but has not been varied here.

[36] Given that $\sigma_L=1$ in these experiments the policy is varied between taxing product innovation by 50% and subsidising it by 100%. The simulation results for the model with high values for y have been presented up to 1.8 due to convergence problems.

[37] A possible specification was given in Note 7 above. With or without policy the model can only be solved numerically and the fact that three policy instruments are being considered simultaneously implies that graphical analysis fails. One cannot plot the value of the objective function against all three instruments simultaneously as graphical analysis is limited to 3 dimensions.

[38] Mathematica 3.0 was used to conduct this numerical search with brute force. A three-dimensional grid was defined and the value of the objective function was computed for the entire grid. It is conceded that this is a very crude and inefficient method and no doubt there are more sophisticated software packages and optimisation methods available. As this method fails to guarantee that the obtained minimum is global, only general impressions are discussed below. The fine grid does guarantee that a local minimum is found.

[39] These policy implications were derived under the assumption that the government weighs all factors in its objective function equally.

[40] These results obviously follow from the assumptions of the model, in particular those that constitute the technology part of the model. It should be noted that technology plays a key role in the composition of relative labour demand by construction. In reality the skill distribution is not strictly sorted and the sorting of high and low skilled over new and mature products is also far from perfect. Moreover, the innovative process may itself be misspecified, as was mentioned in Chapter 6. All these caveats are to be made when the policy conclusions are evaluated.

[41] Note that the model can only switch between zero and perfect substitutability of labour between manufacturing and R&D. The intermediate cases would create a weaker trade-off.

[42] This is not an argument for actually reducing benefit levels per se. A lot of real world policies fall under this category. The outside option and insider power of workers needs to be reduced to reduce their wage claims. All policies that do this are relevant here. Reintegration of long-term unemployed, active labour market policies, enhancing search effectiveness, avoiding poverty traps and stimulating labour participation are a few examples of less controversial labour market reforms that would fall into this category.

[43] The implications of clamping down on low skilled replacement rates exclusively will obviously cause their relative wages to fall.

[44] In practice the problem is of course to first identify high and low skilled complementary innovations before they are made and then adequately time and dose the innovation subsidies. In numerical simulations such problems disappear. One simply computes the required policies to stabilise wages for a given exogenous shock backwards.

CHAPTER 8:

SUMMARY AND CONCLUSION

This book investigated the interaction between technical change and the labour market. Its purpose was to explain key labour market trends in the OECD over the past few decades and to investigate the implications for policy in general and science and technology policy in particular. As work progressed that turned out to be quite an ambitious agenda. In the economic literature there are many ways in which technology has been approached. As bulky as that literature may be, it is dwarfed by the infinite number of contributions in which the interaction between labour demand and labour supply has been analysed. Both strands of literature then naturally also produced a huge amount of policy proposals. An attempt to be complete would therefore have been futile from the outset.

Surprisingly, however, the link from technology to labour demand in general and relative demand for unskilled labour in particular was left virtually unexplored in the literature. The interaction with the labour market and the corresponding policy analysis in light of that link has been all but absent. This book has established first contact between these fields in economic research and concentrated on bringing some of the mainstream ideas on technical change, labour markets and policy together.

Part I started with a rather broad survey of the economics of technical change in Chapter 2. The tools, concepts and ideas developed there were used in Chapter 3 to show how technical change can be modelled as an economic activity. Chapter 4 synthesised these ideas into a model in which endogenous innovation determines the relative demand for high skilled labour. The main conclusion there: The interaction between technology and relative demand is largely determined by the parameters of the innovation function. In plain English that means that returns to scale and knowledge spillovers in R&D are not only crucial in determining the speed or rate of technical change but also play a key role in determining its bias or direction. Consequently these parameters are of crucial importance in explaining labour market trends over the past few decades.

Part II introduced several labour market extensions. Chapter 5 surveyed several mainstream ideas on such issues as labour supply, unemployment and wage formation. In Chapter 6 those ideas were introduced into the model of Chapter 4. The interaction between demand and supply, perhaps surprisingly, hardly played a role in the determination of relative wages. Technology was shown to be the key factor in explaining relative wage behaviour, whereas unemployment could largely be attributed to labour market institutions and wage rigidity. It must be noted that education and shifts in the educational composition of the labour force have not been considered in the model. The long run interaction between supply and demand was not part of the analysis. The strong technology response to exogenous supply shocks does suggest a key role for education as well. Only the demand side of Tinbergen's race between technology and education has been analysed. The extension should rank high on the agenda for further research.

Part III analysed the obviously profound policy implications of these findings. In Chapter 7 it was concluded that technology policy could have serious equity implications. On the other hand there is no trade-off between high unemployment levels and wage inequality, as many and not the least of economists have suggested. Part of a strategy to combat US wage inequality could be the shifting of public R&D funds to development rather than research, such that new general purpose technologies age faster and products move to their mature stage in the life cycle more quickly. That would make wages more equal at virtually no costs to employment. Such policies would probably be inadequate to solve the huge problems of low absolute wage levels for an underclass of working poor but current US policies do not indicate that this is a high priority issue.

In Europe, on the other hand, restructuring social security and benefit systems can bring down unemployment at little costs in terms of inequality. Reintroducing progression into the tax and social contributions system can prevent what income inequality might arise. The model in this book suggests that European ambitions in science and technology are a much larger and stealthier threat to low skilled labour than a well-balanced reform of rigid labour markets.

REFERENCES

Abbott, M. and O. Ashenfelter (1976), 'Labour Supply, Commodity Demand and the Allocation of Time', *Review of Economic Studies*, **43**, 389-412.

Abramowitz, M. (1956), 'Resource and Output Trends in the United States since 1870', *American Economic Review*, **46**, 5-23.

Acemoglu, D. (1998), 'Why do New Technologies Complement Skills? Directed Technical Change and Wage Inequality', *The Quarterly Journal of Economics*, **113**, 1055-1089.

(2002a), 'Directed Technical Change', *Mimeo*, MIT, Cambridge, Massachusetts.

(2002b), 'Technical Change, Inequality and the Labor Market', *Journal of Economic Literature*, **40**, 7-82.

Acs, Z. (ed.) (1996), *Small Firms and Economic Growth*, Vol. 1, Edward Elgar Publishing, Cheltenham, UK and Brookfield.

Acs, Z. and D. Audretsch (1988), 'Innovation in Large and Small Firms: An Empirical Analysis', *The American Economic Review*, **78**, 678-690.

Adelman, I. and Z. Griliches (1961), 'On an Index of Quality Change', *Journal of the American Statistical Association*, **56**, 535-548.

Aghion, P. (2001), 'Schumpetarian Growth Theory and the Dynamics of Income Inequality', Walras Bowley Lecture delivered at the 1999 North-American Meeting of the Econometric Society, Madison, Wisconsin.

Aghion, P. and P. Howitt (1992), 'A Model of Growth through Creative Destruction', *Econometrica*, **60**, 323-351.

(1994), 'Growth and Unemployment', *Review of Economic Studies*, **61**, 477-494.

(1998), *Endogenous Growth Theory*, MIT Press, Cambridge, Massachusetts.

Ahmad, S. (1966), 'On the Theory of Induced Innovation', *Economic Journal*, 76, 344-357.

Akerlof, G. (1982), 'Labor Contracts as Partial Gift Exchange', *The Quarterly Journal of Economics*, 97, 543-569.

Alesina, A. and G. Angeletos (2003), 'Fairness and Redistribution: US versus Europe', *National Bureau of Economic Research Working Paper Series*, No. 9502.

Anderson, E. (2001), 'Is the Unskilled Worker Problem in Developed Countries Going Away?', *Mimeo*, Institute of Development Studies, University of Sussex, Brighton.

Arjona, R., M. Ladaique and M. Pearson (2001), 'Growth, Inequality and Social Protection', *Labour Market and Social Policy Occasional Papers*, No. 51, OECD, Paris.

Arrow, K. (1962), 'The Economic Implications of Learning by Doing', *Review of Economic Studies*, 29, 155-173.

Atkinson, A. (1999), 'Is Rising Inequality Inevitable? A Critique of the Transatlantic Consensus', WIDER Annual Lecture delivered at University of Oslo.

Audretsch, D. (1987), 'An Empirical Test of the Industry Life Cycle', *Weltwirtschaftliches Archiv*, 123, 297-308.

Autor, D., L. Katz and A. Krueger (1998), 'Computing Inequality: Have Computers Changed the Labor Market?', *Quarterly Journal of Economics*, 113, 1169-1213.

Aw, B. and G. Batra (1999), 'Wages, Firm Size and Wage Inequality: How much do Exports Matter?', in D. Audretsch and R. Thurik (eds), *Innovation, Industry Evolution and Employment*, Cambridge University Press, Cambridge.

Baldwin, J. and M. Raffiquzzaman (1999), 'Trade, Technology and Wage Differentials in the Canadian Manufacturing Sector', in D. Audretsch and R. Thurik (eds), *Innovation, Industry Evolution and Employment*, Cambridge University Press, Cambridge.

Barro, R. and X. Sala-I-Martin (1995), *Economic Growth*, McGraw-Hill Publishers, New York.

Bartel, A. and F. Lichtenberg (1987), 'The Comparative Advantage of Educated Workers in Implementing New Technology', *The Review of Economics and Statistics*, 69, 1-11.

Bartik, T. (2000), 'Group Wage Curves', *Staff Working Papers*, No. 00-63, W.E. Upjohn Institute for Employment Research, Kalamazoo, Michigan.

Bean, C. (1994), 'European Unemployment: A Survey', *Journal of Economic Literature*, 32, 573-619.

Beaudry, P. and D. Green (2002), 'Cohort Patterns in Canadian Earnings and the Skill-Biased Technical Change Hypothesis', *University of British Columbia Discussion Papers*, No. 97/03.

Becker, G. (1962), *Human Capital; A Theoretical and Empirical Analysis, with Special Reference to Education*, National Bureau of Economic Research, New York.

Beissinger, T. and J. Möller (1998), 'Wage Flexibility and Employment Performance: A Microdata Analysis of Different Age-Education Groups in German Industries', *Mimeo*, University of Regensburg.

Berman, E., J. Bound and Z. Griliches (1994), 'Changes in the Demand for Skilled Labor within US Manufacturing: Evidence from the Annual Survey of Manufacturers', *Quarterly Journal of Economics*, 109, 367-397.

Berman, E., J. Bound and S. Machin (1998), 'Implications of Skill-Biased Technological Change: International Evidence', *Quarterly Journal of Economics*, 113, 1245-1279.

Berman, E. and S. Machin (2000), 'Skill Biased Technology Transfers: Evidence of Factor Biased Technological Change in Developing Countries', *Mimeo*, Boston University, Massachusetts.

Biddle, J. and D. Hamermesh (1990), 'Sleep and the Allocation of Time', *Journal of Political Economy*, 98, 922-943.

Binswanger, H. (1974), 'The Measurement of Biased Technical Change with many Factors of Production', *American Economic Review*, 64, 964-976.

Black, A. and F. Fitzroy (2000), 'Earnings Curves and Wage Curves', *Aberdeen Papers in Accountancy, Finance and Management*, No. 00-7.

Blanchard, O. (1998), 'Relative Demand Shifts and Unemployment', lecture notes downloaded from http://econ-www.mit.edu on 25-05-2003.

Blanchflower, D. and A. Oswald (1990), 'The Wage Curve', *Scandinavian Journal of Economics*, 92, 215-235.

(1994a), 'An Introduction to the Wage Curve', *Mimeo*, London School of Economics, London.

(1994b), 'Estimating a Wage Curve for Britain, 1973-1990', *The Economic Journal*, 104, 1025-1043.

(1995), *The Wage Curve*, MIT Press, Cambridge, Massachusetts.

Blank, R. (1997), 'No Easy Answers: Comparative Labor Market Problems in the United States versus Europe', *University of Chicago Joint Center for Poverty Research Working Papers*, No. 188, Chicago.

Blundell, R. and T. MaCurdy (1999), 'Labour Supply; a Review of Alternative Approaches', in O. Ashenfelder and D. Card (eds), *Handbook of Labor Economics*, Vol. 2, Elsevier, Amsterdam, pp. 1559-1696.

Bollens, J. (2001), 'Unemployment and Skills from a Dynamic Perspective', in P. Descy and M. Tessaring (eds), *Training in Europe*, Vol. 2, Office for Official Publications of the European Communities, Luxembourg.

Bound, J. and G. Johnson (1992), 'Changes in the Structure of Wages in the 1980's: An Evaluation of Alternative Explanations', *The American Economic Review*, 82, 371-392.

Breshnahan, T. and R. Gordon (eds) (1997), 'The Economics of New Goods', *National Bureau Economic Research Studies in Income and Wealth*, No. 58, London.

Breshnahan, T. and M. Trajtenberg (1995), 'General Purpose Technologies: "Engines of Growth?"', *Journal of Econometrics*, 65, 83-108.

Brown, C., C. Gilroy and A. Kohen (1982), 'The Effect of the Minimum Wage on Employment and Unemployment', *The Journal of Economic Literature*, 20, 487-528.

Cameron, G. (1998), 'Innovation and Growth: A Survey of the Empirical Evidence', *Mimeo*, Nuffield College, Oxford, downloaded from http://www.nuff.ox.ac.uk on 10-12-2002.

Card, D. (1995), 'The Wage Curve: A Review', *Journal of Economic Literature*, 33, 285-299.

Card, D. and J. DiNardo (2002), 'Skill Biased Technical Change and Rising Wage Inequality; Some Problems and Puzzles', *Journal of Labor Economics*, 20, 733-783.

Card, D., F. Kramarz and T. Lemieux (1996), 'Changes in the Relative Structure of Wages and Employment: A Comparison of the United States, Canada and France', *National Bureau of Economic Research Working Paper Series*, No. 5487.

Chang, W. (1970), 'The Neoclassical Theory of Technical Progress', *The American Economic Review*, 60, 912-923.

Colecchia, A. and G. Papaconstantinou (1996), 'The Evolution of Skills in OECD Countries and the Role of Technology', *OECD Science and Technology Indicators Working Papers*, No. 1996/8.

Congressional Budget Office (1996), 'The Incidence of the Corporate Income Tax', *Congressional Budget Office Papers*, March 1996.

Cox, W. (1967), 'Product Life Cycles as Marketing Models', *Journal of Business*, 40, 375-384.

Cronin, J. (1999), 'U.S. Treasury Distributional Analysis Methodology', *U.S. Treasury Department OTA Working Paper*, No. 85.

Diamond, P. (1981), 'Mobility Costs, Frictional Unemployment and Efficiency', *Journal of Political Economy*, 89, 789-812.

Diamond, P. (1982), 'Wage Determination and Efficiency in Search Equilibrium', *Review of Economic Studies*, **49**, 217-227

(1984), *A Search Equilibrium Approach to the Micro Foundations of Macro Economics*, MIT Press, Cambridge, Massachusetts.

David, P. (1969), 'A Contribution to the Theory of Diffusion', *Stanford Center for Research in Economic Growth Research Memorandum*, No. 71.

(ed.) (1975), *Technical Choice, Innovation and Economic Growth*, Cambridge University Press, Cambridge.

Davidson, C. (1990), *Recent Developments in the Theory of Involuntary Unemployment*, Upjohn Institute for Employment Research, Kalamazoo, Michigan

Davis, S. (1992), 'Cross-Country Patterns of Change in Relative Wages', in O. Blanchard and S. Fischer (eds), *NBER Macroeconomic Annual 1992*, MIT Press, Cambridge, Massachusetts.

Davies, S. (1979), *The Diffusion of Process Innovations*, Cambridge University Press, Cambridge.

Dean, J. (1950), 'Product Line Policy', *The Journal of Business of the University of Chicago*, **23**, 248-258.

Dosi, G., C. Freeman, R. Nelson, G. Silverberg and L. Soete (1988), *Technical Change in Economic Theory*, Pinter, London.

Drandakis, E. and E. Phelps (1966), 'A Model of Induced Invention, Growth and Innovation', *The Economic Journal*, **76**, 823-840.

Dunne, T., J. Haltiwanger and K. Troske (1996), 'Technology and Jobs: Secular Changes and Cyclical Dynamics', *National Bureau of Economic Research Working Papers Series*, No. 5656.

Ehlen, M. and H. Marshall (1996), *The Economics of New-Technology Materials; A Case Study for FRP Bridge Decking*, National Institute of Standards and Technology, downloaded from http://fire.nist.gov on 13-11-2002.

Ehrenberg, R. and R. Smith (1996), *Modern Labor Economics; Theory and Public Policy*, Addison Wesley Longman Inc., Reading, Massachusetts.

Fellner, W. (1961), 'Two Propositions in the Theory of Induced Innovations', *Economic Journal*, 71, 305-308.

(1962), 'Does the Market Direct the Relative Factor-Saving Effects of Technological Progress?', in R. Nelson (ed.), *The Rate and Direction of Inventive Activity: Economic and Social Factors*, Princeton University Press, Princeton, New Jersey.

(1966), 'Profit Maximisation, Utility Maximisation and the Rate and Direction of Innovation', *The American Economic Review*, 56, 24-32.

Filer, R., D. Hamermesh and A. Rees (1996), *The Economics of Work and Pay*, 6th Edition, HarperCollins College Publishers, New York.

Freeman, R. (1986), 'Demand for Education', in O. Ashenfelter and R. Layard (eds), *Handbook of Labour Economics*, vol. I, Elsevier, Amsterdam.

(1997), 'Disadvantaged Young Men and Crime', in National Bureau of Economic Research (2000), *Comparative Labor Market Series*, vol. VIII, University of Chicago Press, Chicago.

Freeman, R. and R. Schettkat (2000), 'The Role of Wage and Skill Differences in US-German Employment Differences', *National Bureau of Economic Research Working Paper Series*, No. 7474.

Freeman, C. and L. Soete (1997), *The Economics of Industrial Innovation*, 3rd Edition, Pinter, London.

Galbraith, J., P. Conceicao and P. Ferreira (1999), 'Inequality and Unemployment in Europe: The American Cure', *New Left Review*, No. 237, 28-51.

Gazeley, I. and A. Newell (1999), 'Unemployment in Britain since 1945', *Mimeo*, University of Sussex, Brighton.

Goldin, C. and L. Katz (1998), 'The Origins of Technology-Skill Complementarity', *Quarterly Journal of Economics*, 113, 693-732.

Gomulka, S. (1990), *The Theory of Technological Change and Economic Growth*, Routledge, London.

Greenstein, S. (1994), 'Did Computers Diffuse Quickly? Best and Average Practice in Mainframe Computers 1968-1983', *National Bureau of Economic Research Working Paper Series*, No. 4647.

Gregg, P. and A. Manning (1997), 'Skill-Biased Change, Unemployment and Wage Inequality', *European Economic Review*, **41**, 1173-1200.

Gregg, P. and J. Wadsworth (1996), 'More Work in Fewer Households', in J. Hills (ed.), *New Inequalities: The Changing Distribution of Income and Wealth in the UK*, Cambridge University Press, Cambridge.

Griliches, Z. (1957), 'Hybrid Corn: An Exploration in the Economics of Technical Change', *Econometrica*, **25**, 501-522.

(1979), 'Issues in Assessing the Contribution of Research and Development to Productivity Growth', *The Bell Journal of Economics*, **10**, 92-116.

(1984), 'R&D and Innovation: Some Empirical Findings: Comments', in Z. Griliches (ed.), *R&D, Patents, and Productivity*, University of Chicago Press, Chicago.

Grossman, G. and E. Helpman (1989), 'Endogenous Product Cycles' *National Bureau of Economic Research Working Paper Series*, No. 2913.

(1991a), 'Endogenous Product Cycles', *The Economic Journal*, **101**, 1214-1229.

(1991b), *Innovation and Growth in the Global Economy*, MIT Press, Cambridge, Massachusetts.

(1991c), 'Quality Ladders and Product Cycles', *Quarterly Journal of Economics*, **106**, 557-586.

Guichard, S. and J.-P. Laffargue (2000), 'The Wage Curve: The Lessons of an Estimation over a Panel of Countries', *CEPII Working Paper Series*, No. 2000-21, Paris.

Hacche, G. (1979), *The Theory of Economic Growth. An Introduction*, MacMillan Press Ltd., London.

Hamermesh, D. (1993), *Labor Demand*, Princeton Academic Press, Princeton, New Jersey.

Harrod, R. (1939), 'An Essay in Dynamic Theory', *The Economic Journal*, 49, 14-33.

Hellier, J. and N. Chusseau (2002), 'Growing Inequalities between Skilled and Unskilled Workers: The Technological Bias versus North-South Openness Debate', *Mimeo*, MEDEE Université de Lille 1, downloaded from http://www.univ-paris1.fr on 27-11-2002.

Helpman, E. (ed.) (1998), *General Purpose Technologies and Economic Growth*, MIT Press, Cambridge, Massachusetts.

Hicks, J. (1932), *The Theory of Wages*, MacMillan & Co., London.

Hines, J. (2001), 'Corporate Taxation', *Mimeo*, University of Michigan, Michigan.

Hirsch, S. (1965), 'The United States Electronics Industry in International Trade', *National Institute Economic Review*, 7, 92-107.

Houseman, J. (1999), 'Cellular Telephone, New Products and the CPI', *Journal of Business and Economic Statistics*, 17, 188-194.

Howell, D. (2002), 'Increasing Earnings Inequality and Unemployment in Developed Countries: Markets, Institutions and the Unified Theory', *CEPA Working Paper Series*, No. 2002-01.

Howell, D., M. Duncan and B. Harrison (1998), 'Low Wages in the US and High Unemployment in Europe: A Critical Assessment of the Conventional Wisdom', *CEPA Working Paper Series*, No. 1998-08.

Howell, D. and F. Hübler (2001), 'Trends in Earnings Inequality and Unemployment across the OECD: Labor Market Institutions and Simple Supply and Demand Stories', *CEPA Working Paper Series*, No. 2001-02.

IMF, *International Government Statistics Yearbook*, various issues.

Internet Society (2001), *A Brief History of the Internet and Related Networks*, posted on the website of the Internet Society from http://www.isoc.org on 19-07-2003.

Iyigun, M. (2000), 'Technology Life Cycles and Endogenous Growth', *University of Colorado Working Papers*, No. 00-7.

Jacobs, B., R. Nahuis and P. Tang (2002), 'Sectoral Productivity Growth and R&D Spillovers in the Netherlands', *De Economist*, **150**, 181-210.

Jaffe, A. (1986), 'Technological Opportunity and Spillovers of R&D: Evidence from Firms' Patents, Profits, and Market Value', *The American Economic Review*, **76**, 984-1001.

    (1988), 'Demand and Supply Influences in R&D Intensity and Productivity Growth', *Review of Economics and Statistics*, **70**, 431-437.

Johansen, K. (1999), 'Wage Flexibility for Skilled and Unskilled Workers: New Evidence on the Norwegian Wage Curve', *Labour*, **13**, 413-432.

Johnson, G. (1997), 'Changes in Earnings Inequality: The Role of Demand Shifts', *Journal of Economic Perspectives*, **11**, 41-54.

Jones, C. (1995), 'R&D-based Models of Economic Growth', *Journal of Political Economy*, **103**, 759-784.

    (1999), 'Growth: With or Without Scale Effects', *American Economic Review*, **89**, 139-144.

Jones, H. (1975), *An Introduction to Modern Theories of Economic Growth*, Nelson and Sons, London.

Jones, C. (2004), 'Growth and Ideas', in *NBER Working Papers*, No. 10767.

Jones, C. and R. Manuelli (1999), 'The Sources of Growth', *Journal of Economic Dynamics and Control*, **21**, 75-114.

Juhn, C., K. Murphy and B. Pierce (1993), 'Wage Inequality and the Rise in Returns to Skill', *Journal of Political Economy*, **101**, 410-442.

Kamien, M. and N. Schwartz (1982), *Market Structure and Innovation*, Cambridge University Press, Cambridge.

Katz, L. (2002), 'Technological Change, Computerization and the Wage Structure', in E. Byrnjolfsson and B. Kahin (eds), *Understanding the Digital Economy: Data, Tools, and Research*, MIT Press, Cambridge, Massachusetts.

Katz, L. and K. Murphy (1992), 'Changes in Relative Wages, 1963-1987: Supply and Demand Factors', *Quarterly Journal of Economics*, **107**, 35-78.

Kaufman, R. (1984), 'On Wage Stickiness in Britain's Competitive Sector', *British Journal of Industrial Relations*, **22**, 101-112.

Kenney, H. (2003), 'From Poverty to Prosperity', *Mimeo*, Wits University, downloaded from http://www.freemarketfoundation.com on 25-07-2003.

Kennedy, C. (1964), 'Induced Bias in Innovation and the Theory of Distribution', *The Economic Journal*, **74**, 541-547.

(1966), 'Samuelson on Induced Innovation', *Review of Economics and Statistics*, **48**, 442-444.

Kennedy, C. and A. Thirwall (1972), 'Surveys in Applied Economics: Technical Progress', *The Economic Journal*, **82**, 11-72.

Kiley, M. (1999), 'The Supply of Skilled Labour and Skill-Biased Technological Progress', *The Economic Journal*, **109**, 708-724.

Kim, T., D. Hayes and A. Hallam (1992), 'Technology Adoption under Price Uncertainty', *Journal of Development Economics*, **38**, 245-253.

Kingdon, G. and J. Knight (2001), 'Race and the Incidence of Unemployment in South Africa', *Mimeo*, Center for the Study of African Economies, University of Oxford, Oxford.

Kooreman, P. and A. Kapteyn (1987), 'A Disaggregated Analysis of the Allocation of Time within the Household', *Journal of Political Economy*, **95**, 223-249.

Krueger, A. (1993), 'How Computers have Changed the Wage Structure: Evidence from Micro-Data, 1984-1989', *Quarterly Journal of Economics*, **108**, 33-60.

Krugman, P. (1979), 'A Model of Innovation Technology Transfer and the World Distribution of Income', *Journal of Political Economy*, **87**, 253-266.

(1994), 'Past and Prospective Causes of High Unemployment', *Federal Reserve Bank of Kansas City Economic Review*, **79**, 23-43.

(1995), 'Growing World Trade: Causes and Consequences', *Brookings Papers on Economic Activity*, 1995, 327-377.

Kuhn, T. (1962), *The Structure of Scientific Revolutions*, Chicago University Press, Chicago.

Layard, R., S. Nickell and R. Jackman (1991), *Unemployment; Macroeconomic Performance and the Labour Market*, Oxford University Press, Oxford.

Levitt, T. (1965), 'Exploit the Product Life Cycle', *Harvard Business Review*, **43**, 81-94.

Levy, F. and R. Murnane (1992), 'U.S. Earnings Levels and Earnings Inequality: A Review of Recent Trends and Proposed Explanations', *The Journal of Economic Literature*, **30**, 1333-1381.

Lipsey, R. (1968), 'Structural and Deficient-Demand Unemployment Reconsidered', in B. McCormick and E. Smith (eds), *The Labour Market: Selected Readings*, Penguin Books, Harmondsworth.

Lucas, R. (1988), 'On the Mechanics of Economic Development', *Journal of Monetary Economics*, **22**, 3-42.

Machin, S. (1995), 'Changes in the Relative Demand for Skill in the UK', in A. Booth and D. Snower (eds), *Acquiring Skills*, Cambridge University Press, Cambridge.

Machin, S and J. Van Reenen (1998), 'Technology and Changes in the Wage Structure: Evidence from Seven OECD Countries', *Quarterly Journal of Economics*, **113**, 1215-1244.

Maddison, A. (1987), 'Growth and Slowdown in Advanced Capitalist Economies: Techniques of Quantitative Assessment', *Journal of Economic Literature*, 25, 649-698.

Mansfield, E. (1961), 'Technical Change and the Rate of Imitation', *Econometrica*, 29, 741-766.

(1980), 'Industrial R&D in Japan and the United States: A Comparative Study', *American Economic Review*, 78, 223-228.

(1984), 'R&D and Innovation: Some Empirical Findings', in Z. Griliches (ed.), *R&D, Patents and Productivity*, University of Chicago Press, Chicago.

Mas-Colell, A., M. Whinston and J. Green (1995), *Microeconomic Theory*, Oxford University Press, Oxford.

McCall, J. (1970), 'Economics of Information and Job Search', *The Quarterly Journal of Economics*, 84, 113-126.

Meijers, H. (1994), *On the Diffusion of Technologies in a Vintage Framework; Theoretical Considerations and Empirical Results*, Universitaire Pers, Maastricht.

Mendez, R. (2001), 'Inequality and the Product Cycle', *Mimeo*, Université Paris 1, Paris downloaded from http://eurequa.univ-paris1.fr on 10-09-2004.

Mokyr, J. (ed.) (1999), *The British Industrial Revolution; An Economic Perspective*, 2nd Edition, Westview Press, Boulder, Colorado.

Moore, S. (1995), *The Economic and Civil Liberties Case for a National Sales Tax*, downloaded from http://www.cata.org on 12-06-2003.

Mortensen, D. (1982), 'The Matching Process as a Non-Cooperative Bargaining Game', in J. McCall (ed.), *The Economics of Information and Uncertainty*, University of Chicago Press, Chicago.

Moulton, B. and K. Moses (1997), 'Addressing the Quality Change Issue in the CPI', *Brookings Papers on Economic Activity*, 305-366.

Mühlau, P. and J. Horgan (2001), 'Labour Market Status and the Wage Position of the Low Skilled', *LoWER Working Paper Series*, No. 5.

Muysken, J., M. Sanders and A. van Zon (2001), 'Wage Divergence and Asymmetries in Unemployment in a Model with Biased Technical Change', *De Economist*, **149**, 1-19.

Nadiri, M. (1993), 'Innovations and Technological Spillovers', *National Bureau of Economic Research Working Papers*, No. 4423.

Nash, J. (1950), 'The Bargaining Problem', *Econometrica*, **18**, 155-162.

NBER (1997), *Census Population Survey Monthly Outgoing Rotation Groups*, 1979-1997.

Nickell, S. (1987), 'Why is Wage Inflation in Britain so High?', *Oxford Bulletin of Economics and Statistics*, **49**, 103-128.

Nickell, S. and B. Bell (1995), 'The Collapse in the Demand for the Unskilled and Unemployment across the OECD', *Oxford Review of Economic Policy*, **11**, 40-62.

    (1996), 'Changes in the Distribution of Wages and Unemployment in OECD Countries', *American Economic Review*, **86**, 302-308.

Nickell, S., L. Nunziata, W. Ochel and G. Quintini (2003), 'The Beveridge Curve, Unemployment and Wages in the OECD', in P. Aghion, R. Frydman, J. Stiglitz and M. Woodford (eds), *Knowledge, Information and Expectations in Modern Macroeconomics: In Honour of Edmund S. Phelps*, Princeton University Press, Princeton, New Jersey.

Norton, R. (2003), 'Corporate Taxation', *Concise Encyclopedia of Economics*, downloaded from http://www.econlib.org on 03-07-2003.

Obstfeld, M. and K. Rogoff (1996), *Foundations of International Macroeconomics*, MIT Press, Cambridge, Massachusetts.

OECD (1994a), *The OECD Job Study: Evidence and Explanations*, Part 1, OECD, Paris.

    (1994b), *The OECD Job Study: Evidence and Explanations*, Part 2, OECD, Paris.

OECD (1995), *The OECD Jobs Study: Taxation, Employment and Unemployment*, OECD, Paris.

(1996), *The OECD Jobs Strategy: Pushing ahead with the Strategy*, OECD, Paris.

(1997), *Employment Outlook*, OECD, Paris.

(1998), *Employment Outlook*, OECD, Paris.

(2000), 'Science, Technology and Innovation in the New Economy', *Policy Brief*, OECD, Paris.

(2001), *Employment Outlook*, OECD, Paris.

(2002a), *Benefits and Wages: OECD Indicators - 2002 Edition*, downloaded from http://www.oecd.org on 24-05-2003.

(2002b), *OECD Science, Technology and Industry Scoreboard 2001; Towards a Knowledge Based Economy*, downloaded from http://www.oecd.org on 22-04-2003.

(2003a), *Labour Force Statistics*, downloaded from http://www.oecd.org on 25-06-2003.

(2003b), *Science and Engineering Indicators – 2002 Edition*, OECD, Paris.

OECD-Labour Force Statistics-Database. A detailed description of the data can be found in OECD (2003), Labour Force Statistics, 1982-2002, OECD, Paris.

OECD-STAN-Database. A detailed description of the data was downloaded at http://www.oecd.org on 06-06-2003.

OECD-TBP-Database, A detailed description of the data was downloaded at http://oecd.org on 06-06-2003.

Pakes, A. and M. Simpson (1989), 'Patent Renewal Data', *Brookings Papers on Economic Activity*, 1989, 331-410.

Pencavel, J. (1986), 'Labour Supply of Men; A Survey', in O. Ashenfelder and R. Layard (eds), *Handbook of Labor Economics*, vol. I, Elsevier, Amsterdam.

Persson, T. and G. Tabellini (2000), *Political Economics; Explaining Economic Policy*, MIT Press, Cambridge, Massachusetts.

Phillips, A. (1958), 'The Relation between Unemployment and the Rate of Change of Money Wage Rates in the United Kingdom', *Econometrica*, **26**, 283-299.

Pissarides, C. (1984a), 'Efficient Job Rejection', *Economic Journal*, **94**, 97-108.

(1984b), 'Search Intensity, Job Advertising and Efficiency, *Journal of Labor Economics*, **2**, 128-143

(1990), *Equilibrium Unemployment Theory*, Basil Blackwell Publishers, Oxford.

(2000), *Equilibrium Unemployment Theory*, 2nd Edition, MIT Press, Cambridge, Massachusetts.

Popper, K. (1959), *The Logic of Scientific Discovery*, Reprint Edition (1992), Routledge.

Praag, M. van and A. Booij (2003), 'Risk Aversion and the Subjective Discount Rate: A Joint Approach', *Tinbergen Institute Discussion Papers*, No. 2003-018/3.

Ramsey, F. (1928), 'A Mathematical Theory of Saving', *Economic Journal*, **38**, 543-559.

Rebelo, S. (1991), 'Long-Run Policy Analysis and Long-Run Growth', *Journal of Political Economy*, **99**, 500-521.

Romer, P. (1986), 'Increasing Returns and Long-Run Growth', *Journal of Political Economy*, **94**, 1002-1037.

Romer, P. (1987), 'Crazy Expectations for the Productivity Slowdown', in S. Fisher (ed.), *National Bureau of Economic Research Macroeconomics Annual 1987*, MIT Press, Cambridge, Massachusetts.

Romer, P. (1990), 'Endogenous Technical Change', *Journal of Political Economy*, 98, S71-S102.

Rosenberg, N. (1982), *Inside the Black Box: Technology and Economics*, Cambridge University Press, Cambridge.

Salter, W. (1960), *Productivity and Technical Change*, Cambridge University Press, Cambridge.

Samuelson, P. (1966), 'Rejoinder: Agreements, Disagreements, Doubts, and the Case of Induced Harrod-Neutral Technical Change', *Review of Economics and Statistics*, 48, 444-448.

Sanders, M. (2002), 'Product Life Cycles and Skill Biased Technical Change', *MERIT Research Memoranda*, No. 02-012.

Sanders, M. and B. ter Weel (2000), 'Skill-Biased Technical Change: Theoretical Concepts, Empirical Problems and a Survey of the Evidence', *DRUID Working Paper Series*, No. 00-8, Copenhagen.

Schankerman, M. (1998), 'How Valuable is Patent Protection? Estimates by Technology Field using Patent Renewal Data', *RAND Journal of Economics*, 29, 77-107.

Scherer, F. (1982), 'Demand Pull and Technological Invention: Schmookler Revisited', *Journal of Industrial Economics*, 30, 225-237.

Schimmelpfennig, A. (1998), 'Skill Biased Technical Change versus Structural Change (Insights from a New View of the Structure of an Economy)', *Institute of World Economics Working Papers*, No. 868, Kiel.

Schmookler, J. (1966), *Invention and Economic Growth*, Harvard University Press, Cambridge, Massachusetts.

Schneider, J. and T. Ziesemer (1995), 'What's New and What's Old in New Growth Theory? Endogeneous Technology, Micro-Foundation and Growth Rate Predictions - A Critical Overview', *Zeitschrift für Wirtschaft- und Sozialwissenschaften*, 115, 1-44.

Schultz, T. (1961), 'Investment in Human Capital', *American Economic Review*, 51, 1-17.

Schultz, T. (1975), 'The Value of the Ability to Deal with Disequilibria', *Journal of Economic Literature*, **13**, 872-876.

Schumpeter, J. (1934), *The Theory of Economic Development*, Oxford University Press, Oxford.

Shapiro, D. and D. Wilcox (1996), 'Mismeasurement in the CPI; An Evaluation', in B. Bernanke and J. Rotemberg (eds), *National Bureau of Economic Research Macroeconomics Annual 1996*, MIT Press, Cambridge, Massachusetts.

Sheenan, J. (2002), 'Trends in Business R&D and Government Support for Business Innovation in the OECD', presentation given at the OECD Science and Technology Policy Division, slides downloaded from http://www.oecd.org on 14-05-2003.

Shell, K. (1967), 'A Model of Inventive Activity and Capital Accumulation', in K. Shell (ed.), *Essays on the Theory of Optimal Economic Growth*, MIT Press, Cambridge, Massachusetts.

Siebert, H. (1998), *Economics of the Environment: Theory and Policy*, 5th Edition, Springer Verlag, Berlin.

Smith, A. (1776), *An Inquiry into the Causes and Nature of the Wealth of Nations*, reprinted in E. Cannan (ed.) (1937), Modern Library, New York.

Solow, R. (1957), 'Technical Change and the Aggregate Production Function', *Review of Economics and Statistics*, **39**, 312-330.

Stigler, J. (1961), 'The Economics of Information', *Journal of Political Economy*, **69**, 213-225.

Stoneman, P. (1981), 'Intra-Firm Diffusion, Baysian Learning and Profitability', *The Economic Journal*, **91**, 375-388.

(1983), *The Economic Analysis of Technical Change*, Oxford University Press, Oxford.

Stoneman, P. (1991), 'Technological Diffusion: The Viewpoint of Economic Theory', in P. Mathias and J. Davis (eds), *Innovation and Technology in Europe*, Basil Blackwell Publishers, Oxford, pp. 162-184.

Suplee, C. (2000), *Milestones of Science*, National Geographic, Washington D.C.

Temple, J. (1999), 'The New Growth Evidence', *Journal of Economic Literature*, 37, 112-156.

Teulings, C. and J. Hartog (1991), *Corporatism or Competition; Labor Contracts, Institutions and Wage Structures in International Comparison*, Cambridge University Press, Cambridge.

Thirtle, C. and V. Ruttan (1987), *The Role of Demand and Supply in the Generation and Diffusion of Technical Change*, Harwood Academic Publishers, Chur.

Tinbergen, J. (1974), 'Substitution of Graduates by Other Labour', *Kyklos*, 27, 217-226.

(1975), *Income Distribution: Analysis and Policies*, Amsterdam: North-Holland Publishing Co.

Todaro, M. (1997), *Economic Development*, 6th Edition, Addison, Wesley, Longman Ltd., Reading, Massachusetts.

Trajtenberg, M. (1990), *Economic Analysis of Product Innovation - The Case of CT Scanners*, Harvard University Press, Cambridge, Massachusetts.

Tsur, Y., M. Sternberg and E. Hochman (1990), 'Dynamic Modelling of Innovation Process Adoption with Risk Aversion and Learning', *Oxford Economic Papers*, 42, 336-355.

Usher, A. (1954), *A History of Mechanical Inventions*, Revised Edition, Harvard University Press, Cambridge, Massachusetts.

Vernon, R. (1966), 'International Investment and International Trade in the Product Cycle', *Quarterly Journal of Economics*, 80, 190-207.

Von Weizäcker, C. (1966), 'Tentative Notes on a Two Sector Model with Induced Technical Progress', *Review of Economic Studies*, 33, 245-251.

Walsh, C. (1998), *Monetary Theory and Policy*, MIT Press, Cambridge, Massachusetts.

Xiang, C. (2002), 'New Goods and Rising Skill Premium: An Empirical Investigation', *Discussion Paper Series*, No. 479, University of Michigan, Chicago, downloaded at http: //www.fordschool.umich.edu on 05-05-2003.

Zon, A. van and M. Sanders (2000), 'Endogenous Technical Change and Skill Biases in Employment Opportunities', *MERIT Research Memorandum*, No. 2000-004.

(2002), 'On Growth Frontiers and Labour Market Policies', *Mimeo*, MERIT, Maastricht.

Zon, A. van, M. Sanders and J. Muysken (2001),' Modelling the Link between Skill Biases in Technical Change and Wage Divergence through Labour Market Extensions of Krugman's North-South Model', in P. Petit and L. Soete (eds), *Technology and the Future of European Employment*, Edward Elgar Publishing, Cheltenham

INDEX